Why Me to Tell You?

There is a simple fact about media life that people often ignore. Media life takes place moment by moment, just like any life. Ask anyone trying to function in Hollywood *now*, for instance. Someone with a comic gift. Just try to avoid the aesthetic of the sitcom, for instance; just try. The sitcom is *fact*, just as Napoleon was *fact* in 1804. Before you can rise above David Letterman now, or Jerry Bruckheimer, say, you have to get to be *like* David Letterman or Jerry Bruckheimer. Your capacity for self-expression will have made its mark within a construct that has been ruled by certain still live and kicking social energies.

In 1950 the social life of New York City was the *fact* within which television was developed. Broadway, on the one hand, and Madison Avenue on the other; and yes, with a backdraft of Park and Fifth. Throw in Greenwich Village and you have the real world within which any struggling avatar interested in television *had* to function. I mean, you don't get the MTV-influenced Coke commercials until you have MTV itself, if you get my drift.

I happen to know a great deal about that world. You'll have to trust me on that one.

♦ ♦ ♦

And of course, as of February 1, 1950 (datum for this book), there had been and still *was* this other thing—our victory in World War II. It was that *fact* that had changed our cultural relationship to the rest of the world. We like to think that it is because we are so fascinating as a people that we are—or have been—so successful, but the core of our fascination has been the fact of our Total Sweep in World War II. If Britain had been the *factual* victor, we would have BBCed our way into the media age; if Hitler had won—something else. They didn't; we did; and so we New York–Televisioned our way into the media age (and we call it the "golden age" of television now—not exactly Cicero, but it's what we have). And, as I say, New York television began somewhere—

Prelude and Dedication

Why 1950?

Naturally, a moment matters. Was New York interesting in 1865? Of course it was. The city of Astor, Vanderbilt, and Washington Irving, say. In some ways New York was never more powerful than then—I mean in terms of the dynamism and language intelligence. And on February 1, 1929? You bet. The rock-and-roll financial life of that moment, the booze and Broadway. To a large extent, we—that is, Americans on the face of the earth at this moment—have been working our way back to that legendary electricity ever since. What of media life? Was it more *intelligent* in 1865 than in 1950? Well, yes. Was media life more frenetic, more charged with energy, on February 1, 1929, than it was twenty-one years later? Well, yes it was. However, the moment—I mean the *world* moment—was different. In 1950, America was *about* to be at the height of her power. An interesting moment: Victoria assumes the throne, in a way; Napoleon about to dismember the Holy Roman Empire, in a way. We were *about* to have our most pervasive influence. And another thing: our *microphone* (and Marconi to the contrary notwithstanding, we Americans invented the microphone) was about to become our *camera*.

A LONG INTRODUCTION

Also by George W. S. Trow

The City in the Mist

Within the Context of No Context

Bullies

MY PILGRIM'S PROGRESS

My Pilgrim's Progress

MEDIA STUDIES, 1950–1998

George W. S. Trow

PANTHEON BOOKS ◆ NEW YORK

Grateful acknowledgment is made to the following for permission to
reprint previously published material: *Ayer Company Publishers, Inc.*:
Excerpts from *Adventures of a White Collar Man* by Alfred Sloan
(Ayer Company Publishers, North Stratford, NH, 1941). Reprinted by
permission of Ayer Company Publishers, Inc., North Stratford, NH
03590. • *Doubleday*: Excerpts from *Mandate for Change* by Dwight
David Eisenhower. Copyright © 1963 by Dwight David Eisenhower.
Reprinted by permission of Doubleday, a division of Random
House, Inc.

Library of Congress Cataloging-in-Publication Data

Trow, George W. S.
    My pilgrim's progress : media studies, 1950–1998 /
George W. S. Trow.
        p.   cm.
    ISBN 0-375-40134-2
    1. Mass media—United States—History—20th century.
I. Title.
P92.U5T74   1999
302.23'0973'09045—dc21   98-5967
                                                  CIP

Random House Web Address: http://www.randomhouse.com

Book design by Cindy LaBreacht

Printed in the United States of America
First Edition
2   4   6   8   10   9   7   5   3   1

Acknowledgments

Acknowledgments one, two, three, four, and five go to Bob Gottlieb (acknowledgment number one is for ten years of guidance and conversation; acknowledgment two is for editorial work on this book; three, four, and five are for various reasons, as Lynn Nesbit has taught me to say).

Thank you to: Catherine Cloud; Rudy Wurlitzer and Lynn Davis; Rory Nugent and Elizabeth McFadden; Donald Rosenfeld; Lynn Nesbit and Dan Frank; Winty Aldrich, Sybil Baldwin; Bob and Bo Bo Devens; Ann McIntosh; Honor Moore. And I am remembering, very fondly, Alvin Davis of the old *New York Post*.

in New York City, which had been moving along, moment by moment, like any other place.

I Still Like Ike

The other day I had a thought, and then after I had the thought, I thought, Well, this can't possibly be true, and then I thought about it some more, and it was. True, that is. And my thought was, Well, the president of the United States and the secretary of state, Mr. Clinton and Ms. Albright, don't have any idea of the power base of Dwight Eisenhower—what it was, socially. Well, you might say, what does that matter? My answer to that comes in two parts: one, it's never happened before, not exactly; and two, wasn't it something, that Eisenhower power base, the ease of it? To put these ideas together, I'll take you back to Andrew Jackson, because a Jacksonian Democrat at this point in my argument will object: So why should a president for the people give a hoot about the configuration of the power base of another president? and so forth. Well, it may or may not have been true that Andrew Jackson didn't give a hoot about Virginia planters, or Boston Brahmins, but he knew who they were, and they were around in plenty, to study, in case he felt he needed an update. The remarkable thing about President Clinton's and Ms. Albright's position in regard to Ike's power base is—they don't happen to know about it, and if they wanted to find out, there's really no way they could do it. It's all gone. Ike's power base came in two parts. On top was the Military-Industrial Rolodex, and it was an inert thing; inert, but vastly powerful. The thing under it—let's call it the Country Club Life of the 1920s—the thing it sat on, was, in a way, alive and kicking, and certainly had been very alive and kicking.

Now, most people when they talk about the Military-Industrial Complex evoke large generalizations and *Robert's Universal Robots*, which was a play from the 1930s, and Kafka, things like that. In the old days, images of the Military-Industrial Complex were juxtaposed with images of a strong worker who was unhappy about it. Or a Stevensonian liberal who was unhappy about it. I don't think that way; I think about what it really was, because it was a very specific, very tiny group of men there. You didn't have to generalize; it wasn't going to perpetuate itself; the sons of the presidents of those corporations weren't going to get those positions, and if they were going to get those positions, which they weren't, they weren't going to know what those men knew. It was just an event. There aren't many, you know. An event in the ecology of human social history is a three-step, let's say. In this case, the three-step was: men all from Eisenhower's social background—from the middle class, or rather from the upper edge of the middle class. Steaming out of the late nineteenth century into the early twentieth century—their first step—they came from the Old America, where the automobile was the new thing. They went into the New America, with maximum ambition, and did well in the 1920s—that was their second step.

Alfred Sloan, the famous president of General Motors, is an example of this kind of man. And then the third step wasn't the New Deal, participation in the NRA, or acquiescence in some aspect of the Roosevelt system; that wasn't who they were. The third step was World War II. They got to go full tilt into a kind of business, which was what they knew how to do; production, and no questions asked; patriotism, and no questions asked; command your men, and no questions asked there either. They got to do that at a rarefied level, and they got to do it under the command of Eisenhower and his boss, General Marshall. Now, this can be discussed in terms of natural human phenomena, but why do it? It was an event. It was a three-step event. It happened once. The Old America these men came from is gone, the world of the twenties they went through is gone, and World War II and the Military-Industrial Complex, all of it, gone. A series of American theaters, producing a certain kind of man, and we don't happen to have any of it today. Now, Eisenhower was Guy One in this process—the young man from the upper edge of the middle class who went full steam ahead with ambition in the post–World War I world, and then full steam ahead into World War II. He was the guy who got that right. He was the alpha male of it. And there wasn't a male in that cohort who didn't acknowledge that fact. So that when Ike called on Engine Charlie Wilson or Electric Charlie Wilson, two men of importance who served, respectively, in the General Motors Corporation and the General Electric Corporation, it wasn't like Bill Clinton getting in touch with the two gentlemen who run those corporations now. Those three men— President Clinton and the General Electric man and the General Motors man—haven't been through a one-step together, let alone a three-step. The level of trust existing among those three men is—well, it is whatever it is. And it's a good time to mention the globalization of our economy and the deep unsureness that corporate leaders have that the president of the United States is going to suggest something good for the bottom line. So, in addition to the nonexistent personal trust among these three men, you have an issue problem, an overall "I'm not sure we're on the same side on this at all" problem. Ike didn't have any of that. He made the call, the call was returned, and so forth.

Now, as I say, that system, which I've called Ike's Rolodex— and he had the best Rolodex ever—sat on top of something, and what it sat on top of was, the Du Pont of it. You don't remember 1955; I do. Nineteen fifty-five was the last moment of 1925, socially, in this country. That is, in every city, large and medium, and in most towns, there was a country club, built in the twenties. Were there a couple that went back further than that? Well, let it be. But the vogue was a 1920s vogue. And if in 1925 you went to, say, Terre Haute, Indiana, what you'd see was a group of people living in response to the Du Pont of it. In Terre Haute there was one kind of country club and one kind of person; but they knew that somewhere else it was being done better, and the place where it was being done better was the East Coast, by a small group of families, epitomized by me here in my reference to the Du Ponts. Ike sat on top of a unique cadre of three-step men. Those men controlled the Military-Industrial Complex—and the Military-Industrial Complex, because of the importance of the winning of the war, sat atop that 1925–55 social construct. I like to relate this to the literary history of the century, because I take Ike very seriously as a social historian—he was very astute socially—and there's the famous remark by our famous 1920s men, our justly famous 1920s men, F. Scott Fitzgerald and Ernest Hemingway: "The rich are different from you and me," Fitzgerald said to Hemingway, and he was thinking about Terre Haute versus Du Pont; he was thinking about knowing every possible thing about the country club in Terre Haute, or St. Paul, or wherever, and feeling that it was all in mysterious relation to the mysterious life being led by a tiny group of people. "Yes," said Hemingway, "they have more money." Well, they were both a little bit right, Fitzgerald and Hemingway. You can't quite come down on one side or the other in that argument, but there's a figure bestriding the argument, and it's Ike.

As I say, I have enormous respect for Ike as a social historian, a social man, and I'm quite a good one myself. He knew his man, and he knew the zeitgeist; I don't think he ever made a serious fumble in these two crucial areas. So now let me postulate a theorem about Ike's warning us, as he did, about the Military-Industrial Complex. Well, no one since Washington had ever actually warned us about anything. And yes, I think Ike was warning us about something he didn't quite like, something gone a little rotten in the hyperspace command structure evolved over fifteen years, over twenty years, and I think he was warning us about something else as well. He was warning us about our Social Terrarium, something gone a little rotten in the hyperspace command structure, on the one hand, and on the ground, on the other. I think Ike knew that America had marinated on his watch. There was nothing he could have done about it—his job was to superintend the fighting of that phase of our Eighty Years War we call the Cold War. He wasn't about to open up that fight for our inspection; he knew (as every man at the top knows) how rare it is that one has a reliable command structure, agreed on a common goal—a Command Structure Without a Judas, shall we say; and he wasn't going to dismantle it or open it up for inspection as long as he had the Big Job to do. However, as I say, Ike was astute socially; he saw the command structure get older and older, and he didn't like what he saw coming up. What he was saying at the end of his tenure was: I can *control* Richard Nixon, but I don't know who he is—do you?

Black Roosevelt

I was brought up on the other side of the street. My father came from a Brownstone New York family and was obsessed with Franklin Roosevelt. My father was a Brownstone Liberal as his grandmother, my great-grandmother, had been a Brownstone Progressive dedicated to Theodore Roosevelt right into his Bull Moose days. My great-grandmother was the most important person in my father's life, and so (since I was born in 1943) we were, by 1950, into our fiftieth year, more or less, of our family obsession with the Necessary Correctness of the Roosevelts. You probably don't know what the Black Nobility used to be in Rome. It's a vanished phenomenon, just as the phenomenon I am describing within my family is a vanished phenomenon. I mean, there is the Roman Catholic Church, and of course anyone can belong to it—in fact everyone is encouraged to belong to it, just as everyone is (or was) encouraged to be a Roosevelt-descended liberal—but the Black Nobility are descended from or related to the Italian popes (and all popes used to be Italian). It was felt, within these families, that a certain *thread* of church life was maintained *only* within these families; the thread, of course, was *blood loyalty.* Within the life of the church, with its various aspects, its conflicts, and its tendency to change over time, there was one small, specialized threat guaranteed not to break because it was based on blood.

My father had this notion, and he took it as Job One to pass it on to me. Not for me were any of the freedoms, the promise of which drew ordinary Americans into the Roosevelt fold. My job was to be Black Roosevelt—tinged so deep that no amount of change could change my color.

I remember being taken along on one occasion in the late 1940s to Hartford, Connecticut, where my father was to interview Chester Bowles. Chester Bowles was Black Roosevelt, as far as my father was concerned. Only Adlai Stevenson and Eleanor Roosevelt herself were *as* Black in my father's opinion. (My great-grandmother, an intelligent, homely woman with one cross eye, had been very like Eleanor Roosevelt, both in breeding and behavior.) I waited with my mother in our car while my father did the interview. When he returned he was in a State. Transformed. Clearly, he had seen the pope and the pope had recognized him as Black Roosevelt too.

I should say now that I will be critical of my father in this book, and I will explain in the section below titled "Methodology" why I have let stand some things I might have taken out. My criticism has to do with a Big Topic, and that is the tendency of the Liberal Construct to infantilize its congregation. It was not— is not—a good thing to have been or to be an Adopted Child of Eleanor Roosevelt, forgiven for all the wrong things, and criticized for all the wrong things. I was the son of a man who never grew up and whose grandmother had been very like Eleanor Roosevelt. Two things happened to me at once when I was very young—in 1950, in fact. I was thrust with great force into the deepest tinge of the Roosevelt aesthetic—where the current of infantilization was strongest—and (since my father was deeply and angrily determined never to grow up) I was forced to take responsibility for the male energy in the family. The head of the family as a child, I was forced to direct my life force to the Perpetuation of a Religion of Infantilization.

The Methodology of This Book

I thought you might like to know how I read a newspaper. I read a newspaper differently than you do. The reason is that, starting in 1950, I was told by my father that you couldn't be Black Roosevelt without knowing how. It was all of a piece, my father indicated to me in the strongest terms: gentlemanliness, my family's

history in New York City, New York City itself, the liberal arts—
and the New York newspaper.

There was another ingredient: childish innocence. Innocence with a capital "I" was also part of the mix. One of the freedoms you have that was taken away from me early was the
freedom to choose to read a newspaper or not; the freedom to look
at the sports section and throw the rest away, and so forth. My job
was different: I was to Integrate all of the elements I have mentioned into—Something. Just what, I was not told. But it was
Important. All of the Above Elements had to be part of Some
Whole, and that Whole had to be what *I* was. I had to be Franklin
Roosevelt's Perfect Child or . . . My father had, let us call it, a
tendency toward schizophrenia. If all the fragments he claimed
made up a Perfect Whole did *not* make a Perfect Whole in me,
then he was going to have to look at some things he did not want
to look at.

The process began with the Innocence of the liberal arts. My
father read aloud to me when I was young. *The Wind in the Wil-
lows* was one of the first books he read to me. Toad of Toad Hall.
At the same time, we would look at the New York papers. By the
age of four, although I could not read, I knew what a headline
was, what a lead story was, which columnists were respectable
and which were not (I learned to loathe Westbrook Pegler before I
was in kindergarten), and so on. I learned what the *Times* represented, and what the *Daily News* represented, and the difference
between the *News* and the *Mirror*, and who Old Man Hearst was,
and what was wrong with Roy Howard (head of the Scripps-
Howard chain), and on and on. I was told that *not* to read the
Times was to condemn oneself to second-class citizenship (and
you know, my father was right about that; also, he was right about
Westbrook Pegler). And I was told that the *Sun* was in trouble,
and that *our* newspaper was the *Herald Tribune* (although, for
various reasons, it could no longer command full respect).

My father read the *Trib* aloud to me. We read a nineteenth-
century column for children about Old Mother West Wind (or was
it Old Mr. West Wind, I forget) and it makes me cry to think about it.

Then I was encouraged to Take Initiative and pick a story to follow. The story I picked was in the *Trib* and it had to do with the old Murray Hill Hotel, which was about to be torn down. I followed that story and learned *how* to follow a story (and you should learn how to do this), and that particular story almost made me cry *then*.

So, then, as to the methodology of this book. In considering the course of my life, I came to realize just what I have just told you—that for various strange reasons I became a kind of child-adult in 1950. And that the foci of my child-adulthood were two: my family history in relation to Franklin Roosevelt, and the New York newspaper. It occurred to me that I ought to look at the *New York Times* of 1950. I did. I went to the State Library in Albany, and there it was. I had, of course, never read it before, although the physical object had been in front of me almost fifty years earlier. That in itself was exciting to me. And another thing: I had been developing my ability to parse a newspaper over a very long time, during which time the newspaper had been growing less and less parse-worthy. And here it was, a kind of magical object from a very intense moment in my childhood, still in existence (at first flickering on a screen, then in my hand as a photostatic copy), and I could read it—and fast, and well, and it was not just parse-worthy but *juicy*. So what I did was lay the copies out in front of me, and I made for myself a kind of speed trial. I turned on a tape recorder and read and talked at the same time (I allowed myself a three-minute quick look before I turned on the tape recorder, and I had scanned the pages as I printed them out in Albany). What resulted was a kind of release from Something Intense that had been settling down in me for forty-five years. What I have used from this process I have let stand—there is, really, no way to change it—and I went on to use this technique (though modified) in considering other Mainstream American Cultural Artifacts that relate to the story I am trying to tell, which is the *simultaneous* death of Eisenhower's America and Franklin Roosevelt's Effort.

A Little About Me

I'm a swimmer—and half Irish. If there is a *distanced* tone about my father and his aesthetic; if I talk more often about "my father's family" than I talk about *my* family, it isn't that I don't consider myself a Trow, or that I am uncomfortable with Anglo-Saxon modes and mores (I am comfortable, really with no other), but because all the *matter* I acquired from my father and at my father's urging sits on top of an Irish soul—objective, a little ruthless, at times a little *neutral* on Big Topics like Virtue, Tory or otherwise.

And that leads me to the dedication part of this dedicatory introduction. Elsewhere in this book I will talk about a house called Windy Rock, and the very Old Style family that lived there. It was a house of Deep Probity. The head of the family was called "the Aged P"—P for Pater, Latin for Father. And the family—named Coggeshall—was daunting to me both as to text and subtext. The text would have challenged anyone; the subtext would have challenged anyone who happened, as they say now, to have an Irish soul.

My father presented this family—and this house—as my First School. A difficult challenge, but my luck held. Within this family there was a marvelous woman—an older woman, a maiden lady who was as unlike Eleanor Roosevelt as possible. She was a writer. Her name was Constance Choate Wright, and her books include *Madame de Lafayette* and other good biographical tales. She was my friend. And she let me know that she *liked* my rebellious Irish soul. Thank you, Aunt Con.

Easter, 1997

It seems to me possible that our whole fifty-year postwar period
(and I think of the Second World War in the old style, as having
ended in 1945, on May 7)—it seems to me possible that this
whole period was a kind of test, and where one imagines a test,
one can only mention God as the tester. A kind of test of our
human decency. Here we were, the most interesting human cultural and spiritual experiment ever to have been proposed, and to
some extent implemented, on this planet, constantly ponying up
to stay in the game, which is to say the cultural and spiritual
game, at the very highest level. That is, whenever something
came along that clearly was demanding the top level of cultural
and spiritual fortitude, whether it was the Civil War in the last
century, for instance, or World War II, whenever those ultimate
tests came around, we kept on saying, "You bet, and we'll mortgage the house to stay in the game." We did stay in, and we kept
on winning. However, we kept on not filling in the blanks. All
those secondary, tertiary blanks. We kept on fighting for the farm;
we kept on farming badly. And then we got given a grace period,
one as long and as troubled as any grace period ever was. So,
here are the four ideas I hope my reader will keep in mind as we
march through *My Pilgrim's Progress:* a study of the aesthetic of
Dwight David Eisenhower, a study of the aesthetic of Franklin

Delano Roosevelt, a study of the way the media worked to mediate all our interactions with those powerful, dwindling, one-time-only aesthetics. First, the idea of the grace period. Second, the idea of our being tested. Third, the idea that the powerful aesthetics we were working from—and we'll work very hard in this book to define those aesthetics—were one time only. (We were about to be abandoned.) And fourth, that what we will be discussing in this book are the workings, our unsuccessful workings, within those secondary and tertiary categories, which would have had to have been built up strong for us to win the next and ultimate fight.

In my essay of 1980, *Within the Context of No Context,* I predicted that television would establish the context of no context, and then chronicle it. Well, I'll give myself a little bit of credit here. That began to happen in the 1980s, the mid-1980s, and by 1990 we had reality television, tabloid television, trash TV—many different forms that had suddenly morphed from entertainment into reporting. And if you think it was fun to see that happen, you are wrong. There's nothing fun about being right if what you're right about is the triumph, or temporary triumph, of the inevitably bad. And now we have the next step, which is that media critics, and media institutes, and communications professors at giant journalism schools, and all the rest of it have begun to take an interest—and indeed, they talk about context. And so now I'll give you my overview of what that sort of thing's worth, as it is, at this moment. My Mainstream American Cultural Artifact at the moment is a program I saw on C-SPAN on Easter Sunday of 1997: a panel discussion among the proprietors of a $3.3-million study on violence on television. It was all about ratings, about how do we do this, how do we do that. There was one great gap. The gap was the basic premise, the gap was the foundation, all of this was in midair—well, what is the foundation? This television discussion, reporting on the effects of television civilization—what was this thing it lacked? Well, when the people on this program talked about context, they talked about the context of the television program. Nothing about the context of history, nothing about the context of American social life, nothing that would lend a sense of *sequence* to what's happened in this remarkable television avatar. When they talked about context, they just meant what the producers of the show had created in the way of context. In other words, if the violence was contexted, if the person killing the person was a person who was going to be hung at the end of the program, well, that was one thing; and if it was *gratuitous violence* that was, by the perceptions of the participants, not contexted, that was something else; and that's what their $3.3 million gave them permission to do, and they didn't feel it was their job to mention producers, or deal in any way with the aesthetic history of what they were talking about.

This book is focused on the year 1950, and my friend Dr. Arno Gruen, author of *The Insanity of Normality*, has said an interesting thing. He said that culture, in recent decades, has taken on a life of its own, without reference to the people it is supposed to protect. That's a statement involving two important points. First, Dr. Gruen has said, in his own words, what I've said (sometimes in many words): that the phenomenon of our postwar life has to do with the fact that our culture took on a life of its own, rather in the way of a computer that takes on a life of its own, or a robot that suddenly begins to want to get married and have children, or like that, as they say in the gossip columns. Secondly, he has defined culture as something meant to protect. This is such a fundamental observation that it's invisible. I don't think many people think of culture as something meant to protect. Some people's definition of culture is what people do when they go to a museum, or to the opera. Our other definition of culture is: *My preferences, your preferences,* the sum total of whatever it is we happened to have liked. And if this year we like Debbie Reynolds and *Tammy and the Bachelor,* and last year we didn't, and the year before we liked Nine Inch Nails, and tomorrow we decide to take a look at the Butthole Surfers, well, that's just what we happen to want at the moment, and why shouldn't we?

Why should culture be defined as something meant to protect, and why is it important if culture doesn't have a life of its own, with reference to us—that is, those human avatars who live more or less at its mercy? Well, one simple thing: We know that the military is meant to protect us, right? And that when the military takes on a life of its own, simply becomes enamored of its own high-tech capabilities, decides to develop weapons not of use to anyone but of aesthetic interest to the proprietors of the military, we know that something's got a little out of hand. So we should have a sense, just a simple commonsense sense, that all the avatars of our life ought in some way to be calibrated toward protecting us.

Why focus on the idea of protection instead of *inspiration* or the pleasures of pure mind? Because 99.9 percent of all human projects fail. This one wants to be a doctor, but it doesn't quite happen. That one wants to be a writer, and it never quite happens. So-and-so announces that he's going to move to California and never quite moves. A handsome young woman says that no man is good enough for her except a certain kind of man, and she doesn't get that man; she gets some other sort. It just happens. There are too many of us, and our youthful ambitions are too unrealistic: 99.9 percent of us fail in the height of our ambition, and at some point, early or late, we know it. A protected culture says, "Of course you have. Just relax." And you do, and you find there is something under you. Let's call it a net. You fall from the high wire, and—golly, people have already predicted that possibly you would fall from the high wire, so fall into the net, and then you can regroup, make another, perhaps a better, decision or plan, and there you are. And to continue this high-wire-and-net metaphor, many of the 99.9 percent who fall off the high wire into the net, as they get off the net, back into life, have come to an understanding of the importance of the net, which we will call, let's say, the baseline culture. And as they go into *new plan formation* (more sensible, more adult goals for themselves), they take with them some sense that part of the time they ought to do some volunteer work toward keeping the net in good shape, if only for the sake of their own children. That's how culture's protection works. Well, we don't have that. People fall off the high wire invisibly. There is no net; they crash. They pick themselves up, secretly, in the quiet of their own mind, having had to face some near infinite pain about delusion, and about lack of protection, about abandonment, about no one being there, about nothing being there; and they crawl away from their accident, and when at last they stand up again, if they do, they're a little deformed. And that's a lot of us now. Or when they do find a net, it's not a cultural net, it's a therapeutic net. They give up drugs, and then the philosophy they have is not an overall philosophy of culture, it's an enthusiasm for a particular therapy to get over drugs; and the examples go on and on, and that's fine, but it's not culture. A purely therapeutic fix doesn't help you immediately to reintegrate with history, or with your fellow citizens. It's a personal thing, a good thing, a thing that can help you overcome narcissism in addition to your addiction, and so forth, but it's a personal thing. It doesn't do the job that a protecting culture should do. So to go back for one moment to 1950, the interesting thing about that year is, with television just starting up, and the ancient generation—so I will call them, for although some of the men involved were merely old, the culture they represented was ancient—with ancient culture still in the saddle and destined not to be passed on, even within the families in which it had been exhibited, 1950 is perhaps the last year when you can see culture in definite, immediate, but troubled and conflicted reference to the idea of protection. When I say troubled, I mean, if your protection is formed in large part out of something ancient that you're sick of, and which, in any case, is destined not to be continued (even within the tradition that traditionally embodied it), well, that's trouble. Nonetheless, the relationship of culture to protection is very clear in 1950, and that should be a datum in any of these discussions being held by $3.3-million communications professors.

I made some notes on the C-SPAN program, and I have them sitting in front of me, so, using my usual technique of pursuing what comes to mind, I'll go through them. My first note is "3.3 million dollars," because it just does astonish me that what people ought to be really doing for almost no money, or for free, or just out of their common sense, we've integrated with the study, the colloquium, the what-do-you-think, what-do-I-think, the quantifying thing, all based on a truly flawed methodology. They watched every television program; I think they counted the number of slash marks that a slash-murderer used on a given night, and then watched it the next week to see if the slash-murderer used fewer slashes than on the previous week, and they did all of this stuff—well, they ought to have had just one sharp old screenwriter sitting next to them, to tell them, "Listen, what we do here is we follow the arc of what the audience wants and what our competitor has done, so if you have four slash marks on a given Tuesday, and it raised the ratings, you're naturally going to try five slash marks on Wednesday, and that's how we've been doing it for thirty-five years. And if you can prove to us that you can scare the advertisers by shouting against violence, then we'll get the four slash marks down to three. We'll do what the power of the society says we're gonna do, and that's all we've ever done." They could at least have gotten that far.

My next note says: "No sense of sequence." In analyzing violence on television, it was all treated as though it had been ever with us, like sugar use, as if, naturally we've always had sugar in coffee and tea, and how much are we using now, and what does it do to our energy level, and should we cut down on sugar?—like that. No sense of when sugar was invented, no sense of the sequence of it. And the note I made at this point is, "Like analyzing rock-and-roll on TV—a big subject—without looking at Elvis Presley's appearance on the Dorsey Stage Show in 1956." Well, in 1956, in January, Elvis began to appear on television, and his first appearance was on a program called *Stage Show* with Tommy and Jimmy Dorsey. Tommy and Jimmy Dorsey, who'd been a hit with teenagers twenty years before, were now fifty years old, and the show was corny, and it was corny precisely because we'd been through the experience of the Second World War, which was a very puritanical experience, a military experience, an experience of privation and seriousness. So the Dorseys had cleaned up their act, just as perhaps the perpetrators of violence on television will clean up their act if enough people throw their television sets out their window in protest; for a while they'll clean up their act.

On *Stage Show* the Dorseys presented themselves as something from the hall of fame of popular culture. They had jugglers, they had tap dancers, it was just the standard stuff that adults had grown up on, and Elvis came into that, and anyone who wants to see the moment, and nearly everyone should see the moment, can watch a documentary called *Elvis '56*. Elvis came into it, and you know—I hope you know what Elvis was like when he was twenty-one years old, and he *was* twenty-one—and he wasn't dressed like Liberace, he was dressed to kill, and he *did* kill. He killed *Stage Show,* and everything it represented, in a moment. This has to do with the quality of unexampled people in life, it has to do with the quality of talent, it has to do with the history of Dionysian energy. Of course, there would have been no point in counting everything that was happening in television in December 1955, because in January of 1956 a human avatar of unparalleled power named Elvis Presley was going to change the whole thing forever, and to leave that kind of truth out of a media discussion is simply to have a discussion—well, *worthless* is the word that comes to mind. So, before January 1956, you simply had no Elvis energy. After January 1956, you had a lot. So, we have a marker for rock-and-roll energy on television that we can follow from Elvis Presley's appearance on *Stage Show* in 1956 to the MTV of the moment. Maybe you'll want to choose one of the MTV videos done by Madonna that MTV wouldn't show, that's sort of an interesting marker, because Elvis too, for shaking his hips, was viewed as not acceptable on television, and in recent years there have, in fact, been Madonna videos—oh, she was being raped on an altar or something—also perceived as not being viewable, as going over the line, and if you were to establish that kind of aesthetic marker for a given cultural avatar on television, you could begin to make sense of things. Of course, Madonna was trying to be Elvis. We understand that. We understand it, but the $3.3-million people don't.

As to violence—or to broaden it, hyperactivity—on television, here is another problem these study people are suffering from, because having no aesthetic sense, they don't understand that what characterizes media frenzy at the moment is a sort of hyperactive quality, a kind of unreal, speeded-up violence, which has to do as much with the aesthetic of the people making the product as it has to do with a specific action. You don't get a person in a fist fight very often on television anymore. You get, rather, this quality of frenetic hyperactivity, and that's really what's wanted within the programs, because one wants this kind of hyperactive quality of *click, click, click, click, click* to hold the attention, and the easiest way to get it is with violence; it's hard to get it through dialogue, since most people don't know how to write dialogue. Another way to get it is the car chase. So naturally, what you want as a creator of a successful television popular artifact is the frenetic, the hyperactive, that thing beyond anything people can experience normally in their daily lives, to hold their shallow attention, and the easiest way to do that is violence and the car chase. And that brings me to a suggestion for someone else—it's not my interest, so I won't bother to run it down, but one could make a perfectly interesting attempt to establish cultural markers within the history of television by looking at the car chase, the history of the car chase, and I think that it begins in a film called *Bullitt*, with Steve McQueen; it's certainly more than thirty years old, and in *Bullitt* there was the first car-chase, car-ride sequence that went into hyperspace. It isn't really anything like a realistic car chase of the kind we'd had steadily through the forties, fifties, and into the sixties. In fact, if you look at a 1940s car-chase sequence, it looks wonderfully realistic and old-fashioned. You know, the car speeds up, and you see a cop car over at the side of the road, and he sees the speeding car, and he puts on his siren, and you have a little bit of a chase, and then probably, you know—but in *Bullitt* we went to the next level of hyperactivity. The car rocketed through the streets of San Francisco, up and down hills and past trolley cars, and it really was a moment. I can remember watching that movie at Radio City Music Hall, and it stood out. It was at another speed. It wasn't about a car chase anymore, it was about hyperactivity, the next level of hyperactivity, and my guess is that, starting with that car chase, you can see the increasing level of hyperactivity in car chases, down to *Speed,* for instance, the Keanu Reeves hit, with its out-of-control bus that does this and that and the other, and, once again, it all looks terribly mysterious when put on a television landscape, where one minute you're watching *Frasier* and the next minute you're watching some hyperactive car chase. But *put in the history of popular artifact creation within the context of competition,* it's quite simple. The screenwriters who wanted to be successful in Hollywood, watching *Bullitt,* saw that *Bullitt* was successful because of that car chase. So what if we had three car chases, what if we had four car chases, what if we had ten car chases? It's not that difficult a concept to master. Most people have a will to power that is imitative, and when they see something that works, their imitative mind says, "Well, we'll do that, but we'll do it three times better, or bigger."

Anyway there was no acknowledgment of any of that in this panel discussion of Easter night, and the word *context* was used merely to define the context of the cultural product, without reference to the moment in which the product was designed to have its impact. I'll repeat that, because I think that sums up all my objections to this program. *Context, on this panel discussion, was used to define the context of the cultural product without reference to the moment in which the product was designed to have its impact.* And the reason that I phrased it that way—"the moment in which the product was designed to have its impact"—the usefulness of my approach to this stuff, has two sides, *because you can work back to a rediscovery of the moment* by looking at the cultural product. Once you understand that the car chase in *Bul-*

litt or the violence level in *The French Connection,* the Billy Friedkin film, really was definitive for its moment—in other words, over the line, over the border, for its moment—then you can begin to rediscover the moment. You can say, well, this level of hyperactivity was sufficient to surprise in 1968, or whenever *Bullitt* was released. That gives us a clue as to what 1968 is like.

Three. We're back to discussing the television panel. There was no reference to the television mind. The Cold Child grown up. And I put Quentin Tarantino's name in parentheses here, and the morphing of the television mind into a template for use in movies on TV and elsewhere, and I put *Wayne's World* in parentheses. Because we are in a mannerist, or baroque, period in all of this. In other words—and let's go back to the military metaphor—sometimes an activity goes into a completely self-referential mode; in other words, the military simply has grown to love producing a certain kind of weapon, whether that weapon is useful or not useful; the military has simply decided that this line of weapons research has a life of its own, and that this life can't be stopped or altered, and so forth. You move from a realistic period to a mannerist period to a baroque or rococo period. And so, in this story of television culture having a life of its own without out reference to any notion of protection for the audience—like an advanced missile system that, in fact, won't do any job except advance the aesthetic history of the missile system—you get the creation of something way up in the air within this self-referred culture. And just as you can get a self-referred military mind, which begins to think only in terms of what will advance the history of the military mind, without any reference to the defense of the populace, so within television culture you get the creation of the television mind, which has no reference to anything except itself, and then that television mind begins to create products that refer to that mind. The film *Wayne's World* is plainly about this process. There was no reference to any of this in the violence-on-television study.

My fourth note is "The aesthetic of the hyperactive car chase, from *Bullitt* to *Independence Day,* and its effect on brain-path formation." I'm suggesting this as a study for further analysis—by someone else, not me—but hyperactivity is the really deep subject here, and the really appalling and meretricious thing about this $3.3-million panel discussion was its lack of understanding of the fundamental issue as it affects the minds of young children. To talk about a certain kind of violence as scary to children (Does it cause them to have nightmares?) is just the most minor sort of entry into the subject. The big subject is the history of hyperactivity, the speeding up of things, and again, I know enough about the biology of the human brain to know that what I'm saying is valid (though the specifics of it really ought to be traced by someone who understands it more deeply). The young brain is not a preexisting thing; it's a thing in potential. The brainpaths that get formed are formed, in some sense, by the availability of certain stimuli. So that in an ordinary world—that is, a nonmedia world—a child who, by accident, at the age of three, saw an amazing horse race, for instance, in which two of the horses crashed and their riders were thrown and there was blood and guts and horses and speed all over the place—a child of a certain age would fix on it, and the brain pathways of that child, the appropriate ones, would have been energized and to a certain extent called into existence by that event. The seeing of such a thing, the experience of such a thing, would be viscerally with the child forever.

The other day I was talking with a friend who is seven years older than I am, and we were talking about World War II and our different experiences of it. I was born *during* World War II, so I saw nothing to do with the war itself. My first memory—and it has stayed with me all my life—was of this enormous strange quiet following our victory. Something enormous had just happened; I happened not to have witnessed it, but it had happened; people were living in a kind of quiet, suspended, dignified, tense aftermath, very dignified, black-and-white. Not quite a spirit of mourning, but a spirit of dignity and a little wonder. Those were the first qualities I took into myself. And I've had an interest in dignity and wonder all my life because those were the theatrical qualities available on the stage of life when I first looked around as a three-year-old child. Everyone in reaction to something I happened not to have witnessed. My friend, seven years older, *had* witnessed it, and remembers viscerally the incredible feeling of relief, joy, victory, and astonishment—my friend is a woman, and she had spent all the war with the other women of her family; all the men were gone. She spent her childhood with her mother and her grandmother and her aunts and no men, and suddenly the news came that the men were coming home, that the whole thing was over, and my friend carries with her the sense of that moment. Well, as I say, this is how our brain *is*. We are the beneficiaries and the victims of different theatrical moments in life, and, indeed, a child who at the age of three in 1890 witnessed some sort of enormous horse race in which horses dashed at top speed and collided with one another and riders were thrown and blood was spilled and a horse had to be put down with a rifle and all of that—this remarkable event would naturally have energized the child's mind in a certain never-to-be-altered way, and would have validated, made permanent, some potential brain pathways that otherwise might have been stagnant or nonexistent. Well, every child in America has had those crash-and-burn brain pathways energized and activated. This is something that we must all necessarily understand. There is no child born now who has access to television who does not have those hyperactive pathways energized and validated.

FOLDING THE
NEW YORK TIMES

Folding the *New York Times*

I'm going to skip through some pages and some stories in the full-sized newspapers of February 1, 1950 (though not in the *Times* just now, the other ones). I'm going to leave the tabloid of it out because we know so much about the tabloid now, because we have it again, while we've lost a sense of the variety of the folio newspapers we used to have. One of the things my father taught me when I was young that has proved almost useless is how to fold a folio newspaper, a large-format newspaper like the *New York Times,* so that it could be read in close quarters on the subway in New York. It was assumed that you would read a large-format newspaper, and that you'd be sitting close to your neighbors on the subway, and you had to know how to do it, how to follow the story over from page one to page thirty-two, folding the newspaper while existing in a small, confined space. This skill, which I don't think I have anymore, by the way—I was taught it but I never used it, so I doubt I have it anymore— resembled origami, Japanese paper folding. It really was fairly complicated. My father did it beautifully; he could read content- edly for an hour on the subway, folding and following and moving back and forth. In any case, the variety of what I'm calling the folio newspapers in New York in 1950 has been forgotten, and we have to remember that the television mind hadn't yet formed, and that the newspaper mind was dominant in New York City, and of course New York City, as it had been for some time, was the dominant city in the country as to culture, especially as to mass culture, certainly as to media, and of course as of 1950, the country had assumed a position at the pinnacle.

If you went back to 1920 in New York, as I have said, you found the newspaper business in much healthier shape than it was in 1950. In 1950 the remaining newspapers, the folio newspapers of the day, were the *New York Times,* the *New York Herald Tribune,* the *New York World Telegram and Sun,* the *New York Journal American*—those four. (And I'm pausing to mention a fifth, and that would have been the *Sun,* but as of February 1, 1950, the *Sun,* which was the most old-fashioned newspaper still surviving in New York after the Second World War, had been absorbed into the *World Telegram.* So that as of February 1, 1950, we had four folio newspapers in New York, where just a short few months before we'd had five.) But these four held a position in the culture of the world that they'd never held before. Let's imagine the Boston Latin School, for instance. The Boston Latin School, a public school in Boston, had as its tradition that it educated unprivileged people, young men—and it was for young men only in 1950—on something like a par with the way that privileged young men were educated at boarding schools. A good school, but, in terms of the cultural hierarchy of the world, not as good as Groton, not as good as Exeter, not as good as Eton, not as good as the École Quelquechose de Nantes or any good French school you chose to name, and not as good as the Gymnasium Whoever and Whatever in Germany. Well, in order to understand the position of the newspapers in New York in 1950, in terms of the cultural landscape of the Western world, all you have to do is imagine that the Gymnasium Whatsitsface and the École Quelquechose and Eton and Exeter had all been mysteriously taken off the map. This is what had happened in our Western world. Germany wasn't a factor; no German opinion could be considered, let alone taken seriously; Germany was a defeated nation in disgrace. No German organ of public opinion had wide circulation, or was respected. England was in our thrall. France was in turmoil, resisting our thrall, and if not in our pocket, in our shadow. And the miraculous thing about this discussion of our Western world, which is also to say our world, is that the discussion can stop right there. Russia was an enemy. China, as of 1949, was Communist, and behind what was then being called the "Bamboo Curtain." Japan was, frankly, occupied. There was no world, in the terms I'm using, except for America and her (now moved down five or ten pegs) allies. The world waited for what America would say, and paid attention to whatever America did say. So to return to my metaphor, the newspaper world of 1950, which was the speaking voice of the American media mainstream, was in the position of the Boston Latin School, which had been left standing, and had suddenly become dominant, in a world where, at one time, there had also been a Gymnasium This, and an École de That, and an Eton. So what were these folio newspapers like? The three other ones, apart from the *New York Times*?

The Assumed Dominant Mind

L et's start with the *Journal American,* because it gives us the best idea of how this assumption of the dominant-mind business works in our media life. The issue I'm discussing is always discussed the other way around, from a kind of marketing point of view. In other words, it's discussed in the way that people used to discuss the Packard Automobile. The Packard Automobile is designed to appeal to local bankers: the richest family in town owns a Packard Automobile, whereas the Chevrolet is owned by—and so forth. Marketing talk. And useful, up to a point. The marketing talk about the *Journal American* would be, *designed to appeal primarily to the Irish and also to the Italians,* the Roman Catholics of the city. Well, that's okay, as far as it goes, but how? How is it done? Anyone, after all, would like to be able to appeal to, say, all Irish- and Italian-descended persons in America; that would give you a very powerful marketing position. The question is, how do you do it? Do you just put a pizza pie or a leprechaun on your product and expect it to do the job? No, you can't. These were people who were moving toward a dominant position in the culture. They wanted to be appealed to, and coaxed, and beguiled, and they wanted some piece of information from previous avatars of the dominant culture; that's always what is involved in a certain kind of marketing where information, and even entertainment, is involved. It's a formula. You have to have it; and more than that, you have to embody it. That is, the people who put this thing forward themselves have to be, in a way, the thing they are projecting.

Let me pause here, so we can get a sense of this assumption of the dominant-mind business from our contemporary landscape. Two days ago I saw a contemporary American mainstream artifact called *Real Life* on MTV. It does now what the *Journal American* used to do. On MTV, the assumption of the dominant mind is now the assumption of the dominant mind of rock-and-roll. The people who project this particular cultural artifact, *Real Life,* assume that you, the viewer, are a member of rock-and-roll's civilization, and that certain aspects of that civilization need never be discussed. You've been clued in to them. You *are* them. Then the proprietors of the program take a superior position to that; they know rock-and-roll better, and they know better than you what it has evolved into. The program was interesting, up to a point. There's a kind of information projected about gay people, about African-Americans, about pleasure lovers in Miami, that is new—on televison—and the program takes the point of view that it's giving you, as it says, real life, but of course, it's not giving you real life. It's giving you real life from the point of view of people who embody the assumption that the subtext of American life is rock-and-roll. Absent that assumption, the thing dwindles into meaninglessness, or near meaninglessness, but—it's a powerful assumption.

Now, just for the sake of something like social truth, and to give you a sense of what life would have been like for someone working at the *Journal American* in 1950, let's think for a moment about a person, let's assume that it's a woman, who works for MTV, who is helping to contrive this artifact, *Real Life.* She herself is, must be, a citizen of the civilization of rock-and-roll. If she's not, she won't get it right. She has to know what her audience knows about rock-and-roll, and then two or three things more, and make educated guesses, in the realm of extrapolation, about where all of that, herself plus her audience, can move to. That's who she has to be, to be successful. Who is she as a person? Now, that's not quite anybody's guess; she's got the rock-

and-roll of it, all right, but she belongs to a tribe of people who move quite liquidly through the culture. It might be, for instance, that she's sick of the rock-and-roll of it, it just happens to be where she's placed her cultural investment, and her cultural investment can pay off at MTV and not elsewhere. And as she walks down the street to her job at MTV, to produce yet another episode of *Real Life,* she must wonder about *her* real life. She must wonder, for instance, if she wouldn't rather work for, say, *Vogue.* Part of her does want to work for *Vogue. Vogue* has some mystery for her in a way that the rock-and-roll world no longer has. Perhaps she's feeling almost burned out, or sick of working with kids, or any number of things. And I've met a woman, working for MTV, who was in something like this situation. She was up here in Columbia County, and living in a house, and in a certain way she thought MTV was done, and she was sick of it. Was she wondering if she could get a job with the alumni magazine of her university, for instance, bringing to it a little of the rock-and-roll that she'd come to know, for greater audience penetration, while giving *herself* a bit more quiet in a university town? All of this sort of thing is part of what we're talking about when we talk about the contrivance of the assumption of the dominant mind.

So what were the ingredients of the assumed dominant mind at work at the *Journal American* in 1950? Well, there was a little bit of what we'll call real social authority, and it came in two parts: Broadway-Hollywood and Cafe Society. The *Journal American,* in part because of its link through ownership to William Randolph Hearst, who was one of the gaudiest creatures of this century, reported something like the real deal in those two departments. It wasn't going to offend Mr. Hearst to give you the real deal about how it was at El Morocco; that was a world he wasn't intimidated by. And it wasn't going to offend him to give the readers of the *Journal American* something like the real deal about what was going on in Broadway and in Hollywood. Mr. Hearst had been in long association with motion pictures, and with the actress Marion Davies, and expected to see something like the real deal from that world reported in his papers. He got it from, among others, Dorothy Kilgallen, a woman whose career needs to be studied in depth by the C-SPAN $3.3-million media people, for instance, if they want to know how popular culture really worked and works. Hearst for years got his society stuff from an old-timer named Maury Paul, who was a real character; as of 1950 he got his society stuff from Igor Cassini, an Italian with a mild fascist background who coined the term *jet set* and who trained Liz Smith. (Liz Smith operates in one of the few traditions that have survived from 1950.) The Cassini column was called "Cholly Knickerbocker," and the "Cholly" was an amusing, Preston Sturges–like play on the way upper-class people pronounced "Charlie." There was a little of that in the *Journal American*, a little Preston Sturges. So, Broadway-Hollywood and society.

A third ingredient was embodied by something called the Hearst Headline Service. The Hearst Headline Service wasn't anything at all; it was just a name put on something. The Hearsts also ran the most negligible of all the news-gathering services, the International News Service, which folded, I think, in the 1960s. The Hearsts had to have one of everything, and they didn't mind making up nameplates for what they needed, and so there was something called the Hearst Headline Service, and it gave you the sense that the Hearst ownership had a kind of worldview and a kind of world access, and that, too, had a kind of back-and-forth authority from William Randolph Hearst and his gaudy life. On the one hand, the Hearst Headline Service continued to nourish Mr. Hearst's sense of himself as a world figure (he was still alive in 1950). On the other hand, the paper derived a certain authority from the fact that Mr. Hearst had been a world figure, and this is, of course, an incestuous relationship that all newspaper proprietors seek to manifest, though none did it so well as Mr. Hearst. In any case, the Hearst Headline Service gave you special access. In later days, the younger Bill Hearst would make global fact-finding missions, but he wasn't quite what his old man was, and so he usually had to take along Bob

Considine—usually it was Bob Considine, a real high-level hack who knew the popular energy of it. Considine (who had a column called "On the Line with Bob Considine") gave the readers a sense that "Now the Hearst task force is landing in Moscow, and we're going to talk to this one, and now we're on to—anywhere you like." That was the atmosphere of what I'm describing. The specifics of it were a lot of positive coverage of the pope. There was a sense that the Hearsts knew the pope, and the pope knew the Hearsts, and you, Irish-American and Italian-American Reader, could be sure that, in a way, the pope knew you, because he knew the Hearsts, and—it was like that. The fourth element was the best comics section in New York. "Puck, the Comic Weekly" came out on Sunday, and King Features, the Hearst syndicate, just drenched the newspaper in comics, and it was the best comics section in New York. Between the Mr. Hearst aspect and the "Puck, the Comic Weekly" King Feature aspect, and also the Cholly Knickerbocker aspect and also the Broadway of it— Dorothy Kilgallen—you had a sense of a Vanity Fair for *you*. With Mr. Hearst you had a kind of bus-and-truck Winston Churchill, the Winston Churchill who didn't keep much to ancient, honorable rituals but who partied with you, and that's always been a very attractive energy to have behind you if you want to deal with the public; and that was the *Journal American.*

◆　◆　◆

The *Herald Tribune* was Heartbreak House. It was losing readership and losing authority, and for no particular reason. I say that in a challenging way, because someone who knows the newspaper business will point out a dozen reasons. That it didn't report the news as fully as the *Times* did is the obvious one, but my personal experience is, my anecdotal experience is, that people who switched from the *Herald Tribune* to the *Times* in the 1950s did it for zeitgeist reasons; they did it to escape Heartbreak House. That is, I don't know what the figures are now for how much general news the average reader of the *New York Times* actually reads; the *New York Times* would have to tell me. Is twenty paragraphs a good guess? I have no idea. But I don't think the figure was more than forty paragraphs in 1950. In other words, the average reader of the *Herald Tribune* read forty paragraphs of general news. When he or she switched to the *New York Times*, he or she still read forty paragraphs of general news. The heaping feast of information in the *New York Times* was picked at, not read completely; the move was made because one wanted to associate oneself with the secular, scientific, factual approach of the *Times*. One wanted, if one was a WASP—and my reader will forgive me if a lot of the information in this book is from a WASP point of view; it happens to be the point of view I know best, and it was the dominant point of view at the time. If you were a WASP in 1950, you wanted to move away from your heritage a little bit, and associate yourself with the secular, scientific, factual version of the dominant mind. The other, the older WASP mind, associated with the Anglican Church, for instance, and Groton School, for instance, was a little painful to stay too close to. The *Herald Tribune* still reported the news a little in the spirit of one who'd seen you at St. James Church on Sunday, someone who was professionally suspicious of Mammon, and professionally reluctant to give you sensational information of any kind, lest it damage your soul. The fact is that, because of the A-bomb and the H-bomb, WASPs had to move away from that position if they wanted to participate in the modern world, from a power position. The mere existence of the A-bomb and the H-bomb seemed, on the one hand, to validate the American ruling group as the appropriate ruling group for the world; on the other hand, it undercut the agricultural assumptions of the old WASP ruling group. (This is why, finally and ultimately, the Book of Common Prayer was changed. Not because there were any startling revelations in the new translation, but because some move away from the old agricultural assumptions had to be taken in order that the people who were involved in the ritual not feel completely left out of a world that had experienced the negative epiphany of nuclear weapons.)

I read the *Herald Tribune* in 1950; my father saw to it that I did, and what is more, it appealed to me. It was continuous with what my father was saying WASP civilization was. As I say, there was a daily nature column, which discussed Old Mother West Wind and so forth. I seem to be making fun of it. I don't mean to. It was a very gentle, attractive daily column in which animals talked in a nineteenth-century way, and it was read to me by my father until I could read, and then I read it myself. Also, as I have said, the demolition of the Murray Hill Hotel was a story better read in the *Herald Tribune* than in the *Times*. My grandmother, my father's mother, was a devotee of someone called Clementine Paddleford, who wrote the food column for the *Herald Tribune;* it was my grandmother's firm opinion that the only person writing for the public who could give you a really good recipe was Clementine Paddleford, and all through my childhood I ate spaghetti sauce made by my grandmother from Clementine Paddleford's recipe. We were, it is safe to say, in our souls a *Herald Tribune* family. Indeed, my father's hero in journalism was a man named Stanley Walker, who had been the managing editor of the *Herald Tribune* during the thirties. But it was over, or about to be over.

The other large-format paper was the one I didn't like. And when I was in my first childhood, it was the paper my father worked for. It was the *World Telegram;* after 1950 the *World Telegram and Sun.* My father left, because there was a deadness around that newspaper. It *was* dead. It was the real deal, as to what WASPs—except for the really committed ones—were coming to. It was the paper really read by a certain kind of person working in the advertising business, or working on Wall Street. They bought the *Times* in the morning, but they didn't read much of it. They read the *World Telegram* pretty thoroughly. It was for them. There was no fine and pretty stuff from old-time WASP-dom, and there wasn't the endless factuality and relative high-mindedness of the *Times*. It was what you needed to know to be an effective WASP. It was for WASPs who understood that their education and their background were dominance weapons.

So these three large-format papers, together with the *Times,* represented four different versions of an assumed dominant mind. Now, I'm going to give you a list of groups for whom an assumed dominant mind meant trouble. Some trouble in 1950; much more later on. Number one: committed, visceral liberal arts people—and I don't mean just WASPs here. I mean Jews especially; people for whom books and book learning constituted not just a diversion, or a dominance reference, but a kind of prophetic factor in life. People for whom Thomas Hardy, on the one hand, or James Joyce, on the other, or both, if you were really smart and could make the connection, people for whom the best of the best had real meaning, people for whom the best of the best constituted a kind of evolving bible of our American life. Well, the existence of an assumed dominant mind, with its flatness— even at the *New York Times*—meant trouble; it meant creeping catatonia, creeping illiteracy, which, of course, has come to pass, so I'm not saying these people were wrong, not in any way at all.

Two: many African-Americans. There were many African-Americans in 1950 who possessed culture, and were ready to move through the membrane that had kept them from interacting with the rest of American culture. When people talked about the color line in 1950, they were talking about something real. After all, the people who were talking about it were, by definition, talkers, and probably writers. African-Americans who were talkers and writers in 1950 correctly sensed that the only thing that was keeping them out of full participation in American cultural life was their color. They'd already laid down, well, the blues, for instance, lots of musical avatars, and the Harlem Renaissance. The assumption of a dominant mind in the media—in the newspapers, and then on television—meant big trouble for these people. The odd fact is, that there were many people in the committed liberal arts sector—white people I'm talking about now— who were not just ready to have the membrane pierced as to African-American cultural participation, but who were working for it. But they were not in a power position. The assumed dominant mind was in a power position, and there, African-Americans of the kind I am discussing had no weight, no standing.

We can digress for a brief moment to discuss the Black Power phenomenon. The idea there was that no matter what a black person did, he or she could never pierce the membrane, could never get a fair hearing from white society. That wasn't valid as to the relationship, or possible or evolving relationship, between committed, cultured African-Americans and committed, cultured white people, but that was the relationship between committed, cultured black people and the assumed dominant mind template, which was, in fact, in charge. "How shall we get in the newspapers?" came to be question number one for everyone, and that question came to be question number one for African-Americans.

Three: patrician descendants of the tradition of Washington. There aren't supposed to be patrician people in this country, but there have been, and some of them have been damn useful. General George Patton and General George Marshall were two men who had proved their usefulness to this country, as of 1950. Their descendants were going to find that nothing, *nada*, and *rien* were their portion of the dominant-mind-assumption game. Not in the mix, not in the formula.

Four: nonpatrician descendants of the tradition of Washington. I'm thinking just this moment of a breakfast I had in West Virginia about three years ago. There was a West Virginia man— and I could tell by his face that his family had been here for three hundred years, and that his lineage was spread with the war dead—and there had been a surprise snowstorm (it was already mid-spring), and the man I'm speaking of was ecstatic, no other word can be used, because on account of that snowstorm he'd earned seventy-five dollars plowing people's driveways. He had it in his pocket, and he showed it to me. This is the man, whatever his sins, who is deeply cultured, in American terms. He belongs to Washington. He lives in his own traditional freedom until such moment as he is told to fight for his country, and then he does, and often he dies. That's the deal he's made with the country. This man give no reverence to any assumed dominant mind. As far as he's concerned, there's only one dominant mind in America, the one that belongs to him and Washington. Should our system of assumed dominant mind after assumed dominant mind, right on down to *Real Life,* which is itself based on the assumed dominance of rock-and-roll and Buddy Holly down to the Butthole Surfers—should this system of assumed dominant minds, run by people who are probably sick of the dominant mind they're assuming, should this system run into trouble, *we're* in trouble, on account of this West Virginia man.

Intermezzo: Following a Story

If you know how a newspaper is edited, you can read it quite quickly. The better the newspaper, the faster you can read it, because you can trust the consistent mind of the editors.

I can read the daily *Times* in seven minutes, usually.

When there is a story—or, rarely, stories—to *read*, it can take an hour. But you can *follow* a story in practically no time at all.

Naturally, I am not talking about human interest here, or sports or the stock listings. I *am*, however, including business news.

There isn't much real news, you know.

Most news is in relation to what a government (or a unit of government) is willing to let you know about what it is saying or doing in relation to another government or unit of government. You could spend your whole life reading about the Middle East. You don't want to do that. If there is a car bombing in Tel Aviv, you may want to read it for reasons of your own. What you must do is see what Arafat says *the next day*. You have to get to know the *reporter*. What does the reporter think is going to happen? The clue is in his style, in his selection of quotes. Does he quote the mainstream Professor who thinks that the Peace Process will stay on track anyway? Or does he take you into a violent neighborhood and show you a picture of hopelessness there? I dislike all talk about "bias" and "lack of objectivity" in a reporter. He is there to clue you in to his best assessment; his reading of the *code* of events. He has no way to be objective (other than not to have a personal stake in the argument); he doesn't know the real facts; or if he does, it's so rare as not to be worth the mentioning. He can't read Arafat's mind, or Assad's, or anybody's. In a way, what you value *most* about him or her is his or her *appropriate subjectivity;* his or her feel for events.

I read every word in the paper about Algeria, Ukraine, and Belarus; these are the Underreported Zones. You should get a feel in the paper for what is underreported and what is over-reported. Overreported is Newt Gingrich. One-tenth of one percent of what has been written about Newt will do you just fine. About Algeria, Ukraine, Belarus, you need to read every word; also Shanghai, Chinese billionaires, and the Russian Mafia. Also currency trading. Stories are *boiling* (or seem to be boiling) here. If you have a personal reason to take an interest in a Baby Bell reaching out to form yet another media conglomerate, sure, read it; but be aware that the deal will ravel, unravel, happen, not happen, be consummated or not consummated, be important or not important, and you will have read ten thousand words. Also notice that the news is written in such a way that all these "dramatic" ravelings and unravelings are reported in detail (because they have human interest), but should the thing finally come together, the news will *stop.* Just when you want to know what's going to happen (the president has won the election; what's he going to do?) the news stops.

I never invest myself in a news story. In that I will be different from you. I read nothing about the Equal Rights Amendment during the time it was in the news, for instance. Either it was going to get to be an amendment or it wasn't. There are a *lot* of stories like that. Years in the making; infinite detail; you have no say as to the outcome; it will happen or it won't.

The role of *women in society;* that's another matter. That story I follow. The ERA is just one—was just one—part of that. Asian business; women in society; former Soviet Union; Algeria. These are the four big stories I am following now.

Do yourself a favor. Just wait to see if Al Gore is nominated. Wake up the day after the next Democratic Convention and ask a friend, "Did Gore make it?" My guess is that he will have made it.

Take the fifty-thousand-word investment you were prepared to make on Gore's election prospects and follow another story—Zaire, *par exemple.*

If all you do when you read a newspaper is follow the human interest (the plane crash, the lifestyle, the sports, the celebrity gossip), then you've never really read a newspaper.

Television will not *allow* you to follow a story. Each broadcast is self-contained; television newspeople are embarrassed if they have to remind you that the story existed yesterday as well. They value and love the episodic possibilities within the news. The only exception is Big Human Interest. If it has the quality of a soap opera—O. J. Simpson, or the plane that exploded mysteriously—then they trust it as a story that will have had the dramatic elements necessary for their formula. (That is, they know the story will not let them down. O. J. Simpson will be a celebrity the whole time of his trial; he will be pronounced guilty, and that will be dramatic; or he will be pronounced innocent, and that will be even more dramatic. In other words, from their television-news point of view, the story has *already happened;* it's reliable. It can be trusted not to let *them* down. Television *hates* stories that turn out to be—you know, *disappointing.* No cum shot.)

Take Belarus. This guy who runs Belarus *may* turn out to be our next Big Time Bad Guy. We don't know *now* that he will be; and until he does—who cares, in a way? There are no rules in journalism; no American Medical Association to revoke your license; no Rules of Engagement. If the Belarus guy *does* turn out to be what we will call a *real factor,* we just do an In-Depth Segment, and fast. Dan flies to Minsk and does an interview, and CBS's ass is covered retroactively.

The best example of what I'm talking about as to following a story was the *Times*'s coverage of the Kabila phenomenon in Zaire. I read every word, and for a while it made me proud to

have been a journalist. You could see the reporter struggling with
it. At first it was confusing—to the reporter; you could tell. The
first three stories I read two or three times. We had Rebels, and
we had Refugees. The relationship wasn't clear; it wasn't clear in
the reporter's *style* just who was who—even if, perhaps, it was
clear in his mind.

However, the more the reporter came to understand the *subtext* and *history,* the more the *text* of the story became legible to
him, and to the reader; and the more *elaborate* the story became,
the *simpler* it was to read. One day there was a cum shot: *he*
understood the story; the story made its way into Katanga, and
back to Patrice Lumumba and *into* the question of Zaire's mineral
wealth, and South Africa's role, and so forth. With the reporter's
full participation, the story achieved critical mass. It made this
reader happy.

There Are Four Kinds of Newspapers

And that's all there are.

1. Let's take the tabloid first. In "Following a Story" I have indicated that it is a national disgrace that Americans have not been fully informed over the last dozen of years about the true state of affairs within the former Soviet Union; within Russia of course, Ukraine, and especially now, perhaps Belarus. Journalists are marvelously simple creatures, and the "scoop" has left Russia, and all that is left is ordinary work: you know, inventory, facts, and that hardest job of all, interesting the reader and getting him to follow the story. In the Bad Old Days, Russia wouldn't let us in, and that was a big part of every story reported out of Russia—how journalism in the Soviet Union was under the thumb of the state, and how foreign journalists were spied on, and so forth. Well, it's different now, and we get less, not more.

Yesterday, on the radio, I heard a Story Out Of Russia. A young man is going to drive from Moscow, I think it was, to Vladivostok in his Yugo automobile. *In first gear.* That was the hook. He's a flagpole sitter, this young man with the Yugo automobile, a marathon dancer, a jazz baby in the making (the only information we get about Russia in the movies is on the Al Capone model— guess what, they have Godfathers over there now); and if you'll just think about that man in the Yugo you'll understand all you need to understand about the tabloid model, which owns the aesthetic of the World As We Know It today. The tabloid sensibility knows only one job: to make the world safe for the moment in which it had its hit—the 1920s, the age of Broadway Brevities, the gangster, the flagpole sitter—and now, a Yugo racing across the tundra in first gear.

2. Information for and by the Dominant Mind in a limited sphere. The *Racing Form* is the best newspaper in America, in a way. The part of the public that follows horse racing knows a lot about horse racing, and the people at the *Racing Form* know more. In other words, everything is just as it should be in the impresario-audience department. Readers of the *New York Times* are now a little vague about Winston Churchill—who he was and do we still like him or not—but the readers of the *Racing Form* are *not* vague about Churchill Downs, where the Kentucky Derby is run. Events on the world stage as of 1943 are no longer before us in clarity, but readers of the *Racing Form,* many of them, will recall that Count Fleet won the Triple Crown in that year. Standards have been marvelously set. A mudder is a mudder, and falling back (or making your play) in the stretch has an uncontestably decisive effect on what your reaction is going to be. Everyone knows that the Belmont is the Test For Distance, and that's what's wonderful about the Triple Crown—the distance test has been passed too.

Well, the *Wall Street Journal,* the nation's second-best newspaper, would like you to believe that it is the *Racing Form* for business and finance, and it used to be, but it isn't anymore. They missed a big beat: the game changed; Churchill Downs got dismantled; the mudders began to win on dry tracks, and so forth, and the *Journal* never told us the reason why—or even very much about *how.* Moreover, they continue to run those annoying stories about Mr. and Mrs. Anytown U.S.A. and their reactions to world events (with the idea that marketing executives will find this information enthralling), but Mr. and Mrs. Anytown are back-formed from the aesthetic of the paper; they never rock-and-rolled, they never did drugs or anything, and marketing people skip those stories now. The *Journal* got caught in the Hard Place journalism *does* get caught in. Its job was to honorably gadfly a certain animal. That animal got put on the Endangered Species List. As its gadfly, the *Journal* felt no responsibility to the animal. Gadflies *don't* feel a sense of responsibility; it's part of their integrity that they don't. *On the other hand,* the new species that has taken over the range doesn't respect the *Journal* as *its* gadfly. Enter Bloomberg.

The *Washington Post* is a paper for a company town. People complain that the *Post* is too much like the *Racing Form.* They shouldn't. What they *should* complain about is that the paper of the moment of the mid-seventies had twenty years to make of itself our national newspaper—and didn't do it. Most "good" newspapers—the *Boston Globe,* the *Los Angeles Times,* the *Miami Herald,* et al.—fall into the *Post* category, except that they never will have a chance to be our national newspaper.

3. The *New York Times.* Our National Treasure. Our Marilyn. Our Elvis. In other words: *What We Have.* People who complain *murderously* about the *Times* ought to be shot. We all ought to pray for the continued financial well-being of the Sulzbergers.

4. Papers of the Assumed Dominant Mind. This category has been discussed as it was in New York in 1950, when the job of owning the Assumed Dominant Mind fell to newspaper people. Now, of course, the Assumed Dominant Mind belongs to television and other visual people. The computer people want you to accept the Internet as the new model, or paradigm, but don't count on it. *USA Today* is back-formed from the Assumed Dominant Mind of television.

The Worst of the Worst

The world has been spoiled by wannabes; and the worst of the worst are wannabe writers and thinkers who end up as journalists and won't let go of their typewriters.

This strident sentence is a parody of the Worst of the Worst: Westbrook Pegler as he was in 1950. The Assumed Dominant Game is a dirty game; but, hey—there are lots of dirty games: the English monarchy has been a dirty game for the Irish, and the English language is a dirty game played on those who think it is a language only and not a dominance ritual also. Money has been invented as our new international language just to get away from the dirtiness of the dominance ritual part of language and culture, and when the money game goes down, some Brit will be there to say, "I told you so."

I find that I am surprisingly good as Westbrook Pegler. I will try to keep myself in check.

Short punchy paragraphs are part of the style.

In a boring textbook you have to read many sentences to give yourself the pat on the back that goes with having read a whole paragraph, you ignorant son of a bitch who never read a good book in your life.

But not here.

The dirty part is in this (end of Westbrook parody, by the way): Pegler won't let go of his sparkle and glitter within the Assumed Dominance Structure; he keeps it by making you feel like shit for allowing yourself to be conned by the structure he is energizing. His real place (he lets you know) is within another structure; he *condescends* to appear next to a photograph of a rapist so that you should know that there is something *better*.

Segue to a more serious discussion. A newspaper fails to tell you about real events in Ukraine or Belarus because the writers and editors are not good enough (or brave enough) at what they do to create a story you will be willing to follow. So they dumb it down.

When they dumb it down (oh dear, I feel Pegler coming back to me; he is a persistent presence; just ask Rush Limbaugh), they feel a little contempt for themselves—which they transform, by a magic process known only to themselves, into contempt for *you*.

A Photograph of 1956

M y God she's pretty. THE GIRL of 1956. Here she is. Gauzy
dress—just like a *little* girl; but *she's* not little. She's THE
GIRL.

There were a number of them in 1956. Most of them based on
Dorian Leigh, Suzy Parker's older sister. Suzy was the Christy
Turlington, but for people who valued the Template, the Standard, Dorian had something Suzy didn't have. I saw Dorian Leigh
in the 1970s. I was with Diana Vreeland. I asked Mrs. Vreeland
about Dorian Leigh. "The most tragic story ever told," Mrs. Vreeland said. "She was *perfect* except for one slight *exaggeration*
about the nose. She wanted to change her nose so she could be
really perfect. I begged her not to change it. There is nothing
more boring than *total* perfection. She changed it anyway, against
my advice, and *no one ever used her again.*" (In private conversation, especially, Mrs. Vreeland was likely to exaggerate. I'm sure
people used Dorian Leigh again, but Ms. Leigh did look a little
glum as she sat across from us at that table; as though she knew
she had made a *mistake.*)

Back to the photograph. By 1956, out of all the Cultural
Avatars and Vectors available in 1950, THE GIRL had won.
Authority. (And they had it, those girls; no one today has it.)
They'd won the war, in a way.

It worked for everyone. No endless trouble choosing among

Conflicting and Conflicted Male Avatars; just go with THE GIRL.

Except that it didn't work for young men of my generation; and it didn't really work for the young women of my generation, either. She was *too* perfect. *Too* much authority—and where was the sex, anyway? Did she *fuck*, that girl? And if she did, was it only Cary Grant? *That* level of money and sophistication? And wasn't Cary Grant an *old* guy? We went *On the Road;* we picked up *Howl.* And just think of those sixties girls, the ones in granny glasses and feathers and so on—just the *relief* of being a sexual female *without having to understand how to wear that goddamned gauzy dress.*

Anyway, the Gauzy Girl is standing next to a *piano* in the photograph I am looking at. It's a Wurlitzer piano. The photograph is embedded in a promotional booklet celebrating one hundred years of Wurlitzer production. (German man comes from Saxony to Cincinnati; makes quality musical instruments; reference to Classical Music; company grows and grows; Wurlitzer Organ in movie palaces to go with silent films; organs for the home—"Gee, Dad, it's a *Wurlitzer.*" Sideline in mechanical music: music boxes, carnival musical production, the *jukebox.*) Wurlitzer a little shamed to find that quality musical instrument production—reference to the Education of the Masses—is being *overwhelmed* by *demand for jukeboxes.* In 1956, pride of place in Wurlitzer promotional booklet is held by THE GIRL standing next to a Dignified Piano for the Home; real story is next page: new jukebox, 1956. Enter Elvis.

The current, on-the-face-of-this-planet Rudy Wurlitzer is a good friend of mine. I had this promotional booklet in my files. I gave it to him. (Okay, it's a *color Xerox* of the photograph in the booklet I've been working from here.) He looked through it. Pictures of the big Wurlitzer plant in North Tonawanda, New York; pictures of a fleet of trucks with 1956 guys standing next to them, etc., etc.

"My father took me to tour that plant," Rudy said. "They had a girl—you remember Miss Rheingold? This was Miss Wurlitzer. A local girl; a *real* local girl. We went drinking in some place she knew in her neighborhood. We got sloshed. She was real glad to be with me, and I was *real* glad to be with *her.*"

Anything to get away from THE GIRL IN THE PHOTO-GRAPH.

My Best Friend's Wedding

Well, it's a good movie, an amusing movie, and not *completely* surprising. I mean, there is no evidence of Bob Dylan in it, and God knows there's no Winston Churchill, but it's not *completely* surprising. People who are interested in *conspiracy* and *slanting* and *bias* in our media industries should understand that the script is hidden in obvious places. These industries have a history. Just as there are certain Classic Cars (everyone wishes he had been in on the design of the Cord), so, too, are there Classic Films. *Bringing Up Baby,* for instance; *Singin' in the Rain,* for instance; *The Philadelphia Story,* for instance. You'd be surprised to learn how many studio executives who've just given the okay for *Lethal Weapon XII* are going home to watch *Bringing Up Baby.* The *bias* is in this: just as a Tabloid Sensibility Journalist prays that some Russian guy will drive from Moscow to Vladivostok in a Yugo *in first gear,* so, too, do certain people in the movie business pray for the return of the *To Catch a Thief* audience; or maybe even the *Singin' in the Rain* audience. The demography tremors with certain needs; most are not met. However, whenever the demography half-tremors with a need that has been *met before* (by Rock Hudson and Doris Day, for instance), that need is met way more than halfway. You want to go outside and play in the mud; Mama seems not to notice. You have a Deep Emotional Problem; Mama seems not to notice. You drift toward the piano.

Mama is alert. "Want to practice?" The curtains are drawn. The room is hushed. It's *like that.*

My Best Friend's Wedding shows how *subtle* the movement within a Delivery Template can be. We are still within the age of the Liberated Woman; Julia Roberts is the star. The neo-1950s girl is a little *corny.* Audience identification is, in *theory,* with Julia. But Julia is *learning* in this one. She's Joan Crawford, in a way. Career isn't everything. (The message is slightly fudged. Julia gets to have a Gay Friend; and the focus stays with her at the end; but *next time* she could lose focus at the end; she and her gay friend could be *marginalized;* we could see the neo-fifties girl grind her into well-earned dust.)

Audience surveys show: many of us are ready for a More Organized Moment. We want our 1950s.

Well, we can't have them.

I Mean *Folding* It

Here's how *I'd* do it.

Reconfigure around the *Times*-owned *Boston* *Globe.* (Boston—so attractive, Boston; those *demographics;* those *universities.*)

I'd take it as job one to kill the *Providence Journal* and the *Hartford Courant.*

The current suburban editions (I assume the *Globe* has them) would be subsumed into a new Regional Paper (lots of money spent on flawless delivery).

A new *fringe* edition is produced to penetrate to Fairfield County in Connecticut and Westchester in New York. (No attempt to circulate on Long Island or in New Jersey. Hey, you have to let *something* go.)

The *Globe* is guaranteed to inherit the *Times's* famous national and international coverage; although, golly, no one would expect *all* of it anymore.

That leaves the Big New Twenty-first Century Printing Plant the *Times* has built. *Lucent* it. Spin it off as TIMESINKCORP, with a special relationship to our *Megapolitan Globe.*

Guess what. TIMESINKCORP could print the Arts and Leisure Section, Book Review, etc., for the *Globe's* fringe edition.

Keep the *Times* logo for the large print edition, now culled from our new *Globe.*

THE 1950S

February 1, 1950;
or, Four Avatars of Kingship

M y methodology in writing this section of the book was to look at the *theater* of the front page of the *New York Times* from February 1, 1950 (considering also the rest of the paper that day, and more lightly, the rest of the paper that month). As I say, my focus will be on the theater of the front page, the theater that represented (and also calibrated) the most powerful mind in the Western world. Well, of course, the most powerful mind in the Western world at the time I'm talking about was the mind of Einstein—or someone else like Einstein—but Einstein didn't give us his read on the news every day. He didn't give us his sense of proportion; he didn't display his competency to discuss everything, from sports to the stock market to world politics. My preoccupation, as my reader may know by now, is with the Mainstream, because only the Mainstream flows on. Was there a man far more brilliant than Einstein, alive in 1950, who was thinking thoughts far more useful to us than any we have knowledge of? Possibly—*probably*— but if we don't know who he is, God alone cares about what he said. Einstein himself is a major/minor player in what we're talking about, just as Henry Ford is a major/minor player in the history of our automotive age. Spark something up and your name is remembered; it doesn't mean that you know about everything that flowed from what you started. The starter-upper can tell us what his assumptions were when he did the starting, and he can give us his emotional reaction to the results. Einstein, by the way, did that. The Einstein phenomenon isn't utterly out of keeping with what we call the Nobel phenomenon, which actually relates also to the Ford phenomenon; in other words, certain people—Alfred Nobel, Henry Ford, Albert Einstein—lit a fuse, started a vector. I mean, Nobel literally lit a fuse—he invented dynamite. And then, at another moment, there's some rumination, some reconsideration. I can remember in my time in New York that the Ford Foundation was absolutely dominant in terms of interesting ways to spend money, inventing the new world, nourishing the good, the unlikely, and the beautiful. They had—and have—one of the prettiest buildings in New York. They were at the cutting edge of everything. I always wondered if there wasn't something schizophrenic about that. Here we all were, living under the cloud of the automobile industry, and yet the Ford Foundation was always looking for almost the arcane, in terms of what to do about our social life. It seemed to me rather interesting that the Ford name was comprised of 99.9 percent automobile, and you couldn't escape the market vectors of the automobile, no matter what you did, and then the other one-tenth of one percent, which involved what was quite a lot of money, was looking into every interesting social and liberal arts corner for solutions to our modern social life.

Well, Nobel did that too, with his famous prizes. The Nobel Prizes have had a one-tenth-of-one-percent effect on the history of our technology society; dynamite, as you know, continues to be a hit. So it was with Einstein. The *New York Times,* on the other hand, did come out every day, did display a competency over every subject of interest to us, from sports to the stock market to the ruling of the world, which was really what New York City was all about in those days. Critics since 1950—not during 1950, so far as I know, except in perhaps very obscure corners, or Communist corners—critics *since* 1950, with increasingly loud voices, up to this day, complain of the power of the *New York Times.* "The *New York Times* represents the establishment." "The State Department calls the *New York Times* and suggests that they do this or they do that." "The people at the *New York Times* are much too much in touch with the government." Well, all of this may be true, but the *New York Times* now is about ten percent as representative of the ruling mind of America as it was in 1950, and of course, the ruling mind of America has split up now, into a hundred pieces, and even if you put those hundred pieces together you wouldn't have what you had then. So, when we look at the theater of the front page of the *New York Times*, we're looking at an important piece of theater, and there are two qualities to this theater. One, it is oblique. It uses a newspaper template of reportage; the newspaper template of reportage *is* oblique. It isn't written in the same style as a CIA memo; it doesn't say, "Here are the facts. This man Mossadegh is dangerous and we're going to have to go in and get him"; there usually isn't much inside information, at least not obviously. It's—well, to get a sense of what obliqueness is, in the terms I'm using, you could imagine your own personal life put into a *New York Times* template: the announcement of your domestic problems, the paying off of your mortgage, whatever it is, if it were put into a *New York Times* template, it would be oblique. There would be a formality, a system of arrangement that would give the information of your personal life but not give, perhaps, the visceral quality you know your life has. That is what a newspaper template of the *New York Times* type does; it drains out the visceral. It appeals to your mental configuration.

Now, having said that, I want to say that there's a quality about the theater of the *New York Times* in 1950 that's as clear as water. That is, for some people, for many people, that oblique template of the *New York Times* was a visceral template, in a way. The men, and some women, who did the work at the *Times* had the same mind-set, let us call it, as the people they were reporting on, and when they didn't have exactly the same mind-set (and, perhaps, the men and women at the *New York Times* didn't have exactly the same mind-set as Harry Truman, for instance), they knew enough about the mind-set of the man or woman they were writing about to bring the mind-set of that person into relation to *their* mind-set, and their readers'. Life was hierarchical in those days. People knew who Truman was. They knew what Missouri was. They knew what Truman's background was, and what Truman's background represented, and Truman knew, too, whom he was dealing with—he'd dealt with Roosevelt, after all, and lots of others, and so he knew whom he was dealing with when he dealt with the *New York Times*. Now, the title of this chapter is "Four Avatars of Kingship," for a subtitle I might have added, "Why We Must Forgive What Happened." I'm going to present my theory about the dysfunction of American cultural life in the past almost fifty years, and I'm going to ask you if you don't agree that the four avatars of kingship at work within the theater of the front page of the *New York Times* of February 1, 1950, were almost impossible to reconcile, almost impossible to bring together. If we weren't, in fact, in a kind of double War of the Roses. Four Roses, to use the name of that nice old blended whisky. We had four Roses fighting, and I think you will see why the Rose that won, won.

So, the headlines from the *Times,* the front page of February 1, 1950. We'll just concentrate on the theater, on the effect of the juxtaposition; but before I read the first headline, which has to do with Winston Churchill, I think we'd better have a little about language theory, because you can only discuss Winston Churchill within the context of the history of English-language dominance rituals, and we'll drop the dominance-ritual part from subsequent mentions in this discussion and just talk about the English language. But, every language has a secret moral history, and within that moral history there are dominance questions: who gets to say what when, and how they speak, and how it is received. We won't say much about this, but, in relation to this particular avatar of kingship in the *New York Times* of February 1, 1950, we need to say something.

Winston Churchill was all about his tone of voice. There— I'll leave that there, as a dictum, which, in the parlance of the checking department of *The New Yorker* magazine where I used to work, well, it's something we'll just put on the author, it's not checkable, you can't check it out. It's just on me that Winston Churchill was all about tone of voice. So, here's a little about language and dominance and morals, within the history of the English language. In the history of the English language, in terms of morals, there's a baseline culture. It's a decent yeoman doing his best on a small piece of ground in Yorkshire, say. Oh, going to church, and maybe opening the Bible once in a while, but you have to understand that in societies where religion is established, people don't spend so damn much time reading the Bible; they go to church and let the ritual of the service do that for them. Dissenters, of course, in England were apart from that—that's what dissenters always are, they're people who read the Bible for themselves—well, my yeoman doesn't do that. He goes to church, and what he reads himself is Bunyan's *Pilgrim's Progress,* and *Pilgrim's Progress* is a marvelous book, and, as to the baseline of culture, you can't do much better. Here is the Slough of Despond, there is Vanity Fair, and a yeoman actually spends most of his time, by my perception, dealing with those two problems. A sensible yeoman has already made his decision to stick by his family, raise his children well, do the best he can with the piece of land he's on. He's made his deal with the hierarchy of society, he doesn't fight the Established Church. The two personal battles he has to fight are the Slough of Despond—in other words, the year when the crops don't do well, the year when the lord he likes in the neighborhood dies and the ridiculous son takes over and makes everyone's life miserable, the year when the parson he likes departs and a silly old fool takes over and makes everyone's life in the church insubstantial. That's the Slough of Despond; and of course there's personal tragedy as well. And then there's the question of Vanity Fair. He has his temptations, this yeoman. There's a market town nearby, and he gets to go to the market town, and there are available in the market town all kinds of things that aren't available at home that attract him very much. There are girls there, and there's drink, and there's an opportunity to take the money you got from your hard-earned farming and splurge, and, God knows, splurging is attractive, and why shouldn't I, one day a year—and that kind of thing. That's a big issue for a simple yeoman. So, my yeoman is Baseline English Language Culture, and my yeoman thinks a lot about the Slough of Despond, on the one hand, and what his relationship is to that Slough, and about Vanity Fair, on the other, and what his relationship is to that.

Language has its own hierarchy, and a man who's been to a great English public school, as Churchill had been, and then Sandhurst, as Churchill had been, has considered the Slough of Despond from twenty different angles. He's considered it from the Hamlet angle, for instance, which is pretty much the deepest angle from which you can consider the Slough of Despond. And he knows all about Vanity Fair. He knows about *The Taming of the Shrew,* and he knows *The Tempest,* and *The Winter's Tale,* and *Antony and Cleopatra,* and *Julius Caesar,* and what he doesn't know about Vanity Fair, in a way, isn't worth knowing. So he gets to go to Vanity Fair; he gets to have a few girls, splurge a little, and still avoid the Slough of Despond. Because the yeoman, as he considers the Slough of Despond and Vanity Fair, is thinking that if he splurges in his market town and spends half the money he got from raising his crops over one whole year, he's going to be depressed. In other words, a wrong take on Vanity Fair—and Vanity Fair specializes in wrong takes—is going to shoot-and-ladder him instantly into the Slough of Despond. Well, of course I'm talking here about the secret of aristocracy. Aristocrats get to go to Vanity Fair, apparently, without giving much of a second thought to the Slough of Despond. In fact, all through Congreve, and elsewhere, there are instances of aristocrats who haven't a sou (and who are, indeed, being dunned by their tailor) but whose optimism seems strangely intact. This must always be a mystery to yeomen. Now, these are the two traditional, polar relationships in English moral life. The yeoman's attitude toward the Slough of Despond and Vanity Fair, as against the aristocrat's.

What of language itself? What is its role in all of this? The aristocrat, in order to keep his freedom (and his freedom, first of all, is to go to Vanity Fair and not lose his optimism), has to speak honestly and with authority about the whole construct he lives in. His mind must reflect the real temper of the social construct he has a privileged position in. He must be sufficient in all his social contacts in order to keep his Vanity Fair visa up to date in such a way that it will not diminish his optimism. Of course I'm saying that Churchill did this, and I'm saying that, in our time, Churchill alone did this. Privileged-language people—and I'm going to shift now from the word *aristocrat* to the phrase *privileged-language people*, because aristocrats, in our time, have been privileged-language people. Not all of them, or even very many of them, have been well-born, in the Churchill sense. Privileged-language people need to keep their social information and their language up to date. This is why we're so in awe of the nineteenth-century English novel. The privileged-language mind was, by the nineteenth century in England, very, very complicated; it just wouldn't do to read Shakespeare alone. We were no longer in an Elizabethan phase. The fact is that the yeoman of the nineteenth century, the good one, may well have been still in reference to *Pilgrim's Progress.* His baseline sense of how his life was going wouldn't necessarily have changed that much, if he'd stayed on his piece of land, and if he were content, overall, with the way his soul—his own soul and the soul of his family, his posterity—was going. He might well not have moved on, in language sophistication. The privileged-language person, however, confronting a various world, by now full of quite a bit of mechanization, and expanding contacts with other countries, and all the things we know happened during the nineteenth century, needed to know more. He had to read better, he had to have a new mind, let's say. And the extraordinary thing about the nineteenth century in England is, such a new mind was available, and it was provided, in large part, by the great novelists of that period, and I mean George Eliot, Charles Dickens, and my hero, William Makepeace Thackeray. So Churchill was the one human avatar out of Vanity Fair—and he lived in Vanity Fair. His mother was Becky Sharp, and I know about her because she came from Brownstone New York, the raffish side, the Jeromes. I've seen the house where she was born—in Cobble Hill, is it? In any case, it's off Clinton Street in Brooklyn. It's a very modest house. And I know the house where she grew up; it was a big Mayfair-style house, where the Manhattan Club used to be, on Madison Square. Winston Churchill's mother had a Becky Sharp progress through life. From Brooklyn, to a big, vulgar, fancy house on Madison Square, to Randolph Churchill, to a kind of—how shall I describe him—well, I think Princess Diana has a relation—is it her mother, or—who married a polo player—but Winston Churchill's mother ended married to someone called Cornwallis West, who was a little bit like that, a kind of polo player stud, without much moral information but plenty of presentability, in the bedroom and elsewhere. So, he's one avatar of kingship, in the paper of February 1, 1950: the son of Vanity Fair, Winston Churchill. And the way he appears in the paper is rather remarkable. He's on the front page, but he's not being reported on. He's not prime minister; Clement Attlee is. Churchill is about to run in 1950—I mean he's about to run for his Tory seat in Parliament, in an election called in 1950, and the Tories are about to lose. He's out of power, and he's going to stay out of power for the next unit of time, but he is, categorically, the number-one guy in the world, and he appears in columns two and three of the *New York Times*.

Now, we should know that in the *New York Times* of 1950, there are eight columns, which is more columns than we have now, and that column eight is the column of the lead story—it's way over to the right-hand side, it's where the eye drifts naturally, top right—and that the second lead is column one, and that's left, top left, and that itself is an interesting bit of theater, because the eye's visceral, natural drift is toward top right; that's first lead; and then to get to know that column one is the second lead requires a little knowledge, a little discipline. And that's the nature of the *New York Times* reading mind of February 1, 1950; the natural visceral drift of the eye was acknowledged, but a little bit of discipline was assumed as well. A certain amount of insider's information about how the *New York Times* was edited was assumed; well, that's not assumed by the editors of the *New York Times* today. In fact, the *New York Times* today is seeking to know its reader's mind. Its reader's mind is now a mystery, and the *New York Times* is terrified that the mind of the generation growing up now—the generation that will someday replace its current readers—is a complete mystery. So, rather than assuming, as the editors of the *New York Times* in 1950 did assume, that its readership would make an effort to know how the *Times* was edited, and recognize in this method of editing some echo of their schooling discipline, the *New York Times* now is scrambling to find the parameters of the mind of the people to whom it must necessarily appeal. This is certainly a very different situation, but, of course, it's almost fifty years later now.

In any case, the *New York Times* in those days, as I say, was eight columns wide, and the second lead, which in this case is PRESIDENT SEEKS SEVENTY DAY COAL TRUCE. FACT FINDING BOARD is top left. Next to the second lead are the Winston Churchill columns, and it's not a story about Winston Churchill. It's a serialization of his book *The Second World War*, and the installment of February 1, 1950, came from volume III, *The Grand Alliance; Book I: Germany Drives East*, "Installment 6: The Japanese Envoy." I'm finding a marvelous echo of Dickens here. All of Dickens's novels, of course, appeared first in installments and were later put out in hardcover, and Churchill, the marvelous old boy—and he was boyish till the end; people remarked that he looked like a baby with a cigar in his mouth—wrote in such a way, had such a marvelous intuitive understanding of the Victorian mind, that it could work the other way for him, you could take his done-between-two-covers book and parcel it out in a daily newspaper, and have it read well, all these volumes, books, installments, and so forth. And, I must say, I'm not aware that since 1950 we've had any book serialized in the *New York Times*, and I'm almost able to say categorically that we haven't had any book serialized on the front page. The closest thing we've had is *The Pentagon Papers*, and that was revelation of public documents.

So, I won't read you any of what Winston Churchill wrote. You can go to his book on the Second World War and read it yourself if you want, but he wasn't in office in 1950; he just was, categorically, the number-one guy in the world. He'd been proven right, in a way. People remembered that they themselves, perhaps, had not wanted to go to war against Germany. The English remembered all their social experiments of the 1930s; they remembered that Churchill had been right, and they had been wrong, and so forth. And Americans were aware, in 1950, that they had been, in a way, somewhat submissive to Winston Churchill. It was not the wish of massive numbers of Americans to support the English immediately in their resistance to Germany; we had to be won over to that point of view; and we *were* won over—of course, Pearl Harbor was definitive in that; the Japanese helped in convincing us, but there was a sense in America that Winston Churchill had got what he wanted from us, beginning with the thin edge of the wedge of "Give us the tools, and we will finish the job," which was certainly a piece of salesmanship. Winston Churchill must have been aware that all the tools in the world weren't going to get the job done. He needed America's full participation, but he was smart enough about America, and smart enough about upholding his own leadership role, to put it that way at first, and so we had Bundles for Britain, and then we had Tools for Britain, and then we had Yankee Boys for Britain. And Americans were aware, politically, that they had, finally and ultimately, gone down the road that Churchill had pointed out. Hoover hadn't pointed it out. Lindbergh hadn't pointed it out. We hadn't gone down—there were lots of American roads we hadn't gone down in the 1940s. Finally, if you wanted to go back to, say, 1935; if you took an inventory of all the different roads to the future that various people were pointing out, by 1950 you'd have to say, "Well, actually, we went down the road that old Winston was pointing out, and yes, it was a good road, and yes, we did just fine." So, as an unexampled human avatar, Winston Churchill represented one kingship possibility, very powerful at that moment, destined to become marvelously unpowerful almost immediately. The strange fact being that Winston Churchill's reelevation to office in 1952 represented something of a defeat for him, because his mind, his glorious, old-fashioned mind, was suddenly, obviously, not sufficient to deal with all the social avatars at work in our postwar world.

So, now we'll move to the lead story. The lead story is: TRUMAN ORDERS HYDROGEN BOMB BUILT FOR SECURITY PENDING AN ATOMIC PACT: CONGRESS HAILS STEP; BOARD BEGINS JOB. The second head is: HISTORIC DECISION; the third headline is: PRESIDENT SAYS HE MUST DEFEND NATION AGAINST POSSIBLE AGGRESSOR. The headline is four columns wide, three lines deep—is it eighteen-point type or twenty-four? I'm not sure. Well, what can I say? It was a big moment. I remember this moment. The reason I've chosen this year—and I'll explain at another time why—is, that this is the first moment my mind opened up to the world. It wasn't because of this headline, it was because of an event in my personal life. But I remember this moment. And the H-bomb had an importance comparable, let's say, to the importance of the high-definition television being developed now. You know about high-definition television. Television now has 250,000 points of light; high-definition television is going to have one billion points of light, or something. Your television now is so big; your high-definition television will be incrementally, logarithmically bigger, and it will give a depth of this, and a definition of that, and it's going to be involved with the computer and—in other words, the invention of high-definition television, which is upon us now, tells us that, yes, we live in the civilization of television. It's not going away, and it's not staying the same. It's marching right along. Well, that's what the H-bomb told us. The A-bomb was, for a time, viewed as an unparalleled thing. And of course, for a time, it was unparalleled, because we had it and no one else did. In other words, for a time shortly after the end of the Second World War we were in the position of dominance we are apparently now in again. For a time after the end of the Second World War we were the one superpower, because we were the one country that had this weapon. It was an uncomfortable situation in some ways, but comfortable in another. We were confident we weren't again going to drop the A-bomb, although we *had* dropped it; so we felt, in our own hearts, that nuclear war was not actually a possibility, even if others were fearful of us; it was just an ace we had up our sleeves. Well, of course the Russians developed an A-bomb, which shattered us all to the core, just as it would shatter us all to the core if suddenly now we were to cease, once again, to be the world's only superpower. We're fairly comfortable with being the world's only superpower, we feel we can handle it, but we're not sure other people can handle it, and we don't like the competition. The H-bomb, like high-definition television now (which may be an H-bomb of another kind), tells us that, oh God, not only is this what we *have,* it's what we're *gonna* have, and we can't see the end of it. Is there gonna be an I-bomb after an H-bomb? Is there going to be super-high-definition television, with virtual-reality implants in your brain? We don't know. It's one of those moments when you suddenly discover that the unexampled thing that pushed over the frontier isn't the limit; you're going to march on. And, of course, I'm saying this is the second avatar of kingship, in direct juxtaposition to the Winston Churchill avatar of kingship. This has nothing to do with Vanity Fair, English-language dominance, or morals. This has to do with mechanization, mechanization taking on a life of its own.

So now we'll go to the second lead, which is, PRESIDENT SEEKS SEVENTY DAY COAL TRUCE. FACT FINDING BOARD, and this story is about President Truman and John L. Lewis. John L. Lewis was the head of the United Mine Workers' Union. There was such a person, in 1950, as a mine worker, a coal miner. In 1950, my family's house was heated by coal, not oil. A man came, he came with a ton of coal. You called up on the telephone and you ordered a ton of coal, nothing about a little oil truck coming and pumping 500 gallons of oil in; you ordered a ton of coal. My grandparents lived not far from the New York Central Railroad tracks in Thornwood, New York. The locomotives of the New York Central burned coal. My grandparents painted their house every two years, because the coal dust settled all over their house, and they wanted to keep it clean. There was a coal strike, the coal miners were powerful and militant; they felt they were any man's equal, they didn't like their rate of pay, and the president was in opposition to them. And this is the third avatar of kingship, the decent working people of this country who'd met their test time after time, including service in World War II, and were dissatisfied.

Well, the fourth avatar of kingship is television, and you'll have to trust me—and you won't have any trouble doing it—when I tell you that there is no story on the front page of the *New York Times* of February 1, 1950, that relates in any way, shape, or form to the world being reported on by the C-SPAN $3.3-million panel of communications experts. You might as well be talking about a different country. We are somewhat deceived in this by at least two factors. One, we have all the architecture. Lots of people have houses that were standing in 1950. We're deceived, in fact, by another factor: our fondness for the automobiles of the 1950s. There are still a lot of 1950 and 1956 Chevrolets on the road. People polish them up, they remember the Chevrolet aspect of that civilization, and they think they still have it. The third deluding thing is the movies: we still like the movies from the 1950s. But we don't have that country anymore, and the sooner we realize it, the happier we'll be. In any case, the country we were going to have appears on a back page—and I'm embarrassed to say I failed to take the page number here, but it's a back page of the *New York Times*—it appears in a section called "Programs on the Air," which is itself divided into four sections. The first section is "Morning," meaning radio programs in the morning; the second section is "Afternoon," meaning radio programs in the afternoon; the third section is "Evening," which is evening programs on the radio; the fourth section is combination of television and FM radio, because all the radio being reported in the first three sections is AM. So now, without having looked at it previously, I will just look through the television listings. The first one is *Morning Chapel, Rev. Alfred Barrett.* The second is

Television Shopper, with Kathy Norris, and a guest named Mrs. Campbell. That's all there is, on any television station, in the morning. Afternoon: *Headline Clues: George F. Putnam*—I'm reading the listings in their entirety; 12:30 *Johnny Olsen; Rumpus Room;* 1:00 *Okay Mother: Dennis James*—Dennis James went on and on and on, he may still be alive, as a game show host; *Betty Congdon, guest;* 1:30 *Man on the Street;* 1:45 *Margaret Johnson: Songs;* 2:00 *Homemakers Program; Market Melodies; News Reports; Of Human Interest.* These are all lined up, and I might as well read you the channels at this point: WCBS-TV is channel 2, WNBT is channel 4, WABD is channel 5, WJZ-TV is channel 7, WOR-TV is channel 9, WPIX is channel 11, and WATV is channel 13, and that's what you've got. Now, at 2:15 WATV *Feature Film;* 3:15 *Homemaker's Guide: Fred Sayles, Brooks Stephens;* 3:45 WCBS; *Music and Weather;* 4:00 WCBS *Homemaker's Exchange, with Maggie Waggoner Young.* WJZ *Telephone Game;* WATV *Western Feature;* WABD *Test Pattern and Music;* 4:30 WCBS *Vanity Fair*—how interesting—*with Dorothy Dean, Herman Steinkrauss*—and a couple of other people; 4:45 WPIX *Music;* 5:00 WCBS *Ted Steele Show;* WATV *Junior Frolics;* 5:15 WNBT *Judy Splinters, with Shirley Dinsdale;* WPIX *Mr. Magic, with Norman Jensen;* 5:30 WCBS *Church Wagon—Bob Dixon; Howdy Doodie—Bob Smith*—we'll come back to that; WPIX *Six Gun Playhouse;* WATV *Feature Film;* 5:45 WABD *Time for Reflection;* 5:35 WABD *Camera Headlines.* Evening: 6:00 WNBT *Children's Theater;* WABD *Small Fry Club—Bob Emory;* 6:30 WCBS *Lucky Pup—Puppets;* WNBT *Easy Does It—Johnny Andrews and Francey Lane;* WABD *Magic Cottage;* WOR *The Mystery Rider;* WPIX *Telepix;* WATV *Flim: Burn 'Em Up Barnes—Frankie Darro;* 6:35 WPIX *Ben Gross, Column of the Air;* 6:45 WCBS *Bob Howard Show;* WOR *Time for Beany—Puppets;* WPIX *Jimmy Powers, Sports;* 6:50 WATV *Western Featurette;* 6:55 WNBT *Weather by Wethbee;* 7:00 WCBS *Kirby Stone Quintet;* WNBT *Kukla, Fran and Ollie—Fran Allison;* WABD *Captain Video;* WOR *Comedy Carnival, Film— Harry Langdon;* WPIX *News—John Tillman, George Cray;* and so forth. What I mean is, it wasn't much. And maybe we'll pick up the evening shows later in the month, but I wanted to give you the subtext of what the overall activity looked like. It didn't look like much. But it was going to win. It was going to win, because the other avatars of kingship weren't going to be able to cut a deal, culturally. You put old Vanity Fair together with mine workers on strike, and the H-bomb—well. You had to move on to a new possibility, and we did.

There's one other story on the front page that I'll just use as a kind of coda, because it's striking, as one looks at the paper of February 1, 1950, to see what was destined to be of paramount importance and what was going to go away. The Churchill of it was simply going to go away, and fast; really by 1952, certainly by 1956. Coal miners—well, coal mines were going to shut down; we were going to go the oil route, the foreign oil route. The H-bomb? Well, it looks as though, for a time, we've put it away. I hope that's true. In any case, as to developing a national mind sufficient to encompass the real meaning of the H-bomb, we never tried to do it, and probably it's impossible to imagine doing it. And then, of course, these tiny television listings, which were the seed out of which our national culture of irony and anger was to grow. But there's a story in the fourth column that strikes a chord with me, and it's FRANCE PROTESTS SOVIET RECOGNITION OF HO CHI MINH RULE. Need I say more?

February 1950

Today is September 29, 1997, and this will be Trow's last tape, the last work using this method of mine with a tape recorder that I do for this book, and this section will be placed out of sequence. Which is to say that some of my first work in thinking about 1950 was to think about the front page of the *New York Times* of February 1, 1950, and then I did all kinds of other work, and now, at the very end of this period of consideration, I'm going to go back and look at headlines and some other material appearing in the *New York Times* during the month of February 1950. This process will have had three parts: first, almost a year ago I scanned the whole month, at the State Library in Albany, and photostatted all its front pages and some other things that caught my eye. I had put these things aside, and I just went through them again, in a preliminary way, circling what I thought was interesting, keeping mostly to a linear chronology through the month, and also mostly following the avatars of kingship idea I introduced in discussing the front page of February 1. That is, stories to do with the brand-new world of nuclear physics, the old world of Winston Churchill, and the coal miners, the men. So, let's start. This will be completely free association; I'm not claiming here to be doing anything else. Let my mind wander within its parameters of concern about the events of this month, and here we are, on the second of February, and here's another episode of Winston Churchill's book, in columns two and three, and this is the "Grand Alliance" and "Germany Drives East." This kind of marvelous—it isn't even *late* Victorian—writing; Winston Churchill's hero was a man named A. W. Kinglake, who wrote about the Crimean War, and so right on the front page of the *New York Times*, you get a bit of the early-nineteenth century, early-Victorian writing, making our modern era continuous, in a way, with the Crimean War—with Agincourt for that matter. Next to it, in column one, is

SOVIET ASKS TRIAL OF HIROHITO, OTHERS AS WAR CRIMINALS

And I mention this story not because the Soviets got their way—obviously they didn't—but to remind myself and my readers of the thousands of bad things that didn't happen, and to sympathize, in a way, with our governors, our elected officials, our powerful men. A completely dysfunctional and wrong-minded thing to do, to try Hirohito as a war criminal. We were seeking to occupy Japan, and I know a bit about this, because my uncle, a naval officer, was part of the occupying force. We were seeking to occupy Japan in a most unique way—namely, with a tiny number of people. There was to be no attempt by America to station two billion Americans in Japan to govern the country; the idea was simply to govern the country by using the emperor, for instance, and the established hierarchical forms, and, of course, the threat of our nuclear capability; and also let me remind my reader that for many years during the Cold War it was simply the policy of the Soviet Union to throw any wrench into any gears they saw, and they obviously knew that to try Hirohito as a war criminal would upset our arrangement in Japan, our occupation of Japan; they also knew that it would have a kind of demagogic appeal to some people, perhaps even to American men who'd fought the merciless soldiers of Hirohito. And that introduces yet another subject, which is demagoguery, and how difficult it is to counteract, how difficult it will be for us to counteract in the future, since we've given in to it completely, in our tabloid mentality. Here we are again, in the first days of February 1950, and a headline on the front page is

TRAUBEL, FLAGSTAD SPLIT 'MET' ROLES; BING BARS 'ULTIMATUM' BY MELCHIOR

Well, this is just plain funny, and quite wonderful. Bing, generally forgotten today, was an enormous celebrity in New York in the 1950s; Rudolf Bing was the impresario of the Metropolitan Opera, and the Metropolitan Opera supplied what it doesn't supply today: a kind of celebrity zing of fun—opera stars competing with one another—and it's a front-page story in the *Times*, and, of course, it belongs to the world of Winston Churchill.

Here we are, on I believe February 3. The dateline says February 2, but it probably appears on February 3—and again, it's

MCMAHON PROPOSES 50 BILLION CRUSADE TO HALT ATOM RACE

I'm going to read this story, for the flavor of that moment, the newness of the nuclear problem, and also, it works nicely together with Winston Churchill and Rudolf Bing and the Metropolitan Opera, because I want to remind my reader that a sixty-year-old man in the prime of his powerful life in 1950 would have been born in 1890. He would belong, in a way, to the world of opera, to the old world of Vanity Fair, plus the world of business, plus World War II, and here we have a man of roughly that age and that era, not necessarily that sophistication or background; and the point I want you to address is his reaction to what is old hat to us, the existence of nuclear weapons. He feels, coming out of an older civilization, that we have something like God's judgment before us, and he is suggesting this reaction. "McMahon Proposes 50 Billion Crusade to Halt Atom Race. He Appeals to U.S. to Consider Almost Any 'Bold Step' to Get Accord With Russians. Would Then Extend Aid. Truman Indicates He Will

Not Seek New Talks With Soviet Because of Hydrogen Bomb. The highest Congressional authority on atomic energy, Senator Brien McMahon, Democrat, of Connecticut, warned today that the Soviet Union would not be long behind this country in progress toward a Hydrogen Bomb." I hope you get a sense of the tension of this moment. We live in a moment when the nuclear problem is presented as something having to do with the cleanup of certain kinds of toxic wastes. Here we have the thing just beginning, and there's an atmosphere of terror, and it's terror among older men, men who are not necessarily particularly modern in their sensibility, who do have a considerable amount of masculine force, and also perhaps a record of liberal arts, or even Christian concern about the state of the soul of the world. "Matters have reached the point, he asserted as chairman of the Joint Congressional Committee on Atomic Energy, where a Russian success with the weapon would make it conceivable for 50,000,000 Americans to be 'incinerated in the space of minutes.'" Well, this was quite a new idea in 1950. You know, the idea of tens of thousands, or hundreds of thousands of men being lost in battle on the face of the earth was an idea we'd come to live with, but the idea that fifty million people could die quickly and instantaneously, through technological horror, was new, and it went right to the heart of some people, and they insisted on addressing it as a commonsense issue, like a food shortage, or some other real, on-the-ground concern, and they insisted that it be addressed as such. This contrasted with what was then government policy, and what remained government policy, which was that the thing be approached moment by moment, as a face-off with the Soviet Union.

And here we have "Lauritz Melchior, for twenty-four years a leading tenor of the Metropolitan Opera"—this is a front-page story—"in all the heroic Wagnerian roles, sang his farewell performance last night. After the final curtain dropped on 'Lohengrin,' the Danish-born tenor declared in his dressing room that he would never return to sing while Rudolf Bing, who takes over the management next season, was in control." And again, I just balance that against the nuclear stories. Again, all the people taking part in both the nuclear drama and the Metropolitan Opera drama are Edwardian figures in part of their soul, and that's something we need to remember.

February 3, 1950:

U.S. TO INVOKE OCCUPATION STATUTE IN STUTTGART DENAZIFICATION SCANDAL. MCCLOY'S OFFICE IS EXPECTED TO INTERVENE NEXT WEEK

Now, I'm not going to follow this story. I'm just going to tell you who this man McCloy was, from the point of view of someone growing up in a privileged East Coast background. He was someone not everyone knew about, but we knew about him, and he represented, to us, something above John Foster Dulles. John McCloy was the insider's insider. He was the man who knew all the games in our country. He knew the business game, he knew the power game, he knew, to some extent, the liberal arts game, he was the kind of person—well, when the world was in serious trouble, he was going to be there, and in part of my education and in a big part of my family background there was the idea that you held ten or twelve percent, or twenty percent, or thirty percent of your life possibilities open, so that if, at a certain moment, you needed to help John McCloy in his work, you were available to do that. You would walk into his office and he would know, categorically, that you were the right sort of person, and could be trusted absolutely, and there you would be, helping Mr. McCloy, who never held an elected office, who was always appointed here or there, whose work was always taken seriously, you would be helping him to govern Germany, which is what he was doing at that time.

Now, on February 4, we have a big lead story.

BRITISH JAIL ATOM SCIENTIST AS SPY AFTER TIP BY F.B.I.; HE KNEW OF HYDROGEN BOMB

It is a picture of Dr. Klaus Fuchs, and the subheads for the lead story are: "Two charges made. First Alleges Betrayal of Information in U.S. 2nd Site Not Named. Court hearing is brief. Klaus Fuchs, a Ministry Aide, is Remanded in Custody to Reappear on Friday." The story is by Benjamin Welles, and begins "A senior British scientist who has worked on atomic projects in the United States and Britain was charged here today with having betrayed atomic research secrets." Well, we have these stories today; we have people who—Mr. Aldrich recently was giving secrets, but nothing that we've had recently had the impact that these stories had in the early fifties. As I say, and I think it's worth repeating, the people in this drama were fifty or sixty years old, they were, in some sense, Edwardian people, they had lived through the first half of the century, won the war, only to find themselves in this hyperspace of horror, the idea that after all this time had gone by, the world could be destroyed by pushing a button. And then there were these spy stories, how Russia was approaching parity with us in nuclear horror, and all the time Russia was making it absolutely clear that anytime they could throw a monkey wrench in any gears of ours, they would. It produced a kind of repressed, psychotic terror in these men who had been born in the late nineteenth century, or early in this century, and this legitimate—I'm not saying a word against it—but this legitimate, repressed psychotic terror was conveyed in the *New York Times* of these years.

Another story allied to it:

**CAPITAL IS STIRRED. HOOVER SAID TO TELL BODY
OF SENATORS THAT FUCHS SENT DATA TO SOVIET.
INVESTIGATION IS STARTED. CONGRESSIONAL UNIT
SUBPOENAS GENERAL GROVES—PRESIDENT MEETS
CABINET ON CASE**

And it occurs to me that one thing we don't get in the *Times* anymore is all these small, extended headlines; and, reading them aloud, it occurs to me that you get something of the newsreel feeling of stridency from all these small headlines. I'm going to do it all from the top, because I think, in a way, it was the equivalent in the *New York Times* of the tabloid energy, and it echoed the newsreel, so see if you don't feel that you get a sense of the urgency of the story, just by reading the headlines.

BRITISH JAIL ATOM SCIENTIST AS A SPY AFTER TIP BY F.B.I.; HE KNEW OF HYDROGEN BOMB. CAPITAL IS STIRRED. HOOVER SAID TO TELL BODY OF SENATORS THAT FUCHS SENT DATA TO SOVIETS. INVESTIGATION IS STARTED. CONGRESSIONAL UNIT SUBPOENAS GENERAL GROVES—PRESIDENT MEETS CABINET ON CASE.

This was, for the educated reader of the *New York Times* in 1950, the equivalent of telegraphic urgency, and it gave the paper of that day something it lacks now, which is that vector of power into the reader's mind. The first paragraph of the story, by William White, reads thus: "Dr. Klaus Fuchs, the British scientist held in London as accused spy, had certain basic information dealing with the hydrogen bomb development, and was thus in a position to pass it on to the Russians."

Here we are, all still in early February, and there's a little ad for Winston Churchill; it says, "Read Winston Churchill this week on: Crete, the problem of defense and the 'unique' battle for the island," and so forth. Next to it is a story COMMUNIST CHINA SEEKS CASH HERE IN SECRET CAMPAIGN TO SELL BONDS, and this is just a marker against where we stand with China today. "Chinese and Chinese-American supporters of the Communist-dominated government of China are carrying on a secret campaign to sell in the Chinese community in New York the so-called People's Victory Bonds of the Mao Tze-tung regime, it became known yesterday." It turns out that the amount of sales was in the thousands of dollars.

Here we are on February 7, and here we're moving on to other kingship avatars, not the nuclear physics one, not the Win-

ston Churchill, Edwardian-Victorian one, but the men, and I juxtapose this with something I read in the *Times* yesterday, which is
that the most expensive, high-tech coal mine in Britain has been
shut down by the so-called Labour government, by Tony Blair's
government. That action makes almost no sense, juxtaposed to
this:

TRUMAN INVOKES TAFT-HARTLEY ACT IN COAL STRIKE, NAMES FACT BOARD; 370,000 MINERS OUT, VOICING DEFIANCE

and really, you have to juxtapose this to my other two kingship
avatars—the fading away of the Edwardian aesthetic, which, in
fact, had remained so powerful in the minds of men who had
remained powerful in the first half of the century, to a kind of
whisper of Rudolf Bing, and fights among opera stars—that, on
the one hand—and the astonishing newness of the nuclear
threat, and the fact that the men who were likely to be dealing
with this threat were not people who probably were much at home
with Newton, let alone with Einstein or the bomb. And here you
have, under this, and in the atmosphere of enormous hostility
with Russia, you have three hundred and seventy thousand mine
workers going on strike, something that makes every powerful
person in the country shudder.

Here on February 8:

U.S. RECOGNIZES VIET NAM, TWO OTHER INDO-CHINA STATES

I just throw that in. But here's an interesting story. This relates, in
my mind, to what I saw of extreme liberal arts life as a child
through my father's great hero, Mr. Coggeshall—Allen Coggeshall his name was, the patriarch of the house called Windy Rock
where my father was a kind of adopted son—who took a deep
interest in Henry Wallace, who was probably the most extreme
nineteenth-century figure still available in the twentieth century.

Henry Wallace, who had been FDR's vice president, was still active in politics in the late forties, trying to run for president. It seemed to people of an ultra-old liberal arts bent of a certain kind that this was the last chance for the really good old America, and there was that aspect in the late forties and early fifties, for people who came from an idealistic liberal arts background—the feeling that there was a kind of Armageddon overhead, and that there needed to be a last stand of the real liberal arts. There were reflections of this in the high liberal arts of the time, among writers—you know, Black Mountain, and the Refugees, and that kind of thing. This story is a slightly more mainstream version of that energy, which I don't put in kingship-avatar territory; it's a small trickle, but it is here on the front page, and the headline is

WHOLE COLLEGE ABANDONS CLASSES IN MARATHON OUTBURST OF RELIGION

"Wheaton Ill., February 9: A spontaneous mass confession by 1,500 students of Wheaton College passed the twenty-four-hour mark tonight, and showed no sign of a let-up. All classes were suspended at the Liberal Arts School as the men and women students and the 150 teachers jammed into Pierce Memorial Chapel to proclaim their faith and confess their sins." It's a remarkable thing, from the contemporary point of view; none of these people had allowed themselves to enter radio or movie culture in a primary way, is my guess, and they certainly didn't know anything about television. They were living within the mainstream of America, in a kind of Amish way, and my reader should be aware that there was a trickle of that in American life in 1950. That, of course, seems as out of date from our point of view as—what? As Emerson; and it was *in touch with* Emerson, and the great religious awakening of the nineteenth century—all these things that are just in history books had their last little aurora borealis in the late forties and early fifties, and seem to us infinitely remote.

On the other hand, the next thing I have in front of me is: "It's not history at Bonwit's . . . it's fashion and at Bonwit's you'll find

Dior's American suits, made here to be worn here with an accent truly American, truly of the fifties . . . feminine, rounded lines, straight skirts, not narrow ones, the waist where nature put it, in the middle . . . completely contemporary, shown our way with close little hats, little bouquets, little things at the throat. $250 to $295, in our Suit Salon, Fourth Floor."

This is utterly contemporary, in a way. This is our last American poetry; it's fashion copywriting. It's done differently now, but the ultimate of it has always been Revlon, which was "For lips and fingertips," you know, gangsta rap, in a way. A simple little rhyme, something pleasurable and attractive, and I'm looking at the suit, and it's, you know, it's Dior's new look, and it looks pretty good, and it certainly doesn't have—even though it's almost fifty years ago—it doesn't have that wildly Merovingian feel of the Wheaton College campus erupting in mass confession.

The next one is a Russeks ad: "New from every angle of their Paris-stemming details to their crackling, check-blazed, paper-light fabric, these wonderful designs burgeon forth now in all their fashion glory, bringing a whiff of Spring into the present day."

Well, of course, the present day needed it. This is a whiff of something necessary, after the conflict and horror of the front page. "Envisaging Summer, too, in their all-inclusive scope! Translated by Russeks in the letter and spirit of their French counterparts . . ." (And, of course, the huge deal of those days was the instant copy of French style. Russeks did it; Orbach's did it even better.) . . . they compromise only in American price! Counter clockwise: Balenciaga's Hip-Cuffed Suitdress, at $49.95; Paquin's Pivot Peplum Suitdress at $45.95; Balmain's Pillar-Collared, Side-Drawn Sheath at $45 and Balmain's Tunic Suitdress at $45 All in navy and white checked Pure Silk Taffeta, in sizes from 10 to 16. Third Floor."

This is the top of the ad: "Designed in Paris by Balmain, Balenciaga and Paquin, Translated by Russeks, and Found only at Russeks!"

And the dresses look perfectly good. The next one is an ad for Vim, and in it is a television set with a corny TV cowboy in the middle, and I just circled this because it has to do with—well, odd circumstances allow me to treat all this material with some familiarity, but really, if you were growing up at that time, the things that were being dinned into you were things like "Vim, Vim, Vim, Vim, Vim for Value, Vim, Vim, Vim, Vim, Vim for Value." And another thing, the fact is that all the stories in the *New York Times* in 1950 have this quality of repetition for the *older* generation; in other words, people sixty years old had lived through the First World War, they'd lived through the twenties, they'd read newspapers—movies and radio were probably not primary for them if they were, in fact, sixty years old in 1950— and so, when they read the front page of the *New York Times,* it was part of a continuing soap opera that went back to Bismarck, and the Kaiser, and the end of conventional European civilization in 1918, so that the front page of the *New York Times,* for an educated man of 1950, was, you know, episode eighteen in a drama he had entered as a child. On the other hand the fact is, that for almost everyone of my generation, with the exception of a very few of us who were thrust into the circumstances of another age for odd reasons, the repetition was not the repetition of history, not the ongoing quality of this historical soap opera involving Britain, France, Germany, and so forth, but rather the new repetition of the advertisement. "Vim, Vim, Vim, Vim, Vim for Value, Vim, Vim, Vim, Vim, Vim for Value"—that was to be our repetition.

All of the material I'm talking about, this historical material, was drifting way over our heads. We had no idea who John McCloy was, and how were we to make sense of the atom bomb, and a coal miner, you know, was someone we didn't understand, and whose work we didn't want to continue in, so our repetition, what was going to get drummed into our head, was "Vim, Vim, Vim, Vim, Vim for Value." But, here's something on the other side of the street that was going to get drummed into us, too, and it's a cartoon, and it must be on the editorial page. In any case, it's February 12, 1950, and a big hand with a crayon has just made an emendation in a great remark of Lincoln's. You see the big hand reaching out, crayon in hand, and the great remark of Lincoln's is "that this nation, under God, shall have a new birth of freedom, and that government of the people, by the people, for the people, shall not perish from the earth," and the emending hand crosses out "nation" and instead writes "world," so the two things that entered the life of someone like myself, in the first stages of childhood in 1950, were, on the one hand, the commercial advertisement (and later, of course, television programs), and, on the other hand, this kind of very simple propaganda, one wants to say legitimate propaganda, sincerely meant propaganda. It was a very simple message: that the job of my generation was to take this collapsing history into a new zone, in which, far from merely focusing on the job of keeping America up to Lincoln's standards, we were going to take those standards into the world.

And this brings to mind a personal memory: I had been going through, as part of the process of saying goodbye to a lot of things, some personal papers of mine, and I ran into an essay I wrote when I was eleven, which would put it in 1954, about the United Nations. Now, the United Nations was enormous, and had enormous social prestige then, if you came from New York. The Rockefellers were our primary family in every possible way—the Rockefellers had given the land, and the United Nations buildings were the first really new buildings in New York. There was Lever House, but still, you had this sort of old city that had been built up to the time of the Waldorf-Astoria, say; and then there had been an enormous quiet, and it was all gray; and then suddenly, the color of the United Nations building, and my eleven-year-old's essay on the United Nations is something that would make you weep, possibly, in its idealism, and its silliness.

Next, we just have some pages I've selected from the *Sunday Times Magazine* of February 12, 1950, and this doesn't have so much to do with the stories, just the way the magazine was conducted at that time. It's amazingly gray; I can hardly stand to read the stories now, and people could hardly stand to read them then, but they were published week after week; they were nearly all about foreign policy. My guess is that, among other things, this was a way of using foreign-news material that had been gathered but was too much to put in the regular paper, so the magazine was sort of an outlet for all this extra information, and idealism too. It was a kind of overflow exercise, rather like the "News of the Week in Review." It was daunting to me when I was a child, and, as I say, it still looks a little gray; but, Lord, it was the right thing to do, and it would be the right thing to do now. It would be the right thing to do now to have an enormous overflow of information about Ukraine, Belarus, the Balkans, week after week after week, because, you see, this sort of thing has a secondary effect, even if you don't read it. You are at least *aware* that the *New York Times* is saying you ought to read it, and I'm afraid that has been, and is no longer (but should be) part of the *Time*'s role, to let you know, let us say, that we're terribly sorry you don't like Latin, but Latin exists, and just because you don't like it doesn't mean it's going to go away. This has an important effect on the reader's mind, even if the reader doesn't read the story. Anyway, the specific story here is

ASIA'S CHALLENGE TO US—IDEAS, NOT GUNS. COMMUNISM HAS SOLD CHINA A COPY OF OUR IDEALS. WE MUST PROVE THAT OURS ARE THE GENUINE THING.

That's one side of the way the *Times* wrote for years and years and years about foreign policy, and then the other side, even more valuable:

AGAIN THE SAAR ISSUE. FRANCE AND GERMANY REVIVE AN OLD DISPUTE . . .

Blah, blah, blah—well, it's coal again, isn't it? But the point is that the Saar is one of those places in the world that constantly come up as an area of conflict. Please remember that American soldiers are, at this moment, involved in Bosnia-Herzegovina, which has a long history as a place where people don't get along and over which people have some trouble. The Saar was also a place with that sort of history, and the *Times* made sure that you, the reader, were aware of the ongoing issue of the Saar.

The next thing I have is an advertisement. It is marvelously of its time; it's for a house; it's a kind of Cape Cod, but with a modern picture window. It has three complete bedrooms, and it's for sale for $8,990.00.

The next, February 13, just an update, but again a three-column lead story:

MINERS EXPECTED TO IGNORE TWO U.S. INJUNCTIONS TODAY; CAPITAL TO DELAY PENALTIES

Well, you have to understand that ignoring a Taft-Hartley injunction is really pretty serious business. We don't get people ignoring injunctions, usually; here were three hundred and seventy thousand coal miners, not three hundred and seventy thousand isolated, downsized ex-IBMers, each one with his separate faux-gold parachute, each one isolated in his little family, without real recourse; these were three hundred and seventy thousand big, burly coal miners, all very much in touch with each other, all very much led by Mr. Lewis, all very much a real threat—and remember that a lot of people heated their houses with coal in those days.

Well, here we move right back to our other kingship avatar; it's the second lead, and it must be February 13, because the datelines I'm looking at are February 12:

EINSTEIN SEES BID TO 'ANNIHILATION' IN HYDROGEN BOMB. AS 'ONLY WAY OUT' HE PROPOSES 'A SUPRA-NATIONAL JUDICIAL AND EXECUTIVE BODY'

"On Mrs. Roosevelt's Television Premiere Scientist Declares Arms Race 'Hysterical.' Dr. Albert Einstein, in his first public statement since the decision to proceed with the hydrogen bomb, declared yesterday that 'general annihilation beckons.'" Well, this is way beyond the Nobel Prize, or the Fords establishing a foundation to somewhat ameliorate conditions in the society they vectored us into; this is Albert Einstein saying that something's gone a tiny tad wrong in the world of advanced physics, and where is he saying it? He's saying it on Eleanor Roosevelt's television program. Now, in my family, Eleanor Roosevelt was the first lady of the world for all time, and I was being taught at home that only people of Eleanor Roosevelt's stripe, and that included us, were in possession of the moral authority that our country needed. Of course, our country was no longer enough for our moral authority; we were going to go into the world, à la the United Nations, so have some sympathy for my childhood. There I was, being told that only the Roosevelts really understood, and there, on television—I didn't see it, I'm just reading this for the first time—but on television, Mrs. Roosevelt's television program, Albert Einstein, the man who invented this other mind, the science mind, was saying, you know, something's gone very wrong with it, and he's recommending not careful study, he's recommending a supranational body to deal with this stuff. I'm just saying, put the coal miners in this picture and you get a little sense of the impossibility of our cultural situation at the moment. The elements being put forward here were just too disparate to cohere. Eleanor Roosevelt wasn't in any sense an educated woman—not really. She merely represented a kind of decent American tradition that had got shot upward by the unique quality of her husband's personality. And Albert Einstein was not someone who particularly understood the social history of this country; he was a man who, in quiet, had done very important work that he later saw grow into horror. And these two very finite human avatars are on television, and Albert Einstein is saying that it requires a supranational body of some kind, at a time when people were not going to agree on much of anything, let alone on a supranational executive and judicial body, and three hundred and seventy thousand burly coal miners are defying the Taft-Hartley Act.

So, just in a kind of for-the-record spirit, I'm going to read

Dr. Einstein's address on peace in the atomic era. I haven't read it before; we'll just do it. There's a picture and a headline:

ATOMIC LEADERS WHO WERE GUESTS OF MRS.
ROOSEVELT. THE FORMER FIRST LADY PRESENTING
A SILVER TRAY TO DAVID E. LILIENTHAL, RETIRED
CHAIRMAN OF THE ATOMIC ENERGY COMMISSION

"Looking on are Senator Brien McMahon, left, Chairman of the Joint Congressional Atomic Energy Committee, and Dr. J. Robert Oppenheimer of the Institute for Advanced Study, Princeton, N.J. And underneath a picture of Dr. Einstein: "Dr. Albert Einstein at his home in Princeton Friday, during the making of a film for showing on Mrs. Roosevelt's television program." The text of Dr. Albert Einstein's address on atomic energy and world peace yesterday follows. "I am grateful to you for the opportunity to express my conviction in this most important political question. The idea of achieving security through national armament is, at the present state of military technique, a disastrous illusion. On the part of the United States this illusion has been particularly fostered by the fact that this country"—I'm not going to read it all. You can tell what it's going to say, and I guess what I want to do is give you a sense of the absurdity, socially, of what's being presented as something coherent, something to follow. There's something wonderfully corny about Eleanor Roosevelt presenting a silver tray to David E. Lilienthal, in the same social setting in which Albert Einstein is talking about the beyond-the-beyond-the-beyond-the, and what we would do if we were all a collegial body of scientists like him.

Reality follows the next day:

CHINESE REDS SIGN 30-YEAR ALLIANCE WITH SOVIET
UNION. AIM HELD TO BAR A RESURGENT JAPANESE
IMPERIALISM AND AGGRESSION BY ITS ALLIES. ACCORD
ON RAILWAY, PORTS. PEIPING TO GET THE CHANGCHUN

LINE, PORT ARTHUR, DAIREN AFTER TOKYO
PEACE PACT

And there's a text of that treaty. The story's by Harrison E. Salisbury, one of the better writers for the *Times* for a very long time. Meanwhile the second lead is

STATE ACTS TO RATION COAL; LEGISLATURE GIVES
POWER TO DEWEY TO CUT SERVICES. COAL BOARD
IS CALLED TO ASSIST IN NEW TALKS STARTING
TODAY

And

AUTHORIZATION FOLLOWS BY AN HOUR GOVERNORS
PLEA TO AVERT 'CATASTROPHE'

And this is a severe situation. In our time, the only comparison would be—you know, your license plate is even or odd, and you can buy gasoline only on that day, and that's almost thirty years ago. This was social reality on the ground.

The next is February 16, 1950:

SECRET CODICILS TO SINO-SOVIET PACT SAID TO GIVE
RUSSIA KEY PEIPING POSTS AND LARGE FORCE
OF CHINESE LABOR

Now, I don't think that ever actually happened; I don't think any Russians overtly occupied key posts in Peiping, which is what Peking (now Beijing) was called in those days, and I don't think that a large force of Chinese labor was made available to Russia, not actually. The point is that, again, there's an air of barely repressed panic in the paper at this time, and justifiably so. Let's not expect so much of human beings that they always resist an atmosphere of repressed panic. Next day:

NO ALARM YET, CITY IS TOLD, AS STATE PLANS COAL
ACTION

But there is alarm. Next day:

MODIFIED BROWN-OUT ORDERED AND COAL RATIONED
IN STATE

And there's a picture of someone named Bertram D. Tallimy, and
I know this guy so well—he's about sixty years old, and he's, you
know, he's Mr. Kiwanis, and he's ordering a brown-out, and that's
the social fact of our government most of the time, David Lilienthal to the contrary notwithstanding.

LEWIS ORDERS MEN TO WORK; 'NO PROGRESS' IN COAL
TALKS; CITY BROWN-OUT VOLUNTARY

Well, now, I'm not going to go on and on; we're getting more coal
strike, and the head of the union says go back to work, but it's not
so clear the men will obey, and meanwhile,

CITY FREEZES ALL SOFT COAL FOR RATIONING
TOMORROW; MINERS CONTINUE DEFIANCE

And it's the lead story, three columns' worth.

SALES ARE LIMITED. CONSUMER MAY OBTAIN FUEL ONLY
IN CASES OF PROVED NECESSITY. STATE IS READY TO
ACT. MAY CLOSE ALL NONESSENTIAL ESTABLISHMENTS,
SUCH AS TAVERNS, IF STRIKE LASTS

Well, that really is serious.

Now we're up to February 19, and I'm just looking at the
kind of map I used to look at all during my childhood. It's one of
these Mercator projection worlds, with different countries, and

different blocs in different colors, and this world is about population, and the Soviet Union and China are put in dark colors, and the rest of the world is light. You have Western bloc, population 1.4 billion, Communist bloc, population 721 million; all others, population 115—well, of course, the interesting fact of note here is, the population of the world has more than doubled since 1950. There are more than two people on the face of the earth today for every one we had then; and the population of China and the Soviet Union together is presented there as 721 million. But more important, from the point of view of my memory, is this whole kind of graphing of how many we had, how many they had, how many tanks do we have against the tanks that they have, how many countries do they have against how many countries do we have, and it was all presented as a kind of Monopoly game, in which certain people owned certain blocks of ground, and every time a block of ground was lost, this Mercator map changed, and alarmed you, or heartened you, depending on how that was, and that was just the graphic display of our barely repressed panic.

Here is just a kind of Vanity Fair social note. We'll relate it to the civilization of Winston Churchill, and it relates to my personal history in that in 1949, a year before this, I remember spending a day with my grandparents in which we just drove down through the easy parkways of Westchester County to the North River, and down to the West Side piers of Manhattan, for the simple pleasure of looking at all the ocean liners lined up, and the title is

THE LAST OF THE WORLD'S GREAT FOUR-STACK LINERS THE AQUITANIA IS TO BE DEMOLISHED AFTER THIRTY-SIX YEARS OF SERVICE. NOTED AQUITANIA NEARS LAST BERTH. CUNARD VETERAN QUITS ENGLAND TODAY FOR SCOTLAND, WHERE SHE WILL BE SCRAPPED

And this is—I'm getting a little chill now, because this is where I entered the picture. I entered the picture just in time to see the last twenty-five percent of it disappear. I was a Cunard boy, you know? I mean, I was a boy who had wanted to be on a Cunard liner the whole of his life, and Lord, they were throwing them away by the time I was seven.

So now we have the *New York Times Magazine* from February 19, and I have it because it's the juxtaposition of Winston Churchill and Clement Attlee, and, for heaven's sake, Clement Attlee really was a labor leader; those three hundred and seventy thousand coal miners in America understood that Clement Attlee was on their side, and life at least, was simple in that regard. Again, just from the point of view of nostalgia—and in general I steer clear of that, but,

STARS ON THE RISE

It's from the *Times Magazine,* and it's Julie Harris and Brandon De Wilde appearing as cousins in *A Member of the Wedding,* and the thing to note here is that there was such a thing as a Broadway star on the rise, and it had a different feel from a Hollywood star on the rise, and it was presented as important, which is not something that can happen today.

February 20:

THE GREAT WHITE WAY DIMS OUT AGAIN. THE ONLY ILLUMINATION IN TIMES SQUARE AT 6:50 P.M. WAS FROM STORE LIGHTS AND STREET LAMPS. BROWN-OUT SNUFFS BROADWAY'S GLOW; SPOTTY ELSEWHERE. DARKNESS CLOAKS TIMES SQUARE AS FIRST IMPACT OF COAL STRIKE HITS MANHATTAN

Well, that would be vivid for New Yorkers, to have the coal strike dim Broadway's lights.

UNION, NOT LEWIS, CITED FOR CONTEMPT

And you're getting a sense here, I hope, that of all our kingship avatars, it's the coal strike, which has to do with the immediate needs of people, that's really, finally dominant in the paper during this month, although the issue of atomic annihilation is, in a certain way, more important; and culturally perhaps one can say that the passing of the Cunard phase of our civilization was more important; the *Times* is giving its first notice to "Do we have enough coal to light Broadway today, and what's going to happen next?" In any case, the union, not its leader, Mr. Lewis, is cited for contempt.

COAL PILES LOW, RATIONING BEGINS HERE; COLD GRIPS EAST

And this is four columns wide, this headline in the *Times*. Then we have Winston with his cigar, and Attlee wearing some sort of Birmingham-Loves-You ribbon in juxtaposition on the following page, and then, on February 24, it's reported that Labour is well ahead in British voting, and then Labour has a slim majority on the twenty-fifth, and then it's a very slim majority, but Clement Attlee decides that he can function as prime minister:

ATTLEE CARRIES ON; GOVERNMENT CRISIS MAY BE POSTPONED

This is February 26, and then, again, a Vanity Fair note:

HARRY LAUDER DIES AFTER A RELAPSE

This is: NOTED SCOTTISH COMEDIAN AND SINGER, 79, WAS KNIGHTED IN 1919 FOR HIS WAR WORK—and this runs counter to the demographic sense of this moment. This was the civilization under the civilization that was dominant at the time; everyone who was sixty years old, who'd been through the sequence of events of World War I, and the twenties and thirties, and then World War II, knew damn well who Harry Lauder was, and he'd been knighted in 1919, and he's the *Aquitania,* in a way, being scrapped in Scotland.

On February 27,

COAL PEACE ATTEMPTS FAIL; PARLEY IS
TO RESUME TODAY

And then, on the twenty-eighth, it's a full-page advertisement
that I'm going to read; it has personal meaning for me, because
it's where my father worked in 1950. It's a big ad taken by the
World Telegram because it's just absorbed the *Sun*, which was a
kind of *Aquitania* in the realm of New York newspapers. The *Sun*
had had a long run as an important newspaper, but its day had
set; oddly enough, the architecture is still to be seen in New
York. It's quite poignant; it's near City Hall, the old *Sun* building,
and the clock that the *Sun* had outside its building—and it's a
very fine old building—is still to be seen, and "It shines for all"
was its motto, as I remember, and anyway, you can see for yourself. "More than 600,000 New Yorkers are now buying the *New
York World-Telegram*"; and it says, "Since the *World-Telegram*
purchased the *New York Sun* on January 4, 1950, the five-day
average (Monday thru Friday) circulation of the *World-Telegram*
and *Sun* has been in excess of 600,000"; and it's just, you know,
the modernity of demography we'll end our story with.

Faye

The title of this chapter should really be "More Free Association." We're going to step a little bit further out of chronology and real history into the just-for-fun, but for serious fun. This is a discussion, from another point of view, of the impossibility of our situation in those days: juxtaposing the moment in 1950 when, really, our old rituals had their very last stand, alongside the impossible projections of new rituals, epitomized perhaps by Eleanor Roosevelt and Albert Einstein on television. Mrs. Roosevelt presenting the man with a silver tray, a nineteenth-century gesture that was meant, perhaps, to encompass the world of atomic physics—it just wasn't going to happen with the real social facts on the ground. I will make reference here—actually, I have it, so I may as well read it. Slightly outside our time span is this story. It's December 25—Christmas of 1949—and it's a picture of Pope Pius XII, surrounded by church dignitaries kneeling at the Holy Door at St. Peter's Basilica in the Vatican, and he's inaugurating the Catholic Holy Year, and it's the lead story, and it says:

POPE PIUS STARTS HOLY YEAR JUBILEE
IN ST. PETER'S RITE

And the rite is described. "Pope Pius XII opened the 1950 Holy Year today with a stately ceremony performed under the portico and inside the Basilica of St. Peter's. At 10:35 A.M. the Pontiff, a slim tall figure clad in white and gold, rose from a throne of white silk. Walking a few steps across the portico, he paused in front of a white stucco slab of the Holy Door on the side of the basilica. With a gilded silver and ivory hammer shaped as that of a brick layer, he tapped three times on a small cross embedded in the center of the door. Slowly the panel fell back. The quivering, deep-toned chimes of St. Peter's big bronze bells heralded to the city and to the world the beginning of the jubilee. Their melodious waves spread high over the roofs of the modern homes and ancient palaces, clashing and soon merging with those of Rome's 400 churches."

Well, you know, that's pretty fancy writing for the *New York Times,* and that was the spirit of the moment, in one way. It was the *Aquitania* being scrapped—and please don't think I'm referring here to the religious truth of Roman Catholicism, or anything like that; I'm talking about the ceremony. I'm talking about the hope that the ancient world would still, in some way, be relevant to the modern world. The writer in the *New York Times* himself clearly hopes that this will have been so, since he gives it his most eloquent, heartfelt literary style. There was a hope that some of the *Aquitania* civilization would still be relevant to our modern crisis; that is the sense that I'm trying to give in my analysis of that writing. On the other hand, and secondly, something I just saw while flipping through February 1950's *New York Times*—I didn't bother to photostat it because it was so small and I knew so completely what it meant. A small ad for Norman Mailer's book *The Naked and the Dead,* done in a kind of jagged black-and-white graphic style, completely different from anything else appearing in the *New York Times,* and with a teaser, a slogan, "Have you read *The Naked and the Dead?*" I looked at that, and I smiled, and I knew exactly what it was, because by the time I was at Exeter, in the late 1950s, we had decided that the hope the *New York Times* writer was expressing about the Catholic Holy Year, in terms of ceremony and the relevance of the ancient world, was not a real possibility, that what was real in American life was something else, some emerging social tradition that never reached the pages of the *New York Times* but which we felt in our own life. Something real, something visceral, and something a little negative. We boys decided in favor of Norman Mailer's interpretation of reality, especially the reality presented in his book *Advertisements for Myself,* a very defiant statement of the importance of one's own creative self in this very difficult world.

And then there's this document that I'm juxtaposing in my own mind with the Eleanor-Roosevelt-Albert-Einstein-on-television hyperspace possibility. It's on the entertainment page, it's by Val Adams, and it says, "Glamor girl of the television screen. Faye Emerson Knows How to Turn on Charm to Please the T.V. Audience. The art of playing a 'professional personality' on television is being put to rather strenuous practice by Faye Emerson. Recently she was labeled the 'most overworked guest in television' and has eased up in fear of wearing out her welcome. Now, she says, she turns down three guest-shot offers for every one she accepts. Miss Emerson's own program on the Columbia Broadcasting System Video Network is limited to fifteen minutes once a week, Mondays at 11:00 P.M. If it were presented more frequently, she would have to curtail some of her traveling on the various channels. There are three different panel discussion programs on which she appears at regular intervals, and she knows practically every program moderator in the business by his first name. As something less than a great star of stage, screen and radio, Miss Emerson has made a more resounding impact in television than all the others put together. An analysis of her headway breaks down to female charm presented with careful, lady-like discretion. She just sits and oozes personality. In recent weeks she had taken great delight in asking viewers to vote on whether she should wear low-cut or high-neck gowns. It was perfectly safe for Miss Emerson to raise the issue. She couldn't possibly have any doubt as to the opinions of the male viewers; as for the female viewers, her showmanship was bound to create a lot of talk, to say the least." Smart. "Coupled with Miss Emerson's photogenic qualities is a mental alertness not usually expected of glamor girls. She lays no claim to being a wit or a good story-teller, but conversationally she's in the upper brackets. Although she has definite ideas and positive opinions, she expresses them in a nice easy way rather than the 'now get this!' manner of an army sergeant, a common failing of many career girls who try to sell their intelligence. Apparently Miss Emerson realizes that a man can appreciate an intelligent woman so long as she does not suggest that she is as smart as he is. Actually Miss Emerson is more entertaining when serving as a guest on a TV program than she is on her own show. She opens the CBS show by talking about herself—recounting her experiences of the previous week, telling where she's been and urging all the viewers to run out and do the same. The only catch would appear to be that the average viewer either doesn't have the money or the time or just doesn't give a hoot about making a weekly whirlwind tour. When Miss Emerson finishes telling about the apparent life of a glamor girl, she brings on a guest or two, usually theatrical personalities who relate their present activities and what is coming up next, if anything. Unfortunately, the conversations seldom seem to allow Miss Emerson to show at best advantage. But when she visits other programs such as the panel discussions or question posers, there is less of the fluff and froth and a more meaningful performance. In rehearsal on Monday evenings, Miss Emerson works herself into a lather. She is very emphatic about the way the show should be done and will frequently exclaim, 'I don't like this!' While open to negotiation and compromise, her determination to have things her way is quite evident. During rehearsal she whips along at sixty miles an hour, figuratively speaking, but slams on the brakes and slows down when the show actually goes on the air. Miss Emerson is not particularly enamored of dramatic roles in television, which she has filled on occasions, and terms such work a 'mental hazard.' The grind of rehearsals, the split-second timing and the very rigid routine demanded of the players is more than she cares to endure. Referring to herself as a 'nonconformist,' Miss Emerson implies that in front of the TV camera she prefers to create her own act rather than the prepared assignment of others. As for the near future, Miss Emerson has discussed plans with CBS for a long-term contract whereby she would be given a five-times-a-week television show, but no agreement has been reached. Her present Monday night show comes to the network through an advertising agency. Miss Emerson, who is 32, was born in Elizabeth, La. In her early years she lived in El Paso and Beaumont, Tex. and at the age of 12 moved to San Diego, Calif. Here she graduated from high school and attended San Diego State College for one year. After playing in local repertory productions she was placed under contract by Warner Brothers. Her only Broadway stage appearance came in 1948 when she appeared in 'The Play's the Thing' for about six months."

My overview of the civilization as presented in the *New York Times* of February 1, 1950, is that in World War II, the Germans lost, and Faye Emerson won.

Flair

What seems to be happening is this: after the failure of the 1960s cultural revolution, everyone is busy trying to achieve the stability and prosperity, the dominance of the 1950s, absent all the information available in the *New York Times* of February 1, 1950. I'm thinking of the education of young male children now. The failure of the 1960s cultural revolution to achieve closure, a sense of comedy and tragedy, a sense of sufficiency, and a curriculum sufficient to educate the young, is a big topic. Since the 1970s now appear to me to be a time when the top level of the cultural revolution's survivors began to reinvent for themselves a pre-1950 Jack Warner Hollywood kind of life, I say let's look for a moment at something that was categorically fashionable—the high-mainstream, cutting-edge adventurous life of fashion in 1950, the year we've been discussing. In looking at the Mainstream American Cultural Artifact I'm about to introduce—and I haven't picked it up yet, and I haven't looked at it for ten years, and I don't remember what I saw when I looked at it ten years ago, but my very strong guess is that as we go through this artifact, we will find nothing of what we've been talking about in discussing the *New York Times* of February 1950, except we'll find a contiguousness with the Faye Emerson phenomenon—Faye Emerson, our first personality known for being a personality—because Faye Emerson would have picked up this magazine and been aware of it, and the people editing the magazine would have been aware of her, and of the potential for glamour within television—we'll find a little Faye Emerson, and we'll just find a tiny hint, perhaps, at moments, in the discussion of some piece of avant-garde, whether it's of the past, in the sense of Picabia, or an awareness of Kafka, or something of this kind, we'll find some little echo, perhaps, of that small, challenging, tantalizing advertisement with the tormented black-and-white male head: "Have you read *The Naked and the Dead*?"

So now let's start. The Mainstream American Cultural Artifact in front of me is *Flair* magazine, the New York issue, September 1950—it cost fifty cents. It's green, it's good-looking, it's attractive; I like it. There's the Statue of Liberty, but the Statue of Liberty is against a kind of Mondrian-done-in-waves, Mondrian taken down a peg. As to the modern art of it—that's what glamour does, it takes modern art down a peg, so you like it, and indeed— oh, I've been cheating a bit; that is, I certainly did see the cover when I picked up the magazine ten minutes ago, and, indeed, the way the name "Flair" is done, and it's done in black-and-white up top and then just in black all around the four sides, there *is* a graphic echo of the "Have you read *The Naked and the Dead*?" The cover is kind of interesting, in and of itself. They spent money on *Flair*. *Flair* was the personal project of a woman named Fleur Cowles, who had been the wife of—well, still was, at this time—the wife of Gardner Cowles, who ran *Look* magazine. This was her upscale reward for being the wife of a powerful media man. And she had taste, and she knew what glamour was, and you open the cover, and you discover, if you didn't sense it before, that there's been a hole cut in the cover, so that you can see through to the first page, and on the first page you see what you'd only seen a little of at first, which is this small Statue of Liberty against this Mondrian background of boxy shapes, which now are revealed to be the office buildings of New York. One sees the Empire State Building, and the message it gives you is, first of all, a kind of television-like confusion. The modern art of it really goes away when you open it up. It becomes programmatic.

It isn't just an artist's vision of something, it's an artist of the second rank using motifs developed by artists of the first rank, and he's telling you something, and, indeed, there's a kind of television snow all across the two opening pages. Again, it's attractive, but not quite as attractive as the cover is, and perhaps the reason I think so is that the Statue of Liberty begins to seem just like a black smudge, and we're overwhelmed by the skyline of these colored waves. Rocking onward. First, an ad for Neiman Marcus on the right: "The sealskin cutaway in new deep Matara." The woman is that remarkable person, in such dramatic juxtaposition to Mr. Churchill, Mr. Sumner Pike, Mr. Sumner Anyone—all those men in the *New York Times,* all that H-bomb of it—this is a drop-dead beautiful woman in the Neiman Marcus ad, and one has to notice, first of all, that sealskin wouldn't be allowed now, or fashionable, but the jacket is enormously attractive. This is a world of security and effort. There is no room for doubt here. No atom bomb has dropped on this. This knows what it's doing. Next to it is an ad for something called "Sag-no-mor worsted-wool jersey, by Wyner," and it's a suit, available at Henri Bendel, and this is an ad for the fabric out of which dresses are made—it reminds you of Seventh Avenue. Neiman Marcus reminds you of the retail; the "Sag-no-mor" reminds you of the manufacturing behind the retail. I turn back to an I. Magnin ad on the previous page: more black Alaska sealskin, and, again, the coat isn't allowable now, but, oh, the girl is. Excuse me for calling her a girl, but that's who she was in the fifties; she was The Girl—that's who every woman wanted to be, The Girl, and the one in the Saks ad here has got it. She's got the raised eyebrows, she's got the lips, she's wearing a hat with a veil and carrying a purse in a way that no woman can carry a purse now. The atmosphere here is of utter, complete security, and I have to say that all of the clothes are wearable now, and not ironically. This is "Sophie's close-sheared skirt, curved hip-bone jacket. Significant Fall suit in imported worsted with collar and cuffs of bengaline faille; star-point, button pockets rounding the hips. Elegant afternoon costume in black, gray or navy, regular or custom sizes," and so forth. More secure women. More coats—ah—*Flair* personified: Mrs. William O'Dwyer.

Now, I'm just going to have to pause for a moment. This is quite a lot. I've closed the magazine for a minute, and I just feel I should say what I know about the two women on my mind at the moment. They are Fleur Cowles and Sloan Simpson. Mrs. William O'Dwyer was Sloan Simpson; and Bill O'Dwyer was the mayor of New York City for a time, until things went bad for him; there was this or that trouble and he resigned. After he resigned, a man called Impellitteri was mayor of New York City, and after Impellitteri, Robert Wagner, the father of my friend Bobby Wagner, was mayor of New York City, and I'm thinking at this moment of a chronology I'm having a little trouble with. The first time I saw Gracie Mansion was in 1958, and that was only eight years after the publication of this magazine, and I realize—I've been realizing this for some time, but it's very striking to me now—that the adults I saw in New York City, in what I'll call the Gracie Mansion context, were very mysterious and interesting to me, and that I've spent part of my energy, part of my life, thinking about them and following them. Trying to figure out who they were when I first saw them when I was a young child, coming into the city in 1950 and '51, the time of this magazine, the time we're talking about in this book, and also, as I followed them, their reputations, the story of their lives as they grew older, as my generation moved into cultural prominence.

Sloan Simpson came from Texas. She was a Texas girl who thought just maybe she could be The Girl in New York. Again, forgive me for the use of this phrase, but that's how these women thought. There was such a thing as the Top Girl in New York, and many women and young women thought it was worthwhile to get to be that girl. And by girl, I mean in this case a woman who has a dominance position over all women, and who is attractive, as a girl is, to all men. That was the name of that game, and that was the template off which magazines like *Flair,* and of course *Vogue,* and others, played at that time. We are before the days of "One hundred and one options for you, Miss America"; we are still in the day of certain women, doing certain things, wearing certain clothes. A pecking order. Sloan Simpson was well-born. Money in Texas, but she had an adventurous spirit, decided to become a model, and did. Met Bill O'Dwyer, who was married; he divorced; they took off. He was much older. Bill O'Dwyer ran into his trouble; he was made ambassador to Mexico. My uncle during the fifties was the naval attaché in Mexico. My aunt and my uncle lived in Mrs. O'Dwyer's world. I know quite a lot about her from that perspective. By the time I was a young man, she was corny, by which I mean she had social authority, all right, but it was corny social authority by the lights of my generation. It was a colorful dress on the terrace at Acapulco, with Nada and Nunu and Nell, that group of—whoever. She lived on and on, holding on to that grand duchy. The moment we're talking about, September 1950, would have been the apex of her national social authority. For the rest of her life, she held on to a kind of grand duchy in Mexico, where she got to represent a kind of New York authority for Cafe Society people there. That's her story. Fleur Cowles wasn't too different. *Flair* didn't work out economically; I'm sure that Gardner Cowles knew that it wouldn't, but it really didn't, and I suspect that September 1950 was the appex of Fleur Cowles's authority, too. She was going to show *Vogue* a thing or two, and didn't, and she and Gardner Cowles divorced, and she went to London, where *she* was a little corny. Cornier than Sloan Simpson was in Mexico City, by which I mean, Mexico's very forgiving; there's a sense in which nothing new ever happens culturally there; that's a wildly broad statement, but you can live there in such a way that you don't need to be aware of anything happening culturally, let me put it that way, and you can live in pastels and jewels and a walled compound, and know Nada and Nunu and Nell, and no one can absolutely say that your time has passed. There's a timeless cosmopolitan style alive in Mexico, if you want it. London may be that way now; I don't know London now, but certainly through the 1960s and into the 1970s it wasn't like that. You had the Angry Young Men, you had the Mods, you had the Beatles, and, well, Fleur wasn't that. She was out of it, is what she was, and she did what many women do who've been prominent for a while and then suddenly aren't prominent. She began to represent the higher end of it. She began to present herself as someone who was interested in art rather than glamour. I'm not aware that that was a completely sincere position on her part.

I was in Albany the other day, doing some research for this book, looking at the *New York Times* in the State Library there, and I ended up walking through the State Capitol, because it's such a beautiful old building, it's fun to walk through it, and I remembered something my friend Julius Edelstein told me about my friend Bobby Wagner the first time he met him. Bobby was six. His father was borough president of Manhattan then. It was probably exactly at the time we're talking about, 1949 or 1950. Julius, who later became Mayor Wagner's protegé, at that time worked for Senator—or Governor—Lehman. We'll have to straighten that out. He worked for Lehman, but whether that was—well, Dewey was Governor until '48—I'm just not sure what Herbert Lehman was then, but Julius was an aide de camp to Herbert Lehman, and Mayor Wagner—then, Borough President Wagner—came to Albany for some reason, with Bobby, and he made it a point to introduce his precocious son into all his professional circumstances, from the age of six or seven. And Julius tells the story of going into an office in the State Capitol expecting to see Borough President Wagner, but Bob Wagner had gone elsewhere, leaving young Bobby alone, and the story Julius tells is very poignant, from all our points of view, but certainly from Julius's. He recalls Bobby's graciousness, his adult bearing, and his hospitality. Bobby, dressed in short pants, went across the room, picked up a small dish of nuts, and brought it to Julius, because that's what hosts did when a guest appeared. I'm trying to catch the anthropology of my situation and Bobby Wagner's at Gracie Mansion in 1958, when I first visited there. Here we were, being brought up in very old-fashioned ways to be little gentlemen, and to take an interest in the highest high end of the patriarchal tradition, which, for us, was the tradition of Franklin Roosevelt, and yet the social construct we lived in was the construct of *Flair*. The crown people were fighting for wasn't a masculine crown; it was a feminine crown, and it was the crown of *Flair*.

One Step, Two Step, Three Step, Four Step

It was very striking last night how many people in a celebrated
condition as to their everyday and professional lives as reported in *People* magazine, say, or on the tabloid television
shows, say, seemed to be in what I'm calling an on-the-way-to-a-
first-step position. Madonna, for instance, the biggest name in
the world, in a way, didn't have her film nominated and hadn't
been asked to perform; she called the people up and said, "I want
to sing." Apparently, she doesn't belong to the club, not really.
She's on her way into the club, maybe. If there is a club. That's
the way the whole evening seemed to go. There were people on
their way to having a fully evolved one-step, and there were a few
who were clearly already there, well into their first step. Susan
Sarandon, for instance, appeared with utter confidence. She's
there—well, she's there as a person who's taken one step. What
do I mean by, "One step, two step, three step, four step?" Of
course, my reference here is to F. Scott Fitzgerald's remark that
there are no second acts in American life. You get to try, you get
to succeed, you get to make your point, once. Susan Sarandon.
But there are people who get to take a second step. Or sometimes
a third. I've always been fascinated with the story of the making
of *Gone With the Wind,* what it took David O. Selznick—what he
had to have, what he did have, in order to make that remarkable
film. Selznick was a three-step boy. His father, Louis J. Selznick,

was one of the remarkable anarchs who came out of the nick-elodeon era into the silent-film era. That is, he is exactly comparable to, perhaps not Steven Jobs, but one of Steven Jobs's partners, or— you know the names better than I do, the interesting anarchs who stepped out of wonkdom into prominence for a while in the computer industry. Mr. Wang is one. Wang Computer was the biggest thing in the world in a certain sphere for a while, and then it suddenly wasn't and went away. Well, that was Louis J. Selznick. He controlled stars of high caliber for a while in the silent-film industry, and then suddenly he didn't control the ones that mattered and he went bankrupt. In any case, David O. Selznick, from the time he was ten years old, was brought up in it. He knew the players before there were players, let's put it that way. And I'm not counting that as a step; that's just part of social training. His first step was in the silent-film business. He did well. His second step was in talkies, working at RKO and then at MGM, and he did very well. *Dinner at Eight,* an archetypal film of the thirties, is a David O. Selznick production. His third step was to found his own company, Selznick International Pictures. And from the basis of the two earlier steps, he made *Gone With the Wind.* He had the Rolodex. He had the technical knowledge. He had the expertise. He had the social security. He had the taste. He had the everything of the everything. Built, step by step. A three-step is what *Gone With the Wind* is, and anyone who wants to make anything like *Gone With the Wind* should be prepared to have done two steps already.

So, when we're dealing with President Dwight David Eisenhower, we're really dealing with four steps, not three. We're dealing with winning against one's young fellows from the old America, Middle West division; we're dealing with winning in the cohort competition of the 1920s and thirties; we're dealing with a third step of incomparable success, the conduct of Operation Overlord, the invasion of Europe. Fourth step: president of the United States. I mean, what didn't he know about the America he knew about in 1955? What do I mean by the America he knew about? Well, he couldn't have known, and didn't know, about the psychology of ten-year-old children, say, or even the psychology of twenty-five-year-old men, but as to who held and had held power, and what they were like socially, there was nothing he didn't know. He knew how a given man would take a given order. He knew how a given shitheel would shilly-shally against the order and then, at a later date, acquiesce. He just knew all that. And if the game suddenly shifted from producing the 1955 Chevrolet to something real old-timey, a farmer kicking a clod of clay in a cornfield somewhere, well, he was on top of that, too. And if he were approached by a young Du Pont, whose point of view was, "I've been here, and I've been there, and my family's the richest," well, Ike had sat down with Churchill and Alexander and Roosevelt and Marshall, and he was in a very good position to raise his eyebrow or close a door. Ike is our unique, in modern times, social man.

I'm going to relate one or two or three Mainstream Cultural Artifacts now. I saw the movie *Liar Liar*, with Jim Carrey, the other day, and it's a very funny movie and very much of this moment, and it surprised me. I didn't know that you could craft a movie around a father's love finally revealed and dramatized before his young son. I'm not aware of any American movie that has had this dynamic, not quite. The film isn't about the rediscovery of family life, or the overall human values, or the importance of marriage, although there's a reconnect with the marriage event at the end of the film, nor is it about a man and his children; it's about a man and his son. It's about overcoming narcissism within the context of transgenerational male bonding. That's new. And very much to the point for us, socially, now. An alarming Mainstream American Cultural Event taking place within the same time frame as the release of *Liar Liar* is the *MTV Spring Break* coverage. Thousands, maybe tens of thousands of isolated, working-toward-perfection-and-toward-the-camera human bodies on the beach in Panama City, Florida, hosted by young men and women operating from a deep sense of ironic self-contempt. Of course, the natural reference here for anyone who wants to do a little film juxtaposition is to one of those Annette Funicello movies of the fifties, but that's easy and you can do that on your own. Here we have the audience for all the films the Academy Award people are making, and there's a kind of terrifying balance between the nature of the Academy Award celebration and what's revealed on MTV about the nature of the audience of the films made by the film community. Isolation is the order of the day, almost as though dictated by some event within human ecology.

The Academy Awards are real theater; these are real men and women doing their work; and, looking at this piece of real theater, one can glimpse the real nature of the community they live in. Which is in juxtaposition to how this community is made to appear on television and in magazines, for instance. When *People* magazine does the twenty-five hot young new stars, the magazine supplies the existence of Hollywood, and announces that these twenty-five are now being invited into this place called Hollywood. In other words, it is in the interest of the magazine to posit the existence of something; Hollywood is Harvard. The twenty-five new up-and-comers are the entering class. You envy them; you wish you were at Harvard yourself. That's what a magazine does, and what *Entertainment Tonight* does, for instance. The Academy Award presentation reveals this trick of the magazine and television community to be a lie. There is no Hollywood in the sense the magazines posit. There they are, these young, talented people, already been in two or three movies, already gotten an Academy Award nomination, and they don't look as if they belong. They don't look as if they've had their one-step. There's been no initiation. There's been validation before initiation, always a problem. The people involved mysteriously distrust their own validation. Why should they have the award before they've matriculated? A diploma before entrance? They don't get it. They accept the diploma, they want the diploma, but it seems strange that they should have it before they have a sense of having entered. It looked, the ceremony, like a national bake-off, it looked as though someone had decided that there should be two cooks from every state in the union who should be assembled in the Shrine Auditorium for a given time to be together, to compete to find out who had baked the best cake, and as soon as it was over, everybody went back to wherever they came from and that was it until next year.

And that balanced perfectly the Spring Break phenomenon of jittery, isolated, full of self-contempt, and not particularly sexy—well-sculpted but not sexy—young people in Panama Beach on MTV. It looked as if we'd finally gotten to the end of what I will call our Elvis, or Vitalitarian, period in American life, where you got somewhere by stripping to the waist, showing your muscles, and dancing. My boundaries would be 1956–1997; those would be the time boundaries I would posit for the first existence of Pure Vitality as your best passport. So, understanding that 1956—beginning actually in January of 1956—began the Vitalitarian era, let's go back to the year before, 1955. Well, it was the Year of the Summit, when it was a real summit. Ike met Khrushchev in Geneva, and in those days a summit was more than something with a tag on it; it was a theater in which people sat chewing their nails. "What will these two individual male avatars decide for us?" That, on the one hand; and it's also the year of *The Seven Year Itch*, a Billy Wilder movie with Tom Ewell and the never sufficiently to be praised Marilyn Monroe. And just as *Liar Liar*, with its ferocious interest in father-son bonding, stands just one millimeter beyond the end of the Vitalitarian era, posturing itself, poising itself toward something new, so does the Wilder film give you a sense of what life was like one millisecond before Elvis changed everything. If this were a classroom, or a lecture with audiovisual aids, I would play for you the first ten minutes of *The Seven Year Itch*. The rest of the film begins to be about boy-girl, and with the girl of all time, Miss Monroe, and quite right, but the setup for the film is accurate socially because that's who Wilder was. He was someone who worked, like Alfred Hitchcock, from the real life on the ground that people led and were expected to respond to.

I mention here a film like *The Silence of the Lambs*, which is, in tiny part, related to our real life on the ground but relates

mostly to our deepest psychological fears in fantasyland. I want
to relate the first ten minutes of *The Seven Year Itch* to what I've
been saying about the social structure Dwight Eisenhower controlled, and how that impacted on male inheritance. Ike, I hope
I've made clear, had way, way, way too much. There can rarely
have been a time in human history when so many men found
themselves in vague or direct hierarchical reference to one man,
and the first ten minutes of *The Seven Year Itch* relate to the devolution of white male psychology in our time. The film begins at
the old Pennsylvania Station—now, alas, trashed. It's poignant
that Wilder, who was then an older man, still wants to use a train
station as a background; train stations are such a great background, and this was the greatest of all train stations, and his
social reference is to the construct I've delineated as the 1925–
1955 construct. It's a liberal arts version of it; the Ewell character is, in theory, in the book trade, although he's in a marginal
part of the book trade, but the references are to a version of
country-club living, within all the old, established, hierarchical
forms of Dartmouth to Harvard to Princeton to Du Pont. They're
not laid out *click, click, click,* but that's who the people presented
are. And indeed, the strange, dispirited quality of that construct
is shown. This isn't so much fun anymore. Something's happened. It's still "the best" that we have, it's still about learning in
a way, it's still about being a dominant man in a dominant city in
a dominant culture in a way, but something's happened. What's
happened, of course, is that the world has had a series of psychotic shocks, which have been brought under control only with
enormous trouble, and the people handling these psychotic
shocks are few indeed, secretive part of the time, holding power
we don't have any idea of, actually, controlled by one man: President Eisenhower. In a world of men, only one man really func-
tions in the way that thousands of headmen of villages and towns
once functioned. Only one man has all the necessary information; only one man can take all the necessary action to aggress, to
defend, to make peace, to make war. I mean, within the context of
absolute salvation or absolute destruction, which is what the

terms of the equation were then. Now, we've recovered a little bit of the old hunter-gatherer masculine energy. If you have a regional telephone company under your sway, you can feel you're a real guy, in a way. That's just a parenthetical remark, to bring us back to *Liar Liar*. And why, once again, we have energetic, dominant men, but confused. So Tom Ewell says goodbye to his wife and son at the train station, and the plot of the movie is, will he now take the opportunity of the absence of his wife to be unfaithful to her? But there's another rather poignant aspect to this leave-taking at Pennsylvania Station, which is that he doesn't seem to like his son all that much. His son is rambunctious and wears a spacesuit and a plastic helmet, and when Tom Ewell goes to kiss the son, the son wriggles away and says, "Mommy, Mommy, he's cutting off my oxygen." And the son has a little plastic ray gun, and then Tom Ewell goes home, he closes the doors of an old-fashioned 1955 television set, and says, "Thank God I don't have to watch any more Captain Video or Howdy Doodie."

Hitch and Elvis

L et's rock-and-roll through four important Mainstream American Cultural Artifacts, all by that intuitive genius Alfred Hitchcock. I can't help saying that these films were, to some extent, part of my experience growing up, because they were released during my lifetime, but recently they really became part of my growing up, as I began to understand how intuitively and deftly Alfred Hitchcock dealt with themes having to do with coming to manhood, the nature of manhood, the avatars of wisdom and evil on the face of the earth—themes that, in an earlier generation, had been the province of Thomas Mann. Mann's tracing of the decline in security and decisiveness and manliness within the Buddenbrook family, for instance, comes to mind, and his discussion of that modern Hamlet, Hans Castorp in *The Magic Mountain.* Hitchcock picked up this thread during a time when good and evil were reconfiguring and couldn't so easily be told apart.

My first artifact was made, I was shocked and delighted to realize when I looked at it closely, in 1943—the year I was born. The artifact we're going to discuss here is *Saboteur.* Hitchcock directed the film version of *The 39 Steps* in England before he came to Hollywood, and, as the reader will or will not remember, the Heart of Darkness, the secret place where the undermining of the good in society is going on, is in a remote fastness in Scotland—or is it the north of England? One of those places where very conventional, attractive, flawless people would appear to be living. In *Saboteur,* he sort of takes it to the fortieth step and presents a very alarming milieu, this time in ranch country—is it Nevada? Possibly—where last-gasp patrician WASPs have gone for their Kenya-like experience, let's call it, and there the mastermind of the undermining operation, the saboteur operation, resides, in flawless mimicry of a fine old fellow; but also present, and never again to be present in Hitchcock films so far as I know or can remember at this moment, is an avatar of the old America. He's blind, he's a kind of craftsman person, he's a pianist, he's intuitive and magical and trusting, and to this man the falsely accused man, played by Robert Cummings, comes. It's a very moving, to me, scene, because, as I say, the film was released in the year of my birth, and this kind of character never appeared, as far as I recall, in a Hitchcock film again. Hitchcock was extraordinarily adept at taking the real social landscape and adding his set of values, his intuitions to it; that was always his strength, that he knew the zeitgeist, knew which actors and actresses could present to the audience a sense of the civilization they were, in fact, living in.

And then, of course, Hitchcock crafted the story to give us a little sense of the horror that, of course, has been a part of modern life. The scene from the film that's usually shown when clips of Hitchcock's films are shown in sequence to demonstrate something of his career, and the scene in question is always discussed in visual terms, what a visual genius he was—well, he was certainly a visual genius, but also a thematic genius and an intuitive genius—it's the famous scene at the top of the Statue of Liberty, where the Cummings character is holding on to the sleeve of the saboteur's coat, and the sleeve unravels and then we pan up at Lady Liberty, and the villain plunges to his death, and we have a nice moment of release, because the villain has plunged to his death. Well, this is Hitchcock at his intuitive—oh no, let's say also manipulative—at his intuitive and manipulative best, because every artist wants you to see something, as opposed to something else, and every artist has a text and a subtext. Which is opposed to merely discursive people who tell you in a simple conversation, you know, all their concerns and over and out, and you don't remember anything about it—public-relations writing and so forth—and looking at this movie again, and with the memory of the earlier scene of the last gasp of intuitive, decent, liberal arts America, in the figure of the blind man, looking at the scene at the Statue of Liberty, I noticed simply that, visually, there was a message delivered that was in juxtaposition to the happy ending of the film. The camera holds on the man's unraveling sleeve long enough for one's mind to take the image deeply in, and then, within the same scene, one is shown Lady Liberty, and, when you refer this to your textual mind and reflect that the saboteur has plunged to his death and Robert Cummings is doing just fine, it's a happy ending. Lady Liberty wins, the saboteur loses, and Robert Cummings continues to go forward in life. But visually, the shot seems to be saying, "Lady Liberty's unraveling." The victory in World War II that we're hoping for, and pushing for, even propagandizing for a little, and Hitchcock certainly did a little of that in the movie—and quite right, why shouldn't you, during wartime?—he seems to be saying that, victory or no victory, onward movement for Robert Cummings or not, Lady Liberty's unraveling. I imagine he presented this textual-subtextual juxtaposition as something of a challenge. After all, we still were trying to win the war in '43, and as it was, we did win the war, and we had a grace period to look forward to, so it wasn't in the nature of a doomsaying thing but as a challenge that Hitchcock crafted the final scenes of the movie. On the one hand, Robert Cummings had overcome, and the saboteur was plunging to his death; on the other hand, there was this other thing to think about.

The next Hitchcock movie I want to discuss is *Rear Window,* a movie of 1954, and a good time to mention Hitchcock's brilliant use of American star power. Once again, one of his concerns always was to present to us the zeitgeist we clearly had already given ourselves, and in this he resembled Eisenhower; Eisenhower didn't quarrel with the uses to which we put our Eisenhower America. It didn't occur to him that he could quarrel. He was not in a position to tell Detroit not to put fins on cars. And Hitchcock didn't think he was in a position to tell America which kind of stars they ought to have. He just was awfully good at picking the ones that were useful to him. In this case, the stars were James Stewart and Grace Kelly. I can enter the story directly, because I remember (owing to the circumstances of my upbringing) people in the Grace Kelly–James Stewart mode. James Stewart was presented as a photographer for *Life* magazine, and Grace Kelly is, of course, a stylish blonde, with access to the Cafe Society of it. Oddly enough, I have in mind a particular couple that I saw during my growing up whom I can put in the place of Stewart and Kelly—of course, there were many other such couples; that's why Hitchcock chose to use stereotypical figures, precisely because they were, in fact, dominant on the face of the earth at that moment. The couple I'm thinking of were named Norton and Maggie Mockridge, and Maggie Mockridge was a beautiful, blond, well-born woman, and Norton Mockridge was a newspaperman in New York and later a columnist for the old *World Telegram and Sun*; a little bit of Hemingway, a little bit of Broadway, a little bit of Hollywood. When MGM wanted to make a Doris Day–Clark Gable movie about the newspaper business called *Teacher's Pet,* it was Norton Mockridge who went out to Hollywood and told them what the city room of a newspaper in New York should look like, and the city room he modeled it on was the city room of the old *World Telegram and Sun.* Anyway, I was around people who inhabited the Jimmy Stewart–Grace Kelly model, so this film begins to have more meaning for me. The *Saboteur* movie, in a way, is more poignant for me, because it tells me how embattled, at the moment of my birth, the civilization I care about was, and how much my chances within liberal arts civilization had to do with the winning of World War II, and the grace period we got, especially for young people, during that time. You got permission to ignore all the psychoses that had affected the world for so long, and presume a clean slate, and that's what I did and what a number of people of my generation did—we presumed a clean slate. We were told we could, so we did. Evil had been defeated, evil was not something that—and of course Hitchcock had the different, and correct, view of this—but we were told that evil wasn't something that snaked inevitably through history but rather something that occasionally rose among other, non-American people, and was defeated by honorable people (usually us), and the honorable people, us in this case, got to have our personalities completely validated as functional, competent, and good. And if you're a child and people tell you this, however well you know psychologically it can't possibly be true, you're led to accept what is told you.

But I can remember, at ten, at eleven, at twelve, during the *Rear Window* years, being confused in exactly the terms laid out in the movie, with absolute authority, by Hitchcock. The world was supposed to be about all of us as, on the one hand, completely powerful, functional people, and, on the other hand, we were supposed to be working from a clean slate on the deepest and most serious problems confronting the world. Yet I saw when I was young that, in fact, when you got to the top or toward the top of things, you found, indeed, very flawed but glamorous people, people who were, in fact, not thinking about the kinds of problems that the blind man was thinking about in 1943, not acting intuitively and bravely and in some kind of harmony with nature as that blind man in *Saboteur* was acting, and certainly not taking on impossible tasks. People were acting in a kind of what I've come to call a deutero-Hemingway way: they were preserving their own vitality by being adventurous within the media. The James Stewart character is someone who roams the world, but with a camera, not a gun, and not like Schweitzer, setting up modes of change in impossible places. He's touring the world adventurously in the interest of preserving his masculine independence, but he's doing it with a camera.

The third artifact—and now we're in the heart of Eisenhower country—is *The Man Who Knew Too Much*. Once again it's James Stewart, and it's my private belief that Hitchcock was fascinated,

not by James Stewart himself, but by what James Stewart referred
to culturally. It was something he didn't have in England, and no
other country had it, this kind of straightforward, brave man with
enormous power, in a way, wherever he went, whether he was a
hospital administrator, or a doctor, as he is in *The Man Who Knew
Too Much,* or an automobile executive, or a man on Wall Street—
these American men educated in the liberal arts, but not very
deeply, securely lodged in an American success construct, which
they perfectly understood, and moved forward in with considerable confidence—these men were fascinating, I think, for a time,
to Hitchcock, because Hitchcock was a great man of the theater
and interested in archetype, and this was an archetype you just
didn't find in France, or in England, or anywhere. And of course
the woman is Doris Day and not Grace Kelly, and here you have,
again—and I want to compare Hitchcock at this point to Diana
Vreeland, who was a friend of mine and who was similarly pas-
sive at moments as to the inevitability of vogue—Hitchcock completely accepting the change in social dominance between 1954
and 1957, merely holding a mirror up to what had happened
socially, because, indeed, in those three years, and three years is
a short time, the Cafe Society, *Vogue* magazine—actually, in the
movie it's *Harper's Bazaar*—aspect of America, of New York in
particular, had somewhat declined. In the early fifties there was
still an assumption that what went on at Twenty-One, or this
place, or that place, mattered in some American sense as well as
in a metropolitan sense, that the reference, for nearly everyone
with ambition at all, would be toward New York, toward the center of that Cafe Society writer's life, and that the girl, the big girl,
the girl in the close-up, would be someone with some training
in traditional social matters. By 1957, it's all Tammy and the
Bachelor. We had a new American woman presented to us, and
at her best she was Doris Day, and at her worst she was Debbie
Reynolds. She was enormously powerful, almost arrogantly powerful, not a feminist in any way we would think of feminism now;
on the other hand, she was front and center and central in a way
that, perhaps, women haven't been since. And in the middle of

the movie, in one of what I think of as Hitchcock's *moments of being*, because they happen in his movies in a way that they sometimes happen in books but really very rarely happen in any work of art, and Hitchcock's films are art with a capital A—in the middle of the film, the action stops. It's a little like the old theatrical convention that something or other stops the show; when you stop the show, you do something that is so good or so important that it just doesn't matter that you've dropped the plot for a while; the audience goes into another mode and accepts the event that you've correctly placed within your artwork, and then is happy to pick up the threads of your dramatic action afterward, and in this case the show-stopping moment is Doris Day singing to her young son "Que Sera, Sera, Whatever Will Be Will Be."

Well, this has a lot of meaning for me, especially if I think of myself as I was in those years. The really important parent is presented as the mother. She's the one who understands the world, and, indeed, all through the film she's a lot cagier about things than Jimmy Stewart is, although Stewart acts with traditional, Western masculine bravery, and the two of them triumph over the kidnappers, who are the villains in this piece, although they're kidnappers with a cultural, political plot, to do with a political kidnapping and assassination. The mother is presented as the one with ongoing wisdom information for the young male child. There's no comparable scene where Jimmy Stewart explains the world to his young son, and the point is that Jimmy Stewart, as powerful as he is in a kind of Eisenhower way, as an individual male avatar, isn't going to pass anything on to his son. And it's the woman who sings, the woman is Doris Day, she has a marvelous voice, and it's a very moving scene. People sometimes underestimate Doris Day as a screen presence, as an avatar representer; but she did represent a moment in the history of American womanhood, and brilliantly, and the meaning of the song is—we don't know. What will be will be. And that, it seems to me, is completely in line with the unraveling moment in *Saboteur*. And the intervening scene to mention is: Grace Kelly's big close-up with Jimmy Stewart in *Rear Window*. In *Saboteur* the male figure, Robert Cummings, is completely, in theory, the focus of the piece. He ends up with a blond woman—the actress's name is momentarily escaping me—and it's really his job to educate her, and even bat her around a little, if you know what I mean—there are a couple of little physical restraint tricks played on her to get her to come to what he is perceiving as her senses, and in this, indeed, he has been encouraged by the old liberal arts man, who feels that his niece (because the young woman is his niece) is not getting the point about how life really works: the importance of the aura, the importance of intuition, the importance of trust. Indeed, she is presented as something of a cynical cookie, and, in fact, she's a model, someone whose picture is on a lot of billboards. She's a media girl, and she needs to learn a lesson, and Robert Cummings supplies the lesson she needs to learn, and everything turns out okay in the male-female relationship.

But by 1954, it's the big close-up, and it's a wonderful close-up; it's worth infinite study. You just see Grace Kelly's big face come at you on the screen, and this time *he* needs the educating. He needs to learn that she's capable of acting, and acting bravely, and her power is vaster, in cinematic terms, than the actress's in *Saboteur.* That big close-up is quite something. You don't say no to someone who comes at you when she's Grace Kelly. By 1957, it's shifted again, and not only is the man not teaching the woman a lesson, he's not learning a lesson either. The couple has, in some important way, separated. The kind of—oh, their affection for each other is presumed, but their real bond is within the fact of their parenthood. Their two separate personalities—and they're presented as having two very different personalities—are never to be reconciled. He's not going to teach her a lesson the way Robert Cummings taught his girl a lesson, and he's not going to learn from her how a woman can be this, that, or the other, as happens in *Rear Window;* they're separate, and they're going to stay separate, and finally, it's her point of view from her separate, personal experience that's going to be the informing wisdom for the male child: what will be will be. Now, that, of course, is not traditional Western wisdom, what will be will be. Traditional Western wisdom says: "What will be will be plus me." In other words, yes, there's a flow, but that flow includes my vector, and watch my wake. And that's not Doris Day's point of view in *The Man Who Knew Too Much*, and of course the irony of the title is that although James Stewart is, in one way, the man who knew too much, in another way he's the man who knows much too little. He doesn't understand the personalities, the dynamics, the power relationships among foreigners at all, for instance. He's easily seduced by the English couple, who are functioning within Hitchcock's *39 Steps* mode, and he really can't tell one foreigner from another, although he has luck, and that gets him through. So, that's a part of the unraveling story that Hitchcock was telling, and it's a film in which one hungers for the wise man, the intuitive Western man of *Saboteur*. That would be very healing, but Hitchcock doesn't give him to us, because, by Hitchcock's perception, by my perception, that guy just wasn't around, and Hitchcock just wouldn't introduce human avatars who weren't on the face of the planet, and that was his integrity.

The fourth film is *Vertigo*, and here, the male-female relationship has become a nightmare. *Vertigo* is a nightmare; it's a long dream sequence, and it's over and out for the white guy. Yes, of course it ends this way or that way. The Doris Day figure has now been relegated to girl sidekick status. It's Barbara Bel Geddes, and she wants to be Doris Day for him, but he's gone beyond that. He's gone into something like self-referential madness. He does get to the bottom of the mystery and so forth, and that provides the dynamic for the narrative, but it's a little like—in fact, completely like—the Statue of Liberty shot in *Saboteur*. The text is telling you—just as it said that Robert Cummings is winning and the saboteur lost, and in that sense that everything's all right—the text is telling you that Jimmy Stewart got to the bottom of the mystery and so forth, but the mystery is such a nightmare, such deceit and duplicity, and infinite identity shifting, and the female character is such an interesting, intuitive devil, that we understand that the vertigo of the movie is the vertigo of honorable-white-guy civilization. It's dizzy, at best; at worst, it's locked up for a time in a mental institution.

Now our Mainstream American Cultural Artifact is *Elvis '56*, which happens to be the title of a very good documentary film, narrated by Levon Helm of the Band, about just exactly what happened to Elvis Presley during 1956. It's a very good documentary, but, in my opinion, you can't really know what happened to Elvis in 1956 unless you also know something about all the information I've been talking about. He was in reaction, after all, to the information I've been talking about. Elvis Presley knew there was a kind of Cafe Society life that went on in New York, with people like Jimmy Stewart and Grace Kelly, and he knew that Eisenhower had won World War II and the election, and lots of other things. He was a man on the face of this earth. And the film is moving to me because it shows his vital uniqueness walking—a new kind of old American, innocent, with old American experience, and that's always been our formula, our innocence, plus a unique kind of experience that other people haven't had in other lands—walking, with all of that, plus physical beauty, into *Rear Window*–down-the-drain-land.

I'm particularly moved, for instance, by a segment in which Elvis Presley is interviewed by a man named Hy Gardner, who had a program on television called *Hy Gardner Calling*. Hy was in one place with a telephone, you were in another place with a telephone, he picked up the telephone, and there was a camera at both ends, and you got this modern, Winchellesque take on something. So, Hy Gardner was a bus-and-truck Walter Winchell on the fringes of *Rear Window*–Twenty-One Club stuff, and to him, it is quite clear Elvis Presley is white trash. I don't like that phrase, but it's the phrase that Hy Gardner would have used, I think. A man like Hy Gardner would have had two or three different sets of social perceptions. He would have had a Roosevelt-Eisenhower social perception. I have no idea what his politics or his cultural leanings were, but he would have had opinions about both of those social avatars, and he would have known who was who at the Twenty-One Club. He would have known that a kind of ironic deutero-Hemingway style was called for if you wanted a better table at Twenty-One. He would have known what was going on at the magazine I worked for for so long, *The New Yorker.* He would have known that what we'll call *The New Yorker/Time/ Life* magazine style was definitive, socially, in New York City, and he would have known that Elvis Presley was not someone you could introduce into that society.

Elvis knew it too, of course he did. Every human avatar has a private social life, and Elvis Presley probably all his life felt slighted by the Twenty-One Club of it. Since he never knew too much about the Twenty-One Club of it, he couldn't have known that it was down the drain, and that he had helped put it down the drain. Maybe he did know that. But certainly the welcome wasn't given, and there is a marvelously poignant scene in *Elvis '56* of Elvis walking around Times Square, and the first reason it's poignant to me is, it really is Times Square, I mean, the Times Square of my memory, the predevastation Times Square; and, second, you can see that Times Square was about to go into its devastated phase; and the third thing is what the makers of the film have chosen to put on the soundtrack of Elvis's Times Square walk—and it uses still photographs, and the name of the photographer I'm momentarily blocking, but they're wonderful photographs—the soundtrack plays "Blue Moon," the Lorenz Hart–Richard Rodgers song, and it's just so damn poignant to me. I was in, or adjacent to, the last phases of that civilization, because the Twenty-One Club in the fifties and sixties was some last pale reflection of a Rodgers and Hart–Hemingway point of view, and there's Elvis wandering around at the tail end of it.

Another poignant scene is—actually, it comes back to the Hy Gardner interview—my first poignancy is simply about the juxtaposition of the two men. The content of the interview is not without interest. Hy Gardner is asking him about his film career, and Elvis is acting with extraordinary modesty, and I believe unfeigned modesty, indicating that he knows there's a great deal out here in the world. As far as he's concerned, his singing has just been his card of entry to this civilization; he's here to learn.

That's very much the point of view, and unfeigned, as I say, and that theme is picked up again when he's shown in juxtaposition to Hal Wallis, a minor member of Twenty-One Club–Chasen's civilization, and Elvis shows up on the day of the beginning of the filming of his first film, *Love Me Tender*, having memorized the whole script. He's here to learn. And someone asked him about his experience after the first days of shooting, and he says that he discovered when he showed up that no one was going to tell him anything. That no one addressed his needs as a learner. He was there to provide a certain kind of drop-dead popularity energy, and that was all that was wanted out of him. Well, that was his tragedy. As far as he was concerned, he was on a journey through life, he had a talent that he was unabashed and positive about; he felt that gave him a card of entry into something, and when he got there, no one said a word. He was on his own. And he was lucky, by my perception, to have had Colonel Parker. People say, "Well, he fell into the hands of a charlatan." Well, he was lucky to have just one charlatan, with a consistent, moneymaking point of view. Something much worse might have happened to Elvis, absent that support.

Now, I'll put this all together within my own life story just a little bit. Don't let me get grand with you; I'm not someone who was, from day one, turning himself into a philosophical academic or anything; I was, from day one, someone who was determined to survive, and to pay attention to what was going on around him, period, and when Elvis Presley came along, my heart stood still, to borrow the Larry Hart lyric. The first note I heard from him, I said, "Well, this is it, this is a sufferer like me, this is something new, this is what I want, this is who I am, in a way," and Elvis had that gift. That's why there are so many Elvis imitators. He was Everyman or part of Everyman and Everywoman, at a certain point, and I'll just refer you back to the image of the Billy Wilder film where the young child in a space helmet with a little ray gun doesn't want his father to kiss him and is on his way to narcissism and isolation and who knows that, and also to the Doris Day moment in "Que Sera Sera," the fact that it was a female power that was going to occupy the informed position at that stage in our American history, and of course it's been important to me to have studied the Hitchcock films, for instance, because I now understand that he was a man with the kind of—what would in another civilization at another time have been called a prophetic gift—a Cassandra, who, instead of being a ragtag girl, disrespected, was someone of use to the film industry. He must have been very happy about that. Because the sequence of the four Hitchcock films I've mentioned is in synchronicity with events in my own family and with my relationship with my father.

My father's family was the kind of family that had an aura about it. There had been among them intuitive, brave liberal arts people, of the kind drawn by Hitchcock in the blind man in *Saboteur;* there had been that kind of magical concern with the importance of humanity within civilization, and I met a couple of the people who represented that in my father's family, but they were very old when I was very young, and my father was a notch down from Jimmy Stewart in the aesthetic I've talked about. When I talk about the discrepancies between the blank slate and the deepest concerns and the on-the-ground fact of being a photographer for *Life* magazine in a devolving social construct in New York City, I'm talking about my own experience. And it was also my own experience that by 1957 it was my mother who was the giver of point of view, and not my father. And it is also true that the whole thing ended up in *Vertigo,* and so I'll just end this section by returning to the child in a bubble, the young male child in the space helmet in the Billy Wilder film, and I hope everyone will have observed that there is a story I'm *not* telling here, and that is the story of that child, of that generation. That child is—if he's six years old in 1954, or he might be eight—he's, in any case, a few years younger than I, but my generation, more or less—I'm not telling the story of my generation. I'm indicating that a Vitalitarian experiment began in 1956 with the appearance of Elvis Presley on the national stage, and then the world stage, and that that period is coming to an end now, and that the film *Liar Liar* with Jim Carrey, with its almost maniacal development of a father-son bonding theme, represents the beginning of something new. What it represents is the beginning of a new kind of father-son dialogue, within a context of something like no information. The manic break Carrey makes with his past isn't with a real past, it's with a faux past; there's no honor in the legal profession, there's no Eisenhower of it, there's no Roosevelt of it. There's no anything of it. For all the reasons of dysfunction hinted at in this essay, the Jim Carrey character, who is maybe just two or three years too old to be actually the son of someone in my generation, but who is in a generational position down from my generation, let's say, for all the reasons I've hinted at or outlined or indicated in this section of the book, that proto-adult, pseudo-adult, has no information. He decides, toward the end of the film, that he'll just break through his isolation and focus on his son.

Well, I bet that's going to happen. And I bet my generation comes in for a severe criticism, over time, for its laying down of arms in terms of developing a decent masculine tradition. I think that's inevitable, and justifiable. But I remember what it was like to be half in and half out of a space helmet; to be teased by visions of the power of the past within the context of a very conflicted present, as to masculine tradition, masculine honor, masculine everything, and I can remember what it was when Elvis's voice broke through the deutero-Hemingway of it, the Jimmy and Tommy Dorsey of it, the calcified, pretend dominance of it, and I can see myself lying in my bed in Cos Cob, Connecticut, in 1956, with an old-fashioned 45 RPM record player—it wasn't old-fashioned then—one of those 45 record changers with the big spindle in the middle, listening to an extended-play 45. Extended-play meant that you got four songs instead of two, and I couldn't make use of the automatic record changer, because there was only one song that I wanted to listen to, and it was "Love Me" by Elvis Presley, and the lyric, of course, is "Treat me like a fool, treat me mean and cruel, but love me," and I played it over and over and over, hoping my father would hear.

The 1950s, Concluded

Now I'm going to relate this theater of the *New York Times,* February 1, 1950, to our film discussion earlier: Tom Ewell in *The Seven Year Itch* going to kiss his little son in a space suit bubble and getting rejected by his son with a ray gun, saying, "Mommy, Mommy, he's cutting off my oxygen," or whatever he said—that, on the one hand, and on the other, this series of insights about unraveling presented to us by Alfred Hitchcock, 1943–1958. The two shows I remember from the TV lineup I read to you earlier—and I do remember them—are *Howdy Doodie* and *Captain Video.* And, indeed, those are the two shows that Tom Ewell refers to in *The Seven Year Itch* when he gets home, relieved that his wretched little male child is out of the house for a time, and he can close the television set and not be subject to *Captain Video* and *Howdy Doodie.* So, look at the *New York Times* of 1950 from the point of view of the character played by Tom Ewell. Tom Ewell—oh, let's get literal about it, Tom Ewell seems to be forty-two years old in *The Seven Year Itch,* which was released in 1955, so he was in his later thirties in 1950, so the Tom Ewell character seems to be the kind of guy who'd been maybe to Dartmouth, or Lehigh, but an educated man working unhappily in the publishing industry; and what his book company does in *The Seven Year Itch,* by the way, is to sell classics and put sexy covers on them, which is pretty funny from the point of view of that time. He's shown okaying a cover of *Little Women,* the Louisa May Alcott novel, that has women with big breasts and low necklines, and he's shown telling his assistant that the neckline on one of the Little Women needs to be even lower, and that has something to do with Churchill, you know, something to do with the nature of our respect during the 1940s and 50s for the old country we were forced to become during the Second World War; we were, once again, a country of Little Women and Little Men, but oh we longed for the B movie of it, we wanted the big breasts and the low necklines, so Ewell is shown putting the sexy neckline on the paperback classic.

And what is Ewell's reaction to the newspaper of 1950? Well, what would any of our reactions be to the H-bomb? He had what an educated person's reaction would be. Terror, in a way, deciding merely to go along with what the people who won the war were deciding to do, because what else could you do? What would his reaction to Winston Churchill's book be? Respect, but, oh God, did he really have to read it? He was trained to read it, he was bred to read it; in theory he belonged to the same group of Anglo-Saxon war winners that Winston Churchill belonged to, and Winston Churchill and Franklin Roosevelt were deputizers; they had a marvelous tone of voice, and they specialized in saying, "You, Tom Ewell, Lehigh Class of 19-whatever, you too belong to the ancient patriarchal system of everything, and you have met your responsibilities beautifully, and on we go into a fair patriarchal future." Meanwhile, Ewell is feeling, "Oh, well, really? I mean, my job is, in order to sell this *Little Women* I have to put a low neckline on her, and I have to feel a little ironic about that," but he certainly isn't saying that Winston Churchill didn't do his job, and he certainly is aware that the *New York Times* is putting Churchill's history of the Second World War on the front page. What is his attitude toward the coal strike? Fear. Visceral fear. There's a sense in which Tom Ewell is more afraid of those coal miners than he is of the H-bomb.

Now, those are the father's reactions to three avatars of kingship on the front page, and we've seen his reaction to the fourth avatar, television; he's relieved that his little child is out of the house so he doesn't have to watch the crap. He's also in denial about television. He's aware that television is the cheapest cheap thing in the world. He's also aware that it's gonna win. Because, after all, what is he doing in his job, as he publishes *Little Women*? He's givin' 'em the sex of it. He's givin' 'em rock-and-roll. He can't sell the book without the rock-and-roll. He's in the same business as the television people, but he's in denial about it, which is what's so nice about the gesture of closing the doors on the television. Those old television sets very often were pieces of furniture, and you could pretend you had a Chippendale cellarette or something there instead of a television set. Now, what is the male child's point of view about all of this? Well, first of all, he has absolutely no access to three of the four kingship avatars. I could run it down, but it should be perfectly obvious to you that the young male child in *The Seven Year Itch* doesn't see any way that he could get to understand, let alone be, Winston Churchill; and that he himself would be very reluctant to become a mine worker and would probably be scared stiff of any mine worker he met, although impressed; and that the H-bomb—well, what is a child going to do about the H-bomb? So, three out of the four principal power vectors floating in the theater over the child's head are unavailable, impossible. The fourth avatar is not only available and possible, but geared toward him. He's gonna grow up with it. It's just as stupid as he is. A child growing up with television now must be amazed, impressed, intrigued, frightened, all kinds of things, by the variety of it—how could he ever get to understand television? A child of 1955 watching television would be on a par with television. He is going to grow up with this thing. It isn't any more ambitious than he is. It's for him. Television is the thing that's going to steadily march along with him, be his friend, tell him who he is. When he gets to school, he'll find there was such a thing as the Second World War, but he'll probably avoid it. Too intimidating. He'll have a chance to learn about Winston Churchill, but he won't take that chance. He'll discover the H-bomb, all right, and perhaps he'll be led to take a stand about it, but he won't usually imagine that he can encompass, or be comfortable with, the civilization it represents. It's an issue that he can avoid, and he probably does. And if he takes it on, he says, "We don't want it," and that will be as simple as that. And the coal miners remain the mystery. What will we do about these strong men who work with their hands for their living, doing very hard, dangerous work, and who want more money? That's another issue he'll avoid, if he gets the chance.

Now I'll just tell you a little about *Howdy Doodie* and *Captain Video*, two programs I watched, and relate them to David Letterman and his inability to participate with any effectiveness on the Academy Awards because he just couldn't drop the irony. The Academy Awards require a mild irony, and David Letterman is suffused with irony from head to toe and can't drop it for a minute. A serious adult who watched *Howdy Doodie* and *Captain Video*, but especially *Howdy Doodie*, was thrown into the Slough of Despond. The next generation was going to tell the story; the next generation was sitting in front of a television set, without taking any interest in the H-bomb or Winston Churchill or the miners. And what was on television was geared toward children, and it was at a level three levels down from the previous, horrifying, child-educating level, which was Shirley Temple, say, or the serials in the movies, *The Green Hornet* and *Batman* and all the other serials shown at movie theaters. A Shirley Temple movie was a confection, a phony idea of childhood, something that promoted narcissism even as it seemed to exalt childish innocence. Any serious liberal arts person or even half-serious liberal arts person would have recognized the fact that to educate children on Shirley Temple movies was to give them an education ten levels down from sending them out to work in the garden and reading to them aloud from *Pilgrim's Progress*.

This would have been the position of Edmund Wilson, say. Edmund Wilson was constantly in mourning, as most serious liberal arts people of the late forties and early fifties were—why not mention Robert Lowell, or anyone you want? These men, however modern they were in their literary technique, would have been, in part of their soul, saying, "Oh, my God, the way we're educating our children is inferior to the way a Yorkshire yeoman used to educate his. Far better for the human soul to spend your days working in a vegetable garden, to come in to hear your father read aloud a few lines from *Pilgrim's Progress,* far better for the sake of your soul to do that than to watch a Shirley Temple movie." Well, *Howdy Doodie* was the sub-basement of a Shirley Temple movie. It was about a marionette—and not a very good one—I mean, puppetry is great if it's lively and skillful, and marionettes can be great too if they're lively and skillful. *Howdy Doodie* was barely going through the motions of Punch and Judydom. He was a marionette, all right, just a wooden, fairly ugly little thing manipulated by strings, and I guess children of my generation reacted positively to that, just as children react positively now to the very ugly image of childhood presented in *The Simpsons.* Within the context of television civilization representing itself to itself, one wants to say that *The Simpsons* represents a kind of apotheosis of *Howdy Doodie.* My generation thought of itself as being marionettes, and not very attractive ones or ambitious ones, being pulled by strings, wooden, dressed in a little cowboy outfit or whatever it was; and that's morphed into this awareness-of-evil-and-cynicism business of *The Simpsons.* It's pretty clear how it's worked. Howdy Doodie had a human pal called Buffalo Bob, who was similarly unambitious; he wasn't even a top minor actor, and he had a kind of salesman's voice, full of insincerity, and he talked with the Peanut Gallery—if you wanted to be kind about it, you'd say it would be amateur hour, but why be kind about it? It was something that couldn't get into a Shirley Temple movie, but its advantage was that it was in an advertising medium, and you didn't have to be so good because you weren't asking people to leave their houses and go and buy a ticket; you were simply there, you were a delivery system for advertising, and you were operating in perfect harmony with a generation that was appalled by its lack of access to the real power vectors in its world; and I'll just repeat that because one day soon, everyone's going to want to know the history of the war babies and the baby boomers, and why most of us acted in a culturally dysfunctional way, and the answer is that as children we felt we were marionettes and we were appalled by our lack of access to the real power vectors in the world. The H-bomb of it, the Winston Churchill of it, the coal miner of it, and, through no action of our own, but just mysteriously and magically we got sat in front of these boxes, which spoke to us to perfection. Here you are, a little Howdy Doodie marionette.

Captain Video was both better and worse. It was better in a sense that it really *was* amateur hour. You know, they had a casting call for two days, and they got an out-of-work this one and that one, and they paid them a hundred and fifty dollars a week, and they stumbled around on a television set that must have been a renovated thread warehouse or something, and they had a few papier-mâché rocks, and somebody hid behind a rock with a ray gun, and somebody—I mean, it was unambitious in the extreme. Once again, it's something that no movie studio would have touched with a ten-foot pole, and that's something else one should be aware of in dealing with the social zeitgeist of that moment. You know, this stuff drove movie people to absolute despair. They were in the habit of having the power vector and doing what they wanted; suddenly that was being taken away from them, and the stuff that was clearly destined to be dominant in the culture was stuff that couldn't get on a B-movie lot. You just wouldn't think of it. So, *Captain Video* was friendlier because it was kind of like sandlot ball. You could sort of be Captain Video on your own, if you wanted, and some people did play at Captain Video. But what was worse about it was, it introduced the idea of endless self-reference. You were going to live in television, you were going to be Captain Video. Captain Video was television; you were Captain Video; it was going to be on video; you were going to be a Video Ranger.

The issue of deputization comes in here, just as Churchill and Roosevelt dealt with the older generation as deputizers, saying, "You too, Tom Ewell, are a Roosevelt-type guy, a war-winner–type guy, a Churchill-type guy," because this business of deputizing is a part, has been a part, of our media culture, and Roosevelt and Churchill were both media figures as well as real figures. The deputizing here was to create a nation of Video Rangers. You were on Captain Video's team. That was the appeal of the program. So we agreed to be Video Rangers rather than Churchill boys, or people who were going to be taken into the history of the H-bomb, and led to understand it in all its details, and what the history of mechanization meant from the cotton gin on, rather than be mine workers; we were going to be Video Rangers, and that was going to be that. And the outcome is David Letterman, because the lively thing that was going on, the human, visceral lively thing that was going on in this process, was the development of irony.

As that little child in the spacesuit in *The Seven Year Itch* grew up, three things would become obvious to him. He would be aware that he hadn't been trained to really understand the history of mechanization, and was insufficient in that regard; that he hadn't been trained to be anything like Winston Churchill, and was going to be permanently insufficient in that regard; and that he wasn't actually going to be able to look a mine worker in the eye, and was going to be insufficient in that regard. He was going to be aware that he had been a Video Ranger from the start, and that he was going to have to keep on being a Video Ranger, and that he was going to have to learn to laugh about that. And, also, because he wanted to get married, to be a man in some sense, he was going to have to be serious about something. He was going to have to touch base with some real thing going on in his father, and what he got hold of was the irony in his father. As that little Video Ranger grew up, and looked at who his father really was, as he necessarily was compelled to by the workings of real human life, the real live and kicking thing he'd see in his father would be irony. The irony of being a man who was selling *Little Women* by putting a low neckline on the Little Women. His father had to laugh at himself a little bit as he did it or he wouldn't have been able to do it. So the son said, "Well, I can laugh even louder at what I'm going to have to do." And the evolution of that process is toward David Letterman, who speaks to my generation and the generations one or two decades younger than mine, speaks to us about the experience of never having had a serious reaction, of never having had a moment of true physical exhaustion after a day at work in the mines, of never having had to fight for money sufficient to feed one's family, of never having worked so hard in the mines that he felt he was entirely entitled to a decent living wage. And ditto the Churchill of it, and ditto the H-bomb of it. We were going to have to grow up to be entirely ironic in our visceral reactions to our own manhood.

UNDER THE AESTHETIC OF DWIGHT DAVID EISENHOWER; UNDER THE AESTHETIC OF FDR

Three American Tragedies

America changed forever in the 1920s, and that change wasn't for the good. No doubt other writers have followed the line of mechanization through American history, from the cotton gin to the this to the that, but what happened in the twenties, after the suicide of old Europe in 1918, was simply that America allowed itself to turn its ecstatic energy to the worship of mechanization. Well, it failed, but it didn't fail subtextually. We had worshiped that way—it was what we had done—it's just that then, as sometimes happens in human life, circumstances caused us to retreat somewhat from what we had, categorically, turned into. It's happening now. The Rolling Stones have categorically retreated somewhat from what they had been. The comparison is apt; Mick Jagger was Clara Bow, the "It" girl, but not anymore, now he's a funded citizen. Well, that's what happened to us in the twenties. We were Clara Bow, the "It" girl, and then we had a crash, and a depression, and over us swam an ancient, premechanization American, Franklin Roosevelt, to inform us that we might again be farmers of the soul, of the land. So we retreated from our twenties avatar, but not really. And then came World War II, an unparalleled event, especially in the phase Dwight Eisenhower called the Crusade in Europe. And then we really were somewhere. We were at the top of the heap in a way that no country had ever, in the history of the world, been at the top of the heap. Ancient

Rome? Please—I mean, it was a Mediterranean civilization with not much in the way of mechanization at its command. At another time, many other people will discover how extraordinary the event of our victory, especially our European victory, was, in terms of the real cultural history of this planet. And who were we? We were people who had turned to the worship of mechanization and the exaltation of gangsterism, who'd retreated a little from that under the hyperspace fatherhood of Franklin Roosevelt, who woke up to discover that they were It.

But they couldn't be Clara Bow "It"; they had to be some other kind of "It." So we—they—had to pretend. After all, if you're suddenly proclaimed to be the rulers of the rulers of the rulers, there's no way out of that; if you just *are* that, well, you deal with it. As much as you know that you are still Clara Bow, the "It" girl, who's had a few problems and gone to war and won, the reality of the situation says, "Well, I won. I'm It." And that's a problem. An ordinary American, full of doubts, full of negativity, full of guilt from having worshiped unsuccessfully, probably, the mechanization of the twenties, having fallen quite a bit in the thirties, having been in awe of Roosevelt in the thirties, having felt, "Oh, I must have wanted all the time to be an old-time American like Roosevelt, and now I can be, but I'm not really"—that American suddenly discovers that his children are sending packages of soap and toothpaste to the children of cultivated Europeans, because he's won and they've lost, socially. It was a kind of problem—I mean a problem of ultraprosperity and ultrapower, an attractive problem in a way, but a problem. Let's say it: a peasant in a palace. It's an attractive problem, but it's a problem.

Well, to this problem we had a solution, and his name was Dwight David Eisenhower. At another time, we'll run down his relation to European culture, to any culture; but anyway, there he was. David O. Selznick plus one. Dwight Eisenhower—it was as though David O. Selznick, having taken his three-step to making *Gone With the Wind,* had stepped on, and decided that he was then going to describe his own civilization and had figured out a way to make *Gone With the Wind* for the North. Eisenhower was that great, in male avatar terms. I hope you know what I'm saying here. Of course, the president of Beloit College was smarter; of course, the Olympic athlete of 1948 was more splendid in physical terms; and of course, George Bernard Shaw was still on the face of the earth in 1950. So there were many other heroes to think about, but there was only one story, and that was the story of our American Dominant Tradition, which won in World War II, and Ike was it and then he won again. And I'm mixing my chronology, because, as I say, George Bernard Shaw died in 1950, but maybe that's exactly what I want to say: he died in 1950, and Ike won the presidency in 1952. There was no absolutely competent liberal arts avatar after George Bernard Shaw. Shaw understood the history of this century to perfection and from the point of view of our social life, and from the point of view of the inevitable triumph of mechanization. He just happened to understand that, and he was able to write about it with considerable grace, and the one thing that William Butler Yeats was ever wrong about was Shaw.

Shaw dies in 1950, Ike wins office in 1952, and now you know what I'm saying. With Eisenhower, we're dealing with something after the fact, a kind of Diocletian grace of God to rule over us, for a time, while we figure out who we are, as rulers. Well, we didn't do it. Our national personality at that time wasn't sufficient to rule over Madras, much less the whole Western world. We're proving that now. So, what was it that God gave us permission to do, for eight years under Dwight Eisenhower? He gave us permission to put together experiments. Our World War II victory was an accident, culturally—not an accident militarily, or socially, but an accident culturally. I hope you understand the difference between social and cultural, as I'm using it here. Old Europe was, and still is, culturally far superior to us. Socially, in the 1940s, it was the slum, and we weren't. We'd sold a large part of our soul to mechanization, but the accident of the moment indicated that mechanization equaled military might, and military might was what was required. It was rather as if what was absolutely required at a given moment was that an absolutely beautiful young woman walk into a room and say a devastating thing to a certain very powerful older man, who happened to be feeling very weak at the moment, and she devastated him. It was like that. At another moment, he would have devastated her. In any objective terms, give them both SAT tests and he wins hands down, she barely hits the graph at all. But at a certain moment we were functional and they weren't. Socially. Culturally, life has to do with the education of children. All those *socially* psychotic Europeans. The Germans, the losers, as well as the British, the winners, and the French, as ever, somewhere in between. All those *socially* psychotic, defeated—and I'm including Britain in this too, because they were as much defeated as the French were. Well, they still know how to send a kid to elementary school. They still knew that Goethe was Goethe, Molière was Molière, and Shakespeare was Shakespeare, and it didn't take money to tell a young child that. And defeat, or the kind of strange semidefeat that Britain endured, and certainly that was what it was— people who ruled the world of the nineteenth century were now kowtowing to people from Terre Haute who happened to have x million dollars, it was a kind of social defeat—well, they still in their private moments knew what book to give to their child, and there certainly was some kind of school where some underpaid person still said, "Well, *Tartuffe* is the play that you ought to read, and you shouldn't do this and that; you should do such and the other," so that culture soldiered on, at least at the elementary school level, which is, of course, the crucial level. But they'd been defeated. They were in the depths of negativity. And we, frankly, were not. And so, like the peasant in the palace, we were given eight years to bone up, to back up culturally the position we'd won militarily and socially.

Ike, as I've indicated, was just one guy. I mean, there was this other man, Nixon, who studied him every minute of every day, and married his daughter off to the guy's grandson, or however that worked. He modeled Ike, to use a word from seventies psychobabble. If there was one more thing he could have done to be like Ike he would have done it, but alas and alack Ike was just one guy. He was Balanchine, in a way. Just an extraordinary individual who moved through this, that, and the other. He was Balanchine, only instead of Balanchine, he was Ike. And instead of being the hero, despite all theories of democratic whatever, for a lot of ballerinas and ballet boys, he was the hero, despite a lot of democratic whatever, for a lot of Americans. I like Ike. So, under the Diocletian rule of Ike, and it was a rule, there was room made for a lot of experiments. "You've got the positions; how are you going to get to be the guys and girls who can hold the positions?" was the job, and everyone, in a way, knew it. Ike categorically defeated Adlai Stevenson. I haven't heard Adlai Stevenson's name mentioned in twenty years—I mean, that is literally true. He's vanished from the face of the planet.

Oddly enough, Eisenhower seems also to have vanished from the face of the planet. But no one talks about Adlai Stevenson. Adlai Stevenson was a person about whose shoulders Eleanor Roosevelt's arm was flung. He was the next Roosevelt. He was Mario Cuomo. He was, absolutely, the person legitimately in line to do the job. Confident in every way, including spiritually, and this is a spiritual country. We said, "No thank you." I'm not including him in my list of tragedies. Tragedies one and two, of course, are the Kennedy brothers. And I hope you'll forgive me here if I'm talking about our American history as though it were the history of ancient imperial Japan—a list of emperors—well, anyone who chooses to do such a simple thing as drive on a superhighway or tour downtown Detroit will understand that this country is essentially ungovernable. That we are in any state of law-abidingness is, to me, an absolute miracle. The way we live, the way we're organized, the way we receive our information, all of this is absolutely impossible in ordinary human terms. We require an emperor, and we've been looking for a legitimate ruling aesthetic within which to choose our emperor, i.e., our president. We don't want—we've said a million times—a guy who just knows how to do the job. We call it vision, the thing we require. Well, that's not what we really require. We require an absolutely compelling ruling aesthetic that we can all embrace, so that we may perceive ourselves as governable. That means all things to all people; that's what that's always meant. The traditional system has been legitimate monarchy. The ruler is all things to all people because his father was all things to all people of another generation—it simplifies everything.

Well, we're more complicated. What sort of guy—and I'm sorry, girls, it really does come down to guys in this kind of situation—what sort of guy would compel everyone's attention in such a way as to say, "Yes, he knows enough to govern me and force me to accept his ruling aesthetic as definitive." That's been the question, and our Three American Tragedies take place within that question. Who were the Kennedy brothers? They were bred to be, and were, to some extent, the embodiment of the Roosevelt system. The trouble with Stevenson was, he was Eleanor Roosevelt's idea of the Roosevelt system. He was the real thing as to idealism and, frankly, Franklin wasn't the real thing as to idealism. Franklin was the real thing as to optimism and suffering. Franklin Roosevelt injected a strain of real WASP suffering into the mix and came out on top nearly always—and *that's* what people saw in him. Like Cuomo, Stevenson really did brood. Franklin didn't brood. Maybe Eleanor thought that it was a fault in Franklin that he didn't brood. Maybe Eleanor thought it was a fault in Franklin that he dealt with Walter Winchell. Maybe Eleanor thought, finally and ultimately, that Stevenson was like a favorite son, and kind of an improvement on the father—someone whose idealism was tinged with melancholy. Mothers like a certain amount of melancholy in a son, especially if they've been put in the shade by a husband. Stevenson was, by Eleanor's perception, the ideal son Franklin never had. Well, we didn't want that.

The Kennedys were the embodiment of Roosevelt's will-to-power system, and Roosevelt had a will to power, and a rather extraordinary one. Please look, as you're thinking about Roosevelt, in one of the 1930s social registers. I hope you know what the social register is, and what it represents. It's pornography for

America. It says, just these people count and no others, and that's, of course, not what was supposed to be, although every golf tournament I see on television tells me that Americans secretly want it to be only about these golf courses and no others, and so forth and so on. It's our pornography. We say that each one of us is just as good as the other, and secretly we all want to be one of x number of people who categorically are something, as opposed to nothing. Well, you'll find the Roosevelts there, all right; Franklin and Eleanor didn't take themselves out of it, and they belonged to a lot of clubs, and that's who they actually were, socially. But Roosevelt had a will to power. What did people who said that Roosevelt was a traitor to his class mean? They meant that no one who was in the social register could possibly talk to Walter Winchell. That's what they meant. Winchell was a schemer, a psychotic, a person who knew nothing, a hoofer, and I'm purposely leaving *Jew* out of here, because—and it's not entirely irrelevant, I suppose, but it really isn't the point, he could have been Irish—because lots of people in the show-business construct in which Winchell swam were. He was a jiggling, psychotic show-business figure, and no one in the social register, however much they compromised their conscience in other ways, would have been happy, at that point, dealing with him. Roosevelt did. The Kennedys decided—Joseph Kennedy decided for his sons—that the Roosevelt will-to-power system should be embodied. Now, we should spend just a moment with this concept. If, for instance, someone from an ancient Roman Catholic family suddenly, for the sake of popularity, begins to consort with the world's most famous pro-choice person, well, you run into a contradiction. And that was Roosevelt and Winchell.

Joe Kennedy, the ultimate shrewd guy, was observing all this. Kennedy, as everybody knows, was married to Honey Fitz's daughter. What he didn't know about the politics of Irish Boston was—nothing. He knew everything, and he knew the Brahmins, and he knew what the Brahmins' position was at that moment, and there was a position, and there were such people as Brahmins at that moment, and they did, in fact, inherit the last bit of

Puritan fineness. And he was a shrewd cookie, and he was a will-to-power cookie, and he was a gangster cookie, and he was a Hollywood cookie. And he said to himself—and he wasn't in favor of Roosevelt, particularly—"This guy Roosevelt's got the game. The game is to be absolutely amoral, but to pick up the two big pieces there are left in this Western world, which is the social position beyond the social position beyond the social position, which is England, and then you rocket right along to what the people want out of Hollywood." I view John Kennedy's affair with Marilyn Monroe as a kind of acting out of what his father told him life was. Of course it was Hollywood in the end. Of course it was the people's choice in the end. But you did it from the point of view of someone who knew the Court of St. James.

Now, anyone who thinks the American presidency is about advocacy of issues will have been disabused by the current presidency of Mr. Clinton. There is nothing Mr. Clinton isn't willing to say, or willing to espouse. He has been willing to espouse every issue John Kennedy would have, could have, possibly been conceived to have advocated. It's not a problem for him. He's a great Modeler. He just doesn't know what he is modeling. He's modeling Kennedy; he doesn't understand that Kennedy was himself modeling, and was modeling under the instruction of his father, who was observing how Roosevelt did it. Well, it failed. Why it failed, I do know. It failed because by the time John Kennedy was doing it, the Court of St. James system had, in fact, dropped out of the equation, and no one wanted it. Jackie knew this, by the way. There must have been some considerable disappointment in her husband on that basis. You'll excuse me if I don't run Bobby Kennedy down. It was mostly picking up his brother's baton. He was a different guy. But by that point, apparently, Kennedy For President wasn't a going slogan.

Our third American Tragedy is Martin Luther King. King was Mario Cuomo and Stevenson another way. Oh, he had some Roosevelt will to power, but Cuomo has a will to power, and Stevenson had a little, maybe more than I'm giving him credit for. He was who you wanted it to be, in a way. Old America. We're singing spirituals again. We're having dreams again. Well, that left mechanization entirely out of the question. There was no Hollywood there. There were no gangsters there. There was no World War II victory there. I hope everyone understands I'm being completely nonracist when I say he was Adlai Stevenson another way.

I Like Ike

The Republican party now, of course, is a completely different animal from the one I first remember. Remember, please, that the Republicans had been out of office a long, long time, and in a kind of disgrace, because of the Depression. They were embattled, and when Dewey failed to beat Truman in 1948—and Truman was viewed as a nobody, and Dewey was the fair-haired-dark-haired-district-attorney-governor-of-New-York-can-do-no-wrong type of person—when Dewey went down the tubes, the Republicans were even more embattled, and to give them credit, even more rock-ribbed. A lot of traditional Republican strength at that time had to do with women. Middle-class and upper-middle-class women. We're talking here of 1950, say, so we're talking of women born in 1910, or 1900. Women who had a sense memory—a patriarchal, let's be honest, sense memory—of their fathers, of men who had been born in 1870, say. Those were the values those women cherished, the values of strong, simple, more honorable than not, practical men, born in 1870. Their memory was carried forward by their sons, but it was cherished by their daughters, and those daughters were Republicans, and, by 1950, they were very likely to be Taft Republicans. I'm talking here of Senator Robert Taft of Ohio, and remember there was a heavy Heartland-of-America aspect to the Republican party of those days. The kind of thing people make fun of: big-bosomed ladies with corsages, with a sense of punctilio that they hadn't quite earned. Those people really existed, and they were Republican women, and they had a lot of influence. And they were for Taft. And Taft was Mr. I-earned-the-job, and he had, and he did stand for something, and he had done it, year in and year out, and people believed in him. He was not an inconsiderable man. And then Ike became a Republican.

I just want to discuss the attractive inevitability of visceral reactions, which, of course, is exactly what our political process, especially our presidential process, is about, and I'm going to do it from a personal point of view. I was nine years old when Ike ran for president in 1952. I was born at the height of the war, and every part of my being was in some reaction to that enormous event. I had two uncles, the husbands of my aunts. One, my uncle Martin Morrissey, who was married to my mother's sister, was called Sarge, because he'd been a sergeant in the army and had fought at the Battle of the Bulge. He was very impressive to me. An ordinary American man who had been transformed, had his bravery validated, had served with distinction, and come home to our family content to pick up tools as an automobile mechanic and earn not much money a week. I was very impressed by every aspect of that. My father's sister was married to a military man of a different kind, Captain William Kirten, Jr., of the United States Navy. He'd ended the war commanding, as it was always phrased—and I haven't checked the military records—commanding all the destroyers of the eastern Mediterranean, was how it was put, and I'm sure it was something like that. An elegant man from Lake Village, Arkansas; small-town in part of his thinking; elegant in his behavior. He played the guitar. He had a kind of jaunty officer's chic, I'll put it that way, that went everywhere in those days. It was impossible not to be impressed, and I was. And when Ike ran for president, I went a little crazy. It was just too exciting. It was just too great. What a great guy he was. I got my uncle Martin to give me one of his green caps, the Eisenhower-style cap, and I covered it with Ike buttons. I got my grandmother to get them for me. She was a member of the Young Women's Republican Club of Thornwood, New York. She had access to as many "I Like Ike" buttons as she wanted, and I wanted them, and I got them, and I slathered them on the military hat given to me by my uncle Martin, and went to school every day in it. That's the way young males are. They see a hero, they submit to him. They say, "I like you. I want to be like you."

So let's just see for a moment whom it was I liked, and what the sequence of the life of the man had been up to 1952. I think Ike's a great writer—I mean for a military man. I mean, he sees it. He's given us his Gallic wars in a couple of volumes, *Crusade in Europe* and *Mandate for Change.* I think they'll be much more read in future than they are now. I think they're out of print now, which is a scandal. So I'm just asking you to think of my two uncles, the simple bravery of it, which, of course, Ike had and commanded, and also the chic of that moment, of the American military officer: how he did things, how he cut through psychotic world events with a deceptively simple, powerful aesthetic, and, of course, I'm going to ask you to compare the tone of the 1952 Republican convention, as discussed by Ike, with, well, what we have now. Ike starts his account at the convention. It's the end of the first ballot. Ike writes, "At the end of the first ballot, I had 595 votes, nine short of victory. Taft had 500, Warren 81." I interrupt here to remind the reader that the Warren here is Earl Warren, a candidate for the Republican nomination for president in 1952, and later, of course, appointed by President Eisenhower to the Supreme Court. "Suddenly, the head of the Minnesota delegation leapt to his feet, demanding the floor. He had earlier cast nineteen votes for his state's favorite son, Harold Stassen. The chair recognized him. 'Minnesota,' he said, 'wishes to change its vote to Eisenhower.' It was all over."

Now you have to remember that Ike had just walked into something. Taft had been there for years and years and years, each one of the Taft delegates was someone drenched in experience in Taftism and traditional Republicanism, and Ike simply walked into the convention and walked away with it. "Immediately after the balloting was finished, my first thought was to go to Mamie's room down the corridor to give her the news. It was, of course, a momentous thing, and both of us were somewhat over-whelmed by the future life our imaginations pictured for us. Curi-ously enough, neither of us expressed, and I'm quite sure did not feel, any doubt, other than in fleeting moments, as to the Novem-ber outcome." Well, this is the elegant will to power of Dwight Eisenhower, the military man. The military condescending to Adlai Stevenson. Adlai was just never a factor in Ike's thinking; he'd taken a survey of the battlefield in his own mind, and had correctly decided that the tough part of it was taking away from Robert Taft what Robert Taft was clearly entitled to, in some way, and so his next action, in a military way, is to make a friend of his enemy, and this is how he did it. "After being assured that she was improving in strength"—he's talking about Mamie here; she had been under the weather—"I decided to make a call without delay on Senator Taft, a man whom I respected, and who had, up to this moment, I thought, every right to think of himself as the logical candidate of the Republican Party."

And here, one wants to note again Ike's simple military respect for legitimacy. You don't have any of the current clawing and scheming point of view, which says that the other guy isn't entitled to anything because some position on some issue isn't right, and the other guy deserves to have everything taken away from him because his stand on some particular issue is one developed by the devil, as opposed to your own fine and pretty point of view; Ike goes into it in a military way, sees that this guy is the logical heir to a certain thing, understands that *he's* going to have the thing and not that guy, and shows the proper respect for what's been given to him. "I walked into the room where my friends were still congregated, and informed them of my inten-tion. One or two of them remarked that this would violate prece-dent in such circumstances. I telephoned Senator Taft and asked for an opportunity to come across the street to call upon him. Although his voice indicated surprise, he agreed, and I started on my way, a trip that proved to be far more difficult than I had imagined. As I left my apartment, reporters, photographers, and crowds of the curious began to impede my progress, the press begging for a statement. Police officers detailed to me by the City of Chicago found it almost impossible to get me outside the hotel, but once in the street, our real problems began. I'm quite sure that it took ten minutes to get across the street. Progress through the lobby and the halls of Senator Taft's hotel was equally difficult, and the atmosphere of the crowds noticeably sorrowful and even resentful. I understood their attitude. I sympathized with it. All of them had worked for weeks and months with one purpose in view, to nominate Robert Taft. They wore great Taft buttons and ribbons. A not inconsiderable number of ladies were openly weeping. Finally, we reached the elevator, and I was escorted to the Senator's quarters. The first thing the Senator asked, after I had reached his hotel room, was whether his sons could be present. I agreed readily. . . . In the course of the talk I said, 'This is no time for conversation on matters of any substance; you're tired, and so am I. I just want to say I want to be your friend. I hope you will be mine. I hope we can work together.' Senator Taft's reply was cordial, and matter-of-fact. 'My only problem for the moment,' he said, 'is that for the twenty minutes it took you to get over here, I have been bombarded by requests from photographers for a picture. Would you be willing to have one taken?' We stepped into the hall to face the flashbulbs, and our short chat was over. I returned to my hotel under circumstances much easier than my former crossing. When I entered my apartment, I saw a marvel of communications that had never occurred to me. As I reached the door of my room, my eye was attracted to the television set in the far corner. On it, startled, I saw myself, moving through my own door."

There can rarely have been a man who cut with such effortless ease through the history of his time. It's hard to think of a situation in which Dwight Eisenhower wasn't lucky—so lucky he's become kind of invisible. He was like water. He flowed so easily within the events he dominated that he became indistinguishable from them. And like some natural element, he had no natural

heirs, and established no school. His school, of course, was the
sequence of his own life, and his ability to walk from sphere to
sphere, staying, always one thinks, pretty much the same, and
yet subtly changing. He isn't the Western liberal arts man's idea
of a great man, precisely because there isn't much of suffering
about him, and we presume a certain martyrdom, a certain something painful, we more or less require it from our Western rulers.
He was Confucius's ideal—he had luck—and to enter a Confucian mode for a moment, let's say that it is a wise people who
allow themselves to be ruled by someone with luck. Queen Elizabeth I had it; so did Ike. He'd walked through a charnel house
with perfect composure.

In any case, what I am is a social historian, and one of the
reasons I still like Ike is that the older I get, and the more I know,
the more I'm convinced that Ike was honest with us, as honest as
a ruler can be, and I think his writings are a treasure trove. For
instance, the chapter in *Mandate for Change* I've just been reading from, which is titled "Candidate," is a marvelous example of
Confucian subterfuge, because, of course, he was a candidate—
it's a perfectly logical title for the chapter, but, in another sense,
there hadn't been a candidate like this since Washington. He was
just Ike walking through something. The chapter "Candidate"
ends this way: "The earliest national election that I can recall is
that of 1896, in which William McKinley opposed William Jennings Bryan. As a little boy in Abilene, I had helped campaign
that year by marching in a nighttime parade with a flaming torch
made of a rag soaked in coal oil. Now, fifty-six years later, my
own name was at the head of a Republican ticket." Well, as I read
that aloud, I think, "Well, good for you, Ike." A man who can
write a military memo and has kept in touch with his anima, let's
say, can write a good sentence, and I think the juxtaposition of
Ike walking into his hotel room and having his eye drawn to a
television set in the corner in which he sees himself enter the
hotel room looking into a television set in the corner—that, on
the one hand, and these sentences at the end of the chapter—
well, I think it shows a sense of social history, and a novelist's

sense of social movement. I'll read this passage once again, hoping my reader will get some better sense of the early 1950s by paying attention to Ike's description of his first exposure to politics. "The earliest national election that I can recall is that of 1896, in which William McKinley opposed William Jennings Bryan. As a little boy in Abilene, I had helped campaign that year by marching in a nighttime parade with a flaming torch made of a rag soaked in coal oil. Now, fifty-six years later, my own name was at the head of a Republican ticket."

Now, history doesn't always move in the same way. There are people moving into adulthood, or what is called adulthood now, whose early childhood memories are watching *Gilligan's Island,* and it must not be uncommon, is not uncommon, for a person working in the media factories of the moment to be thinking, "My earliest memory is watching *Gilligan's Island,* and here I am, executive producer of my own sitcom." The media battlefield has been our battlefield, and thinking of this kind is not uncommon, and has not been uncommon for quite some time. Our progress within the mode of television, which I have called the mode of the Cold Child, is something unprecedented in human history. I've written in my book *Within the Context of No Context* that history paused, sat still, and reversed in the early fifties, and Ike caught that moment from the ghost-of-Hamlet point of view; a man of being, a man who never experienced any real conflictedness, gives us a glimpse of our condition from his point of view, which is the point of view of a torch with a rag soaked in coal oil ablaze—that's his childhood memory, very like the kind of vivid, ferocious imagery that old Hamlet's ghost uses when talking to young Hamlet. "You think you're so fine and pretty with your electric lights; you don't remember what a torch was, what it was to soak a rag in coal oil and set it alight." Ike, of course, is gentle about it; he's a man who understands the inevitability of modern movement; he isn't hectoring us about the greater power of his early life, but it's there, and when he spots himself on the television set, sees himself on the television set, he knows it's important. Just at that moment history was changing into demography, but not for everyone, of course—there was, for instance, the stranded, but still human, British aristocracy. I don't say they're still human at the present moment; I'm thinking of 1950. As the modern juggernaut goes along, it has tended to elevate some people into irrelevancy, but those irrelevant people get to keep the sense of being they've traditionally had. Ike was presiding over something. The television moment he described is emblematic of this. He wasn't formed by television—he had already been formed. His being wasn't ever going to be taken away from him, and his personality was such that no one wanted it taken away from him, but he was presiding over a situation in which history was turning into demography, in which judgment—and Ike possessed judgment with a capital *J*—was being drained out of every powerful situation, and marketing considerations were being pumped in. That was what that moment was like.

So, let me refer in this next summing-up section to my own perception that history paused, stopped, and then reversed in the early 1950s, and became the history of demography, became demography (and for most Americans, the younger they were, the truer my formula holds, or held). I want you to think about the dilemma, or existential position, of the young male child in *The Seven Year Itch,* the Tom Ewell film, the young child in a bubble, in a plastic spacesuit, with a little ray gun, growing up in a world where the dynamic thing he was being asked to participate in was television, in a world where history, on the one hand, was never more intrusive, in that he was being told every minute that the world could end if a tiny number of men decided to push a button or go into panic, but where history was, on the other hand, infinitely remote and in the hands of these few men, all of whom had been born in 1890 or 1900. So let me end this section by giving you a sense of sequence from another life story: Adolph Zukor. Seventeen years older than Ike. Like that. Ike was a child carrying a torch made of a rag soaked in coal oil at the McKinley-Bryan election. Nine years later, in 1905, Adolph Zukor was participating in the invention of the nickelodeon. And he didn't just have two or three steps, he had twelve or thirteen.

Out of the theater into the nickelodeon, to the founding of a unit called Famous Players, which was to film stories using great stage stars. Zukor's first star was Sarah Bernhardt. Moving, then, into distribution, through Paramount, which was originally a releasing and distribution organization and not a production organization, forming a studio, a combine. Going into partnership with Balaban and Katz, the great builders of movie palaces in the twenties, marching right along. Then suddenly not marching. Bankruptcy, trouble, Wall Street in charge. Lots of different avatars for Paramount in those years, including a brief period in which Joseph Kennedy was having a say, or making an assessment. And then back in the saddle by the late 1930s. Paramount becoming the studio we now identify with the name and the building and the big *P*. Then, in 1952, watching it all go down the drain, for a time, because of television.

Under the Aesthetic of
Dwight David Eisenhower

I'm looking at a copy of *Adventures of a White Collar Man* by Alfred P. Sloan, Jr., and I'm going to claim for it an enormous position in the history of twentieth-century letters. If I were picking ten books from the twentieth century to be saved for the use of the twenty-third century, this would be one of them. One advantage of the recent sensible decision on everybody's part to decide that industrial civilization is over, one good result of this is that we can look at industrial society in a new way. We are not in it. We don't have to be hopeful about it. Some of us, like myself, feel that we're in a desperate, dissolving situation and that because we have failed to make any reasonable human adjustment to our industrial experience (while at the same time allowing our agricultural and hierarchical and old-fashioned sense of the world to disappear)—some people like myself think that we're in for big trouble. Others do not. At this moment, the phrase *postindustrial society* is widely in use, and people who use it with hope look forward to a more humane, scattered, a more everything world, because of the information superhighway, because of multiculturalism, because of the global economy, and because people don't like to look back. Anyway, the multicultural globalists and I are in agreement that industrial society is at an end, and now is a good time to take a look at our former condition—and in a new way. While we were in industrial society, while it was our terrarium, we each of us had to be hopeful, we each of us had to try to reform it, we each of us had to take our particular strand of the thing and try to keep it lively, make our strands stronger, make sure that it was weaving itself, in potential at least, with the other strands in a new, more hopeful way. This was the Kennedy effort, after all, which was pushing certain vital strands through the Military-Industrial Complex society that Dwight Eisenhower bequeathed us in 1960. But anyway, that's done, so let's look at it a new way.

The man I most respect as a social historian for the first half of this century is John O'Hara. The important story to get is the story of the 1920s, and I'm convinced he got it. His most nearly perfect book is *Appointment in Samarra.* His best evidence is *Butterfield 8.* He took New York City on, and I'm convinced he got it right. Not in terms of storytelling, actually. As I say, *Appointment in Samarra* is a much better story—*Butterfield 8* dwindles toward the end and becomes melodramatic and lots of other things, but the landscape has never been laid out better. He found the points of obsession in his fellow citizens, and got it right. I'm mentioning that because I'm about to propose a software program, something for a three- or four-dimensional computer program for the twenty-third century, creating rooms and realities to depict the first half of the twentieth century, based on the intersecting work of three American men: T. S. Eliot, Alfred Sloan, and John O'Hara. And since I'm developing this software, and get to have a little bit of *inventor's privilege,* I'm buying John O'Hara's social sense as the starting point, and I'm quite capable of arguing down anyone who tells me I shouldn't do that. Start with his list of speakeasies. And to this, one would add his description of the life in those places, the life of Gloria Wandrous, his heroine, and Weston Liggett, his hero, and all the high-energy despair boys who dashed in and out of those speak-easies. All of that intersects with one brief paragraph, or possibly you could expand it to three paragraphs, in Alfred Sloan's *Adventures of a White Collar Man.* Sloan discusses a hotel in Detroit, the Pontchartrain, where the energetic despair boys, the new speeded-up Americans of 1920, were demonstrating their positive, or *non-speakeasy*, energy; we're not at a speakeasy in Sloan's story, we're in one of those hotels built in the first part of this century, where the positive energy of these speeded-up despair boys and girls was in play:

> The Pontchartrain was where motorcar gossip was heard first. New models customarily had debuts there. As word spread that so and so's new Whizzer was parked at the curbstone, the crowd would flock outside to appraise the new rival of all existing cars. Even on ordinary days, when the crowd thinned out of the dining room, the tablecloth would be covered with sketches: crankshafts, chassis, details of motor wheels and all sorts of mechanisms. Partnerships were made and ended there. New projects were launched.

You have to understand that that energy was new. The Whizzer, the idea of the Whizzer, was new, and I like it that Sloan, with his small bit of imagination—his imagination was small but it was present; his powers of social observation were very limited, but they were present—I like it that he knew, and acknowledged that he knew, that society was completely different, that it was speeded up, and he calls the new motorcar that the speeded-up despair boys were revving up for the Whizzer. We are talking of a period here probably just before the First World War, when the automobile was only ten years old, the process that would accelerate so disastrously during the 1920s was beginning, and Sloan had seen it begin. Sloan was a horse-and-buggy boy. He remembered the slow America. He remembered patriarchal forms, and although he would have seen a certain amount of speed in the older industries, among railroad men and so forth, this particular kind of urban buzz, reflected so beautifully in his choice of the name Whizzer, was new, and destined to win. When we talk about the Pontchartrain Hotel in 1910 or 1912, we're talking about the beginnings of television, we're talking about a new energy forming, and Sloan had seen it form. And no man was better at being effortless and frictionless in his forward-moving vector than Alfred Sloan. Interestingly enough, he began in the ball-bearing business. He's somebody who drifted into an enterprise from somewhere else. What is a frictionless man? What do I mean by that? Well, let's go to the opposite. A man is subject to the friction of life depending on his early, absolute commitment to some specific avatar of social reality. Hence, an eighteenth-century English country parson, whose life touched established cultural forms at many different points, all of them well worked out and strong, stands in marked juxtaposition to Alfred Sloan. An eighteenth-century English country parson would have had to worry about every detail of the social life around him, taking some responsibility for the interaction of all his fellow citizens. In what state of grace or fall from grace was the local magnate, whose influence over the surrounding countryside was so great? Was the local magnate behaving well toward his tenants or poorly? If he was behaving poorly, how could the representative of the Established Church work to bring the soul of the magnate to a better state so he would treat his tenants better? That kind of thing, extending down to how the servants were treated in his own house. A life with a lot of friction, very little easy movement forward, and no movement forward without checking out the results on the surrounding community on a moment-by-moment basis. That wasn't Alfred Sloan's position. But he *remembered* that position.

Now I'm going to rock-and-roll with this a little bit. Last night I watched a little QVC, the television shopping channel, and QVC is, of course, a kind of cocaine. It's the pure version of something. In other words, a woman (and QVC is designed to appeal to women, who are on camera far more than men) in the course of a shopping expedition will encounter many things. If she's shopping on, let's not say Fifth Avenue, that's a little too grand, although Fifth Avenue isn't very grand anymore—well, let's *say* Fifth Avenue, actually it makes it better; if she's just finished shopping at Lord and Taylor and has decided to head

uptown to Saks Fifth Avenue at Forty-Ninth Street, she will encounter many things. She will see what goes on in the streets.
She will see, indeed, some homeless people. She will see the
intrusion of electronics stores on Fifth Avenue. She will pass
the New York Public Library with its lions and be reminded of
the existence of books and marble palaces for culture. As she
approaches Saks Fifth Avenue, she will be aware of St. Patrick's
Cathedral just beyond it and all that a cathedral represents in the
history of humankind. Not so the woman watching QVC. I got the
cocaine metaphor from a lecture I once heard given by a countercultural guru who explained that the coca leaf, properly embedded in the culture of certain South American Indians, played a
natural, attractive role in the life of those Indians, so that as they
climbed high up in the Andes and needed extra energy, or extra
something, they could chew a coca leaf and it would become a
natural part of their natural life. This, he said, was in contradis-
tinction to an urban person sniffing cocaine, the distilled product
of the coca leaf. Well, QVC is the distilled product of a shopping
trip. No homeless people, no public library, no electronics stores,
and certainly no cathedral.

So last night I saw something that was remarkable to me. I
saw a very good saleswoman named Kathy Levine taking over
from Joan Rivers. Now, I don't know if this was a temporary
depression on Joan Rivers' part, or if she's just not feeling well
this week, she may bounce back next week, but on this particular
program, Joan Rivers, who for a couple of decades has personified a kind of feminine avidity, never letting the ball fall into
quiet for a moment, always keeping it whizzing along—and my
echo of the Whizzer here is deliberate—jittering around, Joan
Rivers was strangely quiet. Indeed—and I'm aware of camera
position because I work in the film industry—the cameras had
been positioned in such a way that Kathy Levine was now front
and center and Joan was in the background. Not only that—and
it's a fact that *drama* and *karma* will out, even in the most contrived of circumstances, and believe you me, QVC is the most
contrived of circumstances—but the camera seems to have been

ordered not to do close-ups of Joan. Joan's at a low-energy point now for some reason or other—I'm going to speculate on why—but at one point Joan almost insisted, almost shrieked, that the camera should do a close-up, and the camera didn't, at which point Joan turned it into a joke and said, "I guess no close-ups today." Joan looks as if she's on the way out of an unconflicted selling mode, which brings us back to John O'Hara. We do live in a country that changed forever in the twenties. People do whiz in, and then they whiz out. Fitzgerald is the obvious avatar, the author of all those I-love-the-twenties books on the one hand, and *The Crackup* on the other. He's our poet on the subject. Joan, by my perception, has got somewhere. In other words, having finally made a decision ten years ago to be brave and trusting in her entry into classical modes of chic, let's say, all the time bringing those modes down to the costume-jewelry level, some little piece of moral information—and, in fact, if you surround yourself with artifacts from the past, finally and ultimately you begin to wonder a little bit about the past—some little piece of moral information has gotten through to Joan, and she's no longer so completely comfortable whizzing. That's my perception. My clue to that, and I think it was very poignant, and I think Joan Rivers is a kind of poignant neo-flapper, was that when a pair of pansy pins were on display to be sold, Joan, who'd been rather modest in her participation, suddenly became vehement. She found a way into the conversation—and of course the conversation in these selling things is infinitely frenetic, and participates in what I call varied sameness. It's always the same transaction, but there are all these tiny little variations in it, so that the next transaction will be just as appealing as the one you've been through. And it's a certain kind of feminine mode, which has its roots in something very deep and positive, the affirmation of life; this mode is abused for the selling of products. "It's great, it's wonderful, I love it, it's terrific." Those are the words. It's much more hyper than that, and much more varied, but that's what's said over and over again. Finally this refers to what a mother says to a child: "You're great, you're wonderful, it's wonderful." Even if the bombs are dropping, a mother says to a child, "It's gonna be all right, it's terrific, you're terrific." I mean, that's what's supposed to happen, and here it's being done for jewelry. I mean, you've just seen twenty pairs of earrings, more or less of the same aesthetic, and here's the twenty-first pair of earrings, and this twenty-first pair of earrings is even greater, even better, "This is great, you're gonna love this, if you wear it on camera it's gonna pop out, it's gonna be great, it's not one of those ugly things that does this, it's one of the beautiful things that does that, and you're gonna love it so much more because . . ."

Joan, by my perception, as of last night, has lost the heart for all that. She's done it too often. And, on the other hand, some little bit of the real history of beauty, of aesthetics, of hierarchy, of life, has crept into her consciousness in a way that has made her conflicted or bored or a little depressed, perhaps, about the selling process. She's seen too many pairs of earrings, she can't quite stand to say that this twenty-first pair is new, great, and so forth, she perhaps has seen some really good earrings somewhere. But then the pansy pins came on, and she suddenly found a way to get into it, and she said, "Does anyone know where the word *pansy* came from? It has to do with *Pense-moi*, 'think of me.'" Well, I don't know what the history of that is, but that's what Joan said, and she kept on saying it over and over again, "Pense-moi, pense-moi, pense-moi," and it was extraordinarily poignant, and a little crazy. It seemed to me that as she was saying it, she was saying, "Please think about me, please think about me, please think about me, I'm in trouble here." She was, in her mind, entering the non-buy-and-sell mode of it, even as she continued to buy and sell. Perhaps she badly wanted to be taken out of it— she wanted a place where jewelry really *was* fine, and ladies really *were* ladies, and gentlemen gave beautiful real jewels to beautiful real ladies. It was like that, and then came a variety of negative references to herself. She would say, "It even looks good on me." Suddenly, under all of this positive, positive, positive, there was some negative. There was doubt. There was unhappiness, even.

This is all in marked contrast to Joan as she has been. I can remember once—actually I went into a bar to have a drink, and QVC was on, and this must have been two or three years ago, let's say 1994, and Joan was in the position Kathy Levine was in last night. Joan was front and center, Joan wouldn't let the energy drop. If there was any little hint of something that wasn't quite working a mile a minute, Joan was there to fix it. And at her side was a very disorganized, grumpy-looking woman with pale gray-blond hair, and this woman had something that looked like a plastic egg carton in front of her, and I looked more closely at the woman, and, my God, she was C. Z. Guest. Now, C. Z. Guest in 1950—well, you didn't get cooler or chicer, more social or more theoretically inaccessible than Mrs. Guest in 1950, and here on QVC, selling something that I think had to do with starting a garden, because that's been Mrs. Guest's opening to the marketplace in recent years, there was C. Z. Guest. And her hands were fumbling a little bit, she didn't know quite what she was doing, and Joan was picking up the ball for her. And two years later, by my perception, Joan was in the C. Z. Guest position. She'd been there once too often. She'd caught a glimpse of something that wasn't quite right, perhaps, in what she herself had been doing.

I'm going to relate this now to the agreement we all have that industrial society never quite cohered. It was a great experiment, it was a new way for all of us to live together in a more regimented way on the one hand, but in a more anonymous way on the other. That was always the trade-off. Yes, you worked in an assembly line; no, you didn't have to report to the county parson. But industrial society simply didn't cohere. In the process of trying it—during our seventy-year experiment with industrial society— all the credibility, all the believability, all the trance, in a sense, all the *closure* of agricultural, hierarchical life disappeared, but industrial society didn't cohere. So now we have—a clean slate. Nothing—or a clean slate, it is up to us. We are, at long last, the existential men and women that Heidegger and Sartre saw we would necessarily become. And that was what was getting to Joan: "My God, I don't understand."

What's coming to my mind now is a place, a building, 820 Fifth Avenue. It's an apartment house on Fifth Avenue in the lower sixties in New York, and for people who kept track of things like this it was, and may still be, although I don't think the frame of reference for this kind of thing exists anymore, but for a long time it was one of the two best apartment buildings in New York, the other one being on Park Avenue. It really depended whether you wanted to live on Park or Fifth; if you were a little more traditional in your thinking, it was 820 Fifth Avenue. And at the top of this building lived the father of a friend of mine, a man who was the grandson of James Stillman, an ally of William Rockefeller, and hence one of the stewards of Rockefeller money, one of the men who invented the modern flow of money. And the father of my friend was named Chauncey Devereux Stillman, and he was noted, among the people I knew in New York, for his strict adherence to hierarchical, agricultural rituals, including especially the rituals of the Roman Church, to which he had converted. And I want to juxtapose him, however strange it seems, with Joan Rivers. When people have got to a certain point in *life with money*, or *life with the knack that makes for making money*, when people have satisfied themselves two or three or ten times as to their ability to buy, to have possessions, to live in the best apartment house, often, unless they have some extraordinary original streak, some quirky instinct that leads them on into life in some unusual way, often they come to an understanding of what we all now are about to realize, that the ways of making money that we have evolved have destroyed agricultural life on the one hand and not cohered on the other. And this leads people either to a state of conflictedness of the kind that Joan Rivers was showing last night, or to a sudden vehement embrace of older rituals, as was the case with Chauncey Stillman. Alfred Sloan, toward the end of his life, lived at 820 Fifth Avenue. Another famous New York couple who lived at 820 Fifth Avenue were William and Babe Paley, Mr. Paley the inventor of a big part of our media life, CBS. The Paleys were neighbors of C. Z. and Winston Guest on Long Island. I'm indicating a kind of swirl here, which is enormously big and varied, swirling all through all our commercial processes, the billion and one manifestations, to use a Lao-tzu concept, the many monsters, the billion-headed manifestation of it on the one hand, and then the node of it on the other hand. The drift toward the best building on Fifth Avenue and the North Shore of Long Island, either actually or as to state of mind.

So let's rocket right along to T. S. Eliot, who was frictioned and frictionless both, and the record of his poetry is the record of a conflicted man, who now rolled along on easy bearings on the basis of his talent, right up to the tippy-top of who was doing what in England. That, on the one hand, and on the other, he was a man who had felt a kind of friction of nostalgia for a decent masculine life, which was something he found difficult to get for himself. So here's something from "Prufrock," his poem of 1917, and as I read it, I'll ask my reader to keep in mind Alfred Sloan's description of the Whizzer, and that group of energetic new Americans bursting into modernity, with a lot of just-off-the-farm energy, dashing in and out of the Hotel Pontchartrain to look at this or that new model of automobile destined to change the world: "Let us go then, you and I, / When the evening is spread out against the sky / Like a patient etherized upon a table." Well, you can go on and on in this poem and in others of Eliot's, but the terrible thing about Eliot is that there's hardly any point in going on because it's always the same, and it's not so different from what the Sex Pistols said and what a lot of other people have said, "like a patient etherized on a table." "All in all it's just another brick in the wall," Pink Floyd sang as recently as fifteen years ago. When you go out into the real social circumstances of this life with anything like a sensible animal intelligence, you find etherization, you find the wall, you find nothing, *nada,* and *rien.* Well, do you or don't you? Alfred Sloan didn't, but that was because he was a little etherized to begin with. In T. S. Eliot and Alfred Sloan you have two avatars of old America, both a little *parson-like*—Alfred Sloan was, in his personal life, very parson-like. He didn't participate in the Whizzer of it, he controlled the Whizzer of it. He controlled it by being safe, sane, businesslike, honorable, full of probity, but also with quite a patient, perhaps even a sly, will to power. His move through the corporate jungle of twentieth-century America was all too easy to be entirely accidental. He always did the right thing, in a way, and yet at a certain moment he was able to supplant his boss, Mr. Durant, and then at another moment he was able to insist that Pierre S. du Pont serve as president of General Motors while he, Alfred Sloan, got his sea legs, and then he took over from Pierre S. du Pont. So, we're not by any means dealing, when we deal with Alfred Sloan, with an innocent man, but there are no flies on Alfred Sloan, nothing the tabloid press could get to in any way, shape, or form, and the rituals that had formed him were middle-class rituals, allied, I think, to the Methodist Church, but certainly to one of the simpler, more austere forms of Protestant life. He was a little etherized, and he thought that was quite all right, because—oh, forgive me for this—the ether was a kind of lubricant for his vector. What he didn't notice allowed the vehicle to slip along effortlessly.

Eliot, of course, was different. A modern poet, but always aware of the way of acting that the eighteenth-century parson I've described did once have. Aware that one has a human obligation to monitor the results of one's actions almost moment by moment, and aware also that something of healthy masculine nature had been etherized in him. It is likely that what had been etherized in him also made it possible for him to glide forward on his poetic vector, and he must have been aware of this, and to some extent been glad that he had been etherized out of normal life so that he could write his poetry. I thought I was going to quote something from "Little Gidding," but I'm not going to, because I think it's depressing and tiresome. The thing we're all supposed to be in awe of in Eliot is the way he came home. He was out there on the street overturning Victorian and Edwardian and Georgian modes of poetry; he was a rebel, supposedly, and then the miseries of modern life loomed over his head as they now seem to loom over the head of Joan Rivers (and as at another point, they loomed over the head of Chauncey Stillman, the grandson of James Stillman), and just as Joan Rivers seems to have entered into kind of a little depression or conflictedness, and just as Chauncey Stillman entered into the Roman Church, so—when the nature of the trouble of modern life made full or fuller impact on Eliot—did T. S. Eliot begin to decide to take seriously the modes of the eighteenth-century parson, the Established Church, the Church of England.

I like Sloan better. Here's why I like Sloan better. It has to do with a piece of theater. My assumption is that this century is a failure, a great big disaster, and that we're not really going to need access to T. S. Eliot's *"reconciliation"*—to the idea of an Anglican, upper-class, Mandarin point of view—because that civilization has gone. The technical worth of the poetry is something for someone else to judge, but my guess is that without that English urge or ability to reintegrate with Anglican, upper-class, Mandarin, neo-control-group, standard setting, without that urge or that access, the poetry will be less interesting in the future. I like this Sloan story better. Sloan's book, *Adventures of a White Collar Man,* was published in the year 1941. We don't have the month for it, but the book doesn't indicate a battle going on just this second. It was certainly written pre–Pearl Harbor. Awareness of war but not in war is the feeling I get from the book.

Here is Mr. Sloan writing. Again, he is talking of Durant, who put General Motors together in the early years of the century, starting with the Buick, and one of the things I like about this book is its way of giving us a real line of continuity in a way that Eliot's life doesn't. Here is Alfred Sloan, who saw the automobile business arise from the horseless carriage and Mr. Olds to this moment when he's writing in 1940, say, or early 1941, probably 1940. He has seen almost every car that was ever made up to that point, and he's discussing Mr. Durant, who was one of the eccentric geniuses who got the business going, and he's describing an event:

> Mr. Durant was truly a pioneer. One of the happiest
> moments of my business life occurred a few months ago

UNDER THE AESTHETIC OF DWIGHT DAVID EISENHOWER   169

in Detroit at the time of the completion of the twenty-
fifth millionth car produced by General Motors. To us,
it was a momentous occasion. We had worked hard,
with no limitations on time and effort. We had sacri-
ficed everything to the cause of making General Motors
what it had become, and we felt we had every reason
to be proud of our accomplishment. A big celebration
had been arranged. We gave a dinner to the men and
their wives who had served the corporation for twenty-
five years. *There were over a thousand present. That in
itself was interesting and impressive. Then we staged a
pageant, showing the evolutionary development of General Motors.* A sample of one of the very earliest automobiles was on exhibition, as well as one of today. And Mr.
Kettering [the inventive, technical genius at General
Motors], in his inimitable way, told us about how the car
of 1960 would look and act. Mr. Durant was present,
having made a special trip from New York to attend the
celebration. I asked him if he would be willing just once
more to take part in a General Motors affair. He said he
would, and gladly, so, in due course, I had the pleasure
of presenting him to the audience. (*Emphasis mine*)

Now that—that celebration around the making of the twenty-five
millionth General Motors car (which seems to have taken place
in the year 1940)—is a real piece of American theater. It's a
marker in our real history in a way that the poetry of Eliot isn't.
Twenty-five years after that dinner, in 1965, I was a protocol
guide at the New York World's Fair. I've described this experience in *Within the Context of No Context.* My time spent at the
World's Fair, which was time spent working for Robert Moses, the
head of the Fair Corporation, was transforming for me, as they
say. I didn't just see the fair once or twice, I saw it every day for
two summers. I think I saw more of the fair than any other living
person, or it seems possible that I did. I don't know anyone else
who had the guide job for two summers running, and certainly

the people from our office had more access to the pavilions of the fair than anyone else. As someone working for the Fair Corporation you could walk in and out of pavilions at will, and so we did. And the mention of the *pageant* at the 1940 General Motors dinner is poignant for me. I can see it in my mind's eye. I can see one thousand vital Americans, in some assembly hall, mesmerized by the idea that General Motors had built twenty-five million automobiles. I'm aware (because I think *demographically*) that in 1940, a sixty-year-old man at that dinner would have been born in 1880. He would have been thirty-four years old when the First World War broke out. That dinner in 1940 was, in some ways, a nineteenth-century dinner. A forty-year-old would have been born in 1900. A thirty-year-old would have been born in 1910. It would have been a pre–World War I dinner, full of the energy of old preindustrial, preregimented industrial—I will make that distinction—*preregimented industrial America.* It would have been a dinner for farm boys, I almost want to say, of heirs of some older social system, who had burst out of their older social system into the promise of modernity, and had had as a reward something stupendous—the achievement of twenty-five million automobiles, and the technical achievement of an automobile in 1940 that made the automobile of 1900 look like a bicycle. It must have been an exciting time, and, according to Alfred Sloan, there was a *pageant.*

Twenty-five years later, at the New York World's Fair, I saw a pageant. It wasn't at the General Motors Pavilion. The General Motors Pavilion had resurrected its "Futurama Ride," which had been a hit at the '39 World's Fair, just about the time of Sloan's dinner, and which caused quite a stir because it projected into the future the same kind of enormous progress that had taken place in the recent past. The next twenty-five years will be as astounding to us as the last twenty-five years, was the message of the Futurama Ride in 1939, and that ride was resurrected for the '64–'65 fair, and it wasn't particularly impressive. What was impressive, new, and popular, and what was a kind of pageant in a way to be absolutely compared to the General Motors pageant of 1940, was the Carousel of Progress at the General Electric Pavilion. Just as the pageant at the General Motors dinner in 1940 showed the history of General Motors, so too did the Carousel of Progress at the General Electric Pavilion show the history of America, through the history of General Electric. No human persons participated in this pageant, no astounding event was celebrated; rather, the carousel was a mechanical device. The audience moved from quadrant to quadrant on this carousel. That was supposed to be the astounding thing, that, instead of the stage revolving, which could easily have been arranged for, the audience moved. The grandstand revolved, and there's something novel in that. I'm thinking at this moment of *A Chorus Line*, the play of the 1970s in which the narcissism of modern life was used as a form of theatrical energy. At the General Electric Pavilion in 1965, as later in *A Chorus Line*, the audience was being told, in this age of demography, that *its* movement was what was important; that was the way the spotlight fell.

What went on on the unmoving stage of the General Electric Pavilion in 1965, well, it was a pageant of automatons. So now, sympathy for Mr. Eliot here—*etherized*, indeed, was the right word for it. Progressive catatonia, progressive mechanization, automatons—Disney automatons, one has to say. I am, as I've said elsewhere, a man who has acted as though from an unbroken family tradition, who has made sense of his life by developing an ability to analyze mainstream American cultural artifacts. I'm going to end this sequence of writing with my personal favorite Mainstream American Cultural Artifact, a series of paragraphs from an article in the *Continental Monthly,* "a magazine devoted to literature and national policy," from March 1864, a magazine published by my great-great-grandfather, John F. Trow, but I'll swirl around before I get there. Sloan's book, *Adventures of a White Collar Man,* was published in 1941. And as I say, my guess is that it was written in 1940. Those years, 1939–1941 are particularly interesting to me because the aesthetic I was raised in, or under, was formed in those years. My parents were courting; they were married in May of 1941. This was the world I was born into.

I was born on September 28, 1943, I was in my mother's womb during 1943; the world I was to be born into, the landscape I was to be born into, was taking shape in 1939 and '40. I feel, almost viscerally, that pageant of the history of General Motors that took place in 1940. I feel it reverberating in me. I know those cars; those were the first cars I saw, the cars of the late thirties and early forties. I remember the attitude people had toward automobiles. When I see one of those automobiles, the masculinity of them—the sinuous masculinity of them, one wants to say, the steel so thick, the mechanism so simple, the steering wheel so assertive and so like something on a boat, the way one sat so high in the seats and looked through a windshield that in some cases had been divided by a metal strip down the middle, the anthropomorphism of those automobiles, where the headlights looked like eyes and the grill looked like a mouth—this is all fundamental to me.

So I'm going to start with something I didn't see myself but which I know of, it has been described to me. My parents, courting, not yet married, went over to Windy Rock, the Coggeshall place which was a real piece of old Brownstone New York that had taken root in southern Westchester, and they were assembled there for the purpose of going to watch, from what promontory I'm not sure, from somewhere on the property or perhaps from somewhere on the Choates' property, Pink House, the progress up the Taconic Parkway of King George VI and Queen Elizabeth to a famous picnic at Hyde Park, and sympathy for my parents here, because we all live in a theater. Sympathy first of all for my mother, who came from a lower-middle-class Irish Catholic and Protestant family, who had a natural ambition to be among the movers and shakers of this world, and here she was, with a young man who categorically came from a Brownstone grand duchy, and she was being taken, for a time, to be with the citizens of this grand duchy in order to watch the progress of the king and queen of England up the Taconic Parkway to Hyde Park, where they would have a picnic with FDR and Eleanor Roosevelt. Quite a piece of theater for a young Irish-American girl, and rather heady for the young man from a collapsed Brownstone family who was giving her access to it. A little like taking a modern girl backstage at a Rolling Stones concert. Not a bad metaphor at all—it's all there, the success beyond anything, the thing everyone you know is in reference to, and you get to see it, up close and personal, from a patch of land that seems to refer to a dominant old civilization, the most dominant, the most honorable, and all the people you're with act from a point of view of social ease. Toward Franklin and Eleanor, certainly, but toward the king and queen of England as well. A poignant moment of theater for my parents, and for me. So, what was I doing at the World's Fair in 1964 and '65? I was scouting, I was looking, I was trying to find out what it was my parents were talking about. I kept it up decade after decade. I didn't know what I was doing, I just kept at it. What was there, back then? Well, I explored every social tradition that either of my parents had ever touched. It was my job. And then one day my father handed me this copy of the *Continental Monthly*, "devoted to literature and national policy," and I found in it an article. It begins on page 351. The pages are sequential through various numbers of this magazine, and the name of the man who wrote it is not on the article, but I believe it will be in the—yes—it is by Mr. John A. French. And I ran into this paragraph, at which time my view of what I had been doing was transformed.

Before the world was thickly settled and the nations established, it was held that the power of a nation consisted in the extent of its dominions, so that while the individual strove for wealth of agriculture, manufacture, or commerce, the state despised such low pursuits and turned its attention to increase of territory. But when, after the fall of Rome, it was found that the earth was too fully peopled, and national power too well established for such means of strength, attention was turned to another source of power, in the cultivation of a people's own resources, and increase of its wealth. Wealth is obtained by the addition of mental power to physical products, increasing their value for supplying the wants of man, so that attention to physical comfort and prosperity, which was despised by the brave nations of antiquity, is now the leading object of government. Treaties are made, wars are declared, rebellions break out, not on account of national glory or right, but in consideration of cotton manufacture, facilities of commerce, or freedom of trade. Nations, as well as men, are absorbed in the same great pursuit, adding mind to matter for production of wealth. From this undue attention to physical prosperity spring certain subordinate causes, which, upon examination, are found to be the exact differentia of modern times. The characteristics which distinguish our age from all others are the very ones which have been found so destructive to pre-existing civilizations. The first characteristic of this kind is the abundance of outward knowledge. In the pursuit of wealth, the ocean, the desert, the isles of the sea have been ransacked for commodities to gratify the desires of man. And, in order that nature may be pliable for the same purpose in the hands of the artisan, its laws have been studied with the greatest success. The bowels of the earth, the depths of the air, the prison of the Arctic seas, have all been subject to the same strict scrutiny in this design. The knowledge thus obtained comes pouring in by lightning and steam, and is scattered over the world within the reach of the poorest by means of the printing press. The man of today is a citizen of the world. He seems to be ubiquitous. It is as though he had a thousand eyes and ears, and, alas, only one mind. Thought has two conditions. First, knowledge as food and stimulus, second, time for distributing and digesting that knowledge. But the first is so superabundantly fulfilled that it completely obliterates the second. Knowledge comes pouring in from all quarters so rapidly that the man can hardly receive, much less arrange and think out, the enormous mass of facts daily accumulating upon him. The boasted age of printing presses and newspapers, of penny magazines and penny encyclopedias is not necessarily the age of thought. There is a worldwide difference between knowledge and wisdom. The one consists of facts as they are, the other as facts as they may be. The one sees events, the other, relations. Any schoolgirl could state facts today about the world and the universe which would make old Socrates stare in astonishment, and yet he lived a life to which hers is the dream of the day moth.

When I first read that, I was astounded. Was I involved in some multigenerational, genetic thing quite beyond my understanding? Well, I think, yes, and I think that in the next century, either people will have lost all memory and will start from scratch, or they will integrate with a multigenerational view of their experience. The failure of modernity means, among other things, that we will either start from scratch with nothing or we will find that we are necessarily connected with who we were before the process got rocking and rolling.

One thing modern life does is to obscure our karmic relationships. The man who left the farm, whatever farm it was, the farm in Minnesota, or the farm in Sicily, to go to Detroit in 1905, let's say, to begin whizzing in the automobile industry, was confident that he had put his karma behind him. He was here to ride in the automobile. Nothing like it had ever been seen before on the face of the earth. How could one imagine that one's old karmic relationships were still alive and kicking when this thing from outer space, almost, was so powerful, promised such success, and was destined, everyone saw, past a certain point, to dominate? What parish priest, what owner of two thousand acres, could claim that he was free of the civilization of the automobile? And yet the evidence of my life is that we clear our karma, or else. You swim fast enough, long enough, and you find something that tells you what you've been doing, and why.

John Fowler Trow was part of an experiment, one wants to say, greater than the automobile experiment. The experiment of modern printing. The experiment of the penny press, the experiment of everything like that. He began his experiment in New York City in 1833. In 1864, we were in the Civil War. There were draft riots in New York City. Life was not so simple. The population of the city had grown exponentially between 1833 and 1864. I have no record of John Fowler Trow's reaction to these events, but he was not an insensitive man, and he must have felt them. And here, in a magazine, published by him, with his name on the cover, is a discussion of the problem of the civilization he himself had helped to invent and was continuing to invent. I give him higher marks than Alfred Sloan. For Trow to do this was a little like Sloan hectoring or allowing for the possibility that maybe the automobile was doing some bad things as well as some good, presenting a problem as well as an infinite opportunity. That you never got out of Sloan. The etherization had moved apace. If you were going to be successful at General Motors, in the way that Sloan was, you were going to be unconflicted. If you were going to be unconflicted, you were not going to allow the other possibility to come into view. I said that I have been a scout, looking everywhere for clues as to what was going on in my parents' conversation. I've said that this was a matter of survival with me. It also was a matter of something else. It was a matter of holding on to confidence. My way of judging was simple: if it's not etherized, and it touches my family tradition at any point, I want it, whether it's life in an automobile repair shop with the energy my Irish-American grandfather had when he repaired automobiles, which he did, whether it's that or it's lunch looking over the Hudson with an old aristocrat, I want it. Because it's alive, and if it's alive it gives me confidence. And if it gives me confidence, it gives me the ability to swim on, and clear the karma.

Under the Aesthetic of FDR

So now I give you an overview of my life with FDR, which is a somewhat ironic title for the history of my Brownstone New York family and its mental involvement with FDR. Please understand that all groups feel a strong affinity with powerful people who perfectly reflect their own experience. This is well understood; the appeal of John Kennedy to Irish-Americans would be an instance. A fellow like oneself who makes it to the top is appealing. And if one's group has been in eclipse, and one of one's fellows makes it to the top, well, that holds out all kinds of promise and optimism. So it was with my family and the Roosevelts. My Brownstone Trow New York family had gotten swamped in the Belle Epoque by the robber barons. From being people of almost the highest status in New York City, sometime in the 1880s they went to being merely middle-class, upper-middle-class people in the city, at a time when the definition of middle-class and upper-class and upper-middle-class was being redefined. This process has been discussed with authority by Edith Wharton. My great-grandmother Cora Welles Trow was part of that process. In 1880, at the time of her marriage, she would have been perceived as being an upper-class woman of old New York. By 1886, when my grandfather was born, she would have been perceived as being an obscure person who had roots in the old city. During the 1880s, New York City was redefined socially. The important name here is Alva Smith Vanderbilt, a story for another time, but it's been well documented, the transformation of the city socially in the 1880s, and again, Mrs. Wharton is our best witness. My great-grandmother swam out of her Brownstone Madison Square heritage into the new world, and quite bravely, but, as all people do, she kept a memory of who she had been, who her family had been, and what values had been held or talked about in her family, and she was an enormous fan of Theodore Roosevelt's. In his Bull Moose period as well as before. A loyal partisan of Theodore Roosevelt's. In Edith Wharton terms, it's not inappropriate to mention that around the corner from the house where my great-grandmother grew up, near Madison Square, was the Fifth Avenue Hotel, and that the Fifth Avenue Hotel had been built by Amos Eno (a famous New Yorker of his day), and that the grandson of Amos Eno was Gifford Pinchot, who was the brain trust behind all of Theodore Roosevelt's conservation efforts, a big part of his game plan, and an influence in his attitude toward the rich men of his day. So my great-grandmother would have felt an affinity with Theodore Roosevelt and Gifford Pinchot. Here were people from her New York, who had swum bravely into a modern world and yet kept their values. My great-grandmother was the primary influence in my own father's life, and my father, when I was young, told me many times the story of being taken by his grandmother to see Theodore Roosevelt's house in the East Twenties in New York, and so forth.

The most coherent experience of Old New York I had growing up was not in my own family—my own family really only existed in my father's mind at that point—but at Windy Rock, the echo-of-Old-New-York house I mentioned in my dedicatory introduction. Windy Rock was, in turn, a part of something else—a Joseph Cornell box of New York social history: the Choate house next door—then public land—and the Pocantico Hills in the distance. As to my father's head, his head had been informed, to the extent that it had been informed, by the strong opinions of his grandmother, and he was determined that what was in his own head should be real for me, and so I entered a story that had essentially ended. My father was in a position many men are in. He felt embattled, and he felt that only if his man won would he be anything other than embattled. His man was Roosevelt, Franklin; and Franklin connected to Theodore; and Theodore connected to his grandmother; and his grandmother connected to a dominant tradition in New York; and if all these things continued to be true and vital, and if all these things were accepted by me, his son, to be true, then everything was all right; if any part of that was wrong, then everything was wrong, with a capital *W.* So, the little patch of Old New York in Westchester called Windy Rock was the patch of ground I knew that was alive and kicking on the earth, and which represented the aesthetic my father said was most important in the world. It was a matter of survival for me. This thing must be true, or I'm a dead dog, and the difference between having one patch of ground to work from and having no patch of ground to work from is the difference between night and day. And I did have one patch of Old New York to work from in my project to survive my father's obsession.

And it was alive and kicking, this moral tradition of Old New York, on that patch of ground named Windy Rock, until 1948, until the defeat of Henry Wallace in the election of 1948, and I was five years old at that time and had no way of knowing who Henry Wallace was, of course, but I had a visceral connection to it. Mr. Coggeshall, the head of the family at Windy Rock, was a supporter of Henry Wallace's, and when he died in the early 1950s, my father had what I never saw him have before or again, a strong emotional reaction. I can remember the phone ringing in our house in Cos Cob, I can remember my father going to answer it, I can remember my father dropping the phone and running through the dining room and then the living room of our house, upstairs, to weep. Mr. Coggeshall had died. This moment impressed me so much. This was my father showing emotion; my father didn't show emotion. This was what was important to my father, this was how to please my father, to enter this moment, whatever it was. This was how to make an emotional connection, which was what I was in the process of being denied. And to be fair to my father, one should say there are different kinds of people on the earth; I happen to be a very emotional person, a person for whom a soul connection is essential; without a soul connection I don't see the point. My father, on the other hand, was not like that. And another kind of son would have had none of these reactions, and none of this story would have been told, and perhaps my father would have been better off with another kind of son, but he didn't get another kind of son, he got me, and that's life too. So this moment was of crucial importance to me, this event, the death of Mr. Coggeshall.

In terms of social history, I juxtapose it with another moment when my father discussed with me Mr. Coggeshall's involvement in the Henry Wallace campaign of 1948. My father was by then a practicing journalist, working in New York, for the *World Telegram*. He said that Mr. Coggeshall had invited him to a fund-raising party at Windy Rock, and he told me that the Wallace campaign was viewed by Mr. Coggeshall as of paramount importance, something where the history of a certain kind of moral concern would be settled. I don't think that Mr. Coggeshall was particularly pleased to be involved in this campaign; he felt that it was his moral duty, a do-or-die thing. He did it, he supported Wallace, he gave a fund-raiser at Windy Rock. My father said he attended this fund-raising dinner because of his strong loyalty to Mr. Coggeshall. And my father told me, "When I went out into the kitchen, every Communist in New York was there." And my father was in a position to know who those men were, and I believe it. I'm telling this story up front, because I think really one should date the end of Old New York and its moral involvement in the history of this country at 1948, with the Wallace campaign. With its insistence on preindustrial values, its attempt to make visceral the line of talk Roosevelt was talking. It was over after that, Adlai Stevenson to the contrary notwithstanding. My personal point of view about this, what interests me from the point of view of a five-year-old in 1948, is that my father didn't let go of his obsession then, or even allow it to be slightly modified, not, at any rate, in relation to me. Or perhaps he even liked the fact that he was pushing me into something he knew had died. Perhaps things had gone that far with him then. In any case, the fact of his weeping at Mr. Coggeshall's death convinced me that it was of paramount importance to me, as his son, to make visceral what my father said was true. I rebelled against this at different times because I sensed that what I was asking myself to do was impossible. But I did constantly regroup to make yet another effort to do the job.

One sad note about my father and then onward toward my position in this moment. People who live in their heads grow worse over time. Whatever the system was that was reasonable to start with—because all narcissists or self-involved people begin with systems that make some sense in terms of the moment when the system was adopted—all such systems grow corrupt over time, and finally this system in my father's head turned from system to cinder, some small black thing, and the importance of this system-to-cinder story for my fellow citizens is simply this: my father's system was actually fabricated. However, it perfectly mimicked the overall system of Franklin Roosevelt in that it was partly Old New York and partly people's journalism—Walter Winchell, one might say tabloid, over-the-heads-of-everybody-else-to-where-the-people-are. And of course, in 1948, when my father clearly saw that the real moral force of Old New York was over, he had somewhere else to turn. The journalism of it, the newspaper of it, was flexible enough to carry him through. He never admitted this to himself; he never said, half my system is now over and it's just this other thing. In fact, he was in deep denial about that, and the process of denial indeed caused what had been a system to turn into a cinder. A very unhappy thing for me to watch, and it is a very unhappy thing for me to understand that something like this process had been steadily at work in the social history of New York during all the time I was at work in New York.

Now to my overview of where your author is at this moment. In my lifetime, I have seen both the social systems I grew up under dissolve. The Roosevelt social system and the Eisenhower social system are both gone. It makes me sad because I don't understand my country anymore. These were the two great alternatives in my life. I thought it was plenty to try to understand both.

◆ ◆ ◆

Now we're going to do a little in-depth cultural work here. The Mainstream Cultural Artifact is the *New York Post* of Wednesday, February 6, 1952. I don't have the whole paper here, but I think one day I'll just march through that paper from beginning to end, because I suspect that I'm the only person on the face of the earth who can do it. I'm the only person who understands who Dolly Schiff was on that day and Paul Sann and Jimmy Wechsler and Earl Wilson and Leonard Lyons, and I bet I'm the only person who can place the theatrical ads correctly in context with the movie ads within the theater of that day's paper. But for today, we'll just stick to the headlines and the front-page story. The front page—I'm looking at it now—the front page of the *New York Post*, February 6, 1952, first of all, there's a big seven over on the right, and it says, "Blue Final" and then there are two dots. Well, the two dots are the key to telling which edition of the paper it is. You got a different dot as you moved along, so this is the second edition the *Post* put out that day, it's called "the blue final," but they change it around, the next one could have been the final blue, or whatever. In any case, it's the second edition of the paper put out that day. On the left, there's a box that says, "Late News, Wire Photos, Comics," which is a wonderful old twenties thing, the wire photos. Newspapers are lazy in their templates; things survive for decades after they're already old; *wire photo* was a 1920s phrase, any hip person in 1952 would have changed that word. It no longer meant New, New, New. *Wire photo* was something from the twenties that had just been allowed to survive as a promotional thing into the fifties. "Five Cents in New York City and the Suburbs; Ten Cents elsewhere in the U.S.A." Then, near the dateline, it says "Cloudy and colder," that's the weather, and there again you have the tabloid front page as a kind of telegram to you, a survival from the twenties. The bulletin aspect of the daily paper, which had been so new in the twenties, was, if not stale by the fifties, well known. And then you have, on the front page, a picture of King George VI, who has just died, and Queen Elizabeth II, not yet crowned, but anyway she's now the queen, and the headline is KING DEAD—LIZ QUEEN. Now inside is the story my father was born to write. The headline is EDWARD'S LOVE OF WALLIS GAVE RULE TO GEORGE, by George Trow. "When handsome, dashing King Edward VIII spurned his crown for 'the woman I love,' the task of being ceremonial ruler over a quarter of the globe fell upon a quiet, unassuming family man, with a stammer, and deep sense of duty." Well, that's my father. He's a little bit writing about himself; the writing is boy's-book writing of 1920. "Ceremonial ruler over a quarter of the globe," that's how my father really thought. "Quiet, unassuming family man with a stammer," well, that's him. His megalomania, his tabloid self, his belief that he was also King George VI as well as Roosevelt and Churchill, it all came together, and it's all as phony as baloney can be.

And now I'll just direct your attention, to take a little of the weight off my poor, cancerous, dying father, and remind you of another Mainstream Cultural Artifact from the fifties, to a movie called *Roman Holiday*. *Roman Holiday* takes advantage of the vogue for Princess, then Queen, Elizabeth. And there was such a vogue. People forget the very simple fact that World War II rescued, for a while, the British monarchy from irrelevance. Once again, the world was about honor, the world was about bravery, the world was about who should be king, the world was about legitimacy. Suddenly into the 1950s came something everyone wanted to believe in. The young queen. And so there was a movie that made use of the vogue for a young princess-queen, because anytime the real social energy in the world gets above a certain level, there is a movie to take advantage of that energy; I hope everyone understands that that's the way it works. The media business is filled with people who launch themselves into action wherever energy gets to a certain kind of critical mass. There are very few really imaginative Mainstream Cultural Artifacts; the work of Fellini and Antonioni and Buñuel, for instance, stands apart from this process, but that's rare, very rare, hen's-teeth rare. People were interested in this young woman who was going to be, and then was, queen of England; there was a movie to take advantage of that interest. In the movie, she's made a princess of some mythical kingdom, but it can only be Queen Elizabeth that's referred to because the kingdom is presented as being relevant as well as reminiscent, and, well, you can postulate the Dutch, maybe, but I don't think that works.

Audrey Hepburn plays a princess soon to be queen. And the movie is all about the ongoing necessity for royal dignity. Well, that was over and done with thirty years before, but World War II put it back on the map. The king had picked up his scepter and done his job. It was necessary for royal persons to stick to their knitting for the good of their people. And so, the story about a princess who, for one day, escapes the drudgery of her ceremonial rounds and takes wing with a journalist, played by Gregory Peck, a kind of deutero-Hemingway-style 1920s journalist, grown up a little, had relevance and was a hit. And the climactic moment of the movie is at the end, when the princess is *receiving* (after her day's holiday), is giving a great *darshan*—the climactic moment is the one in which the journalist, revealing his better self, his honorable self, his civic self, returns to the princess some photographs that he might have published and made a lot of money from, but he too is a citizen of the world of pride and honor and wouldn't think of doing such a thing, and that's your movie.

Well, that was a moment of the early 1950s, that was a real social moment. At the last moment, we did all draw together, and kingship and queenship did matter, and we all did stick to our knitting for the common good—but of course, it was nonsense. It had nothing to do with ritual or the way the world was really working; it had to do with what had happened for a very few years. So my father was right on the money for that moment. That was just exactly the style of that moment. "Ceremonial ruler over a quarter of the globe." And so we have existed in our horribly conflicted cultural life through all this century. At the last moment (every once in a while) it's *deutero-Churchillian* "over a quarter of the globe," taking pleasure in the thought of someone who rules over untold millions of polyglot whatever; meanwhile, we've done everything we can to get free of it, to split that apart. It's not so terribly complicated a conflict to analyze, it's just that our mind has not cohered around our dilemma.

◆   ◆   ◆

So, let's rock-and-roll with this. Not quite free-associate; my mind doesn't work that way. I just trust the circularity of it. Let's start, anyway: the Beatles, 1965. Before the Beatles' 1965 album, you have the Beatles as aspiring popular culturalists. Afterwards, you have something else. That's an important marker. The Beatles' 1965 album is the pivot point. You don't have *Revolver* yet, but you have a lot more than "yeah, yeah, yeah." Everyone should understand the sequence of the Beatles Family Story. The Beatles family—because it is one—goes back to Jack Kerouac and Neal Cassady. We won't do that quite yet, it would make our rock-and-roll too complicated. But there they are, all those little Beatles, and they're boys who want to get free of something, and to something. They want to get to American freedom; they don't understand that American freedom is itself horribly complicated and conflicted—but they know where it is, it's Elvis and the Beats. They're the Beatles. There's also a kind of *Less Than Zero* thing about being the Beatles; they're not quite the Beats. They're a little less, there's a kind of Bret Easton Ellis about the whole Beatle phenomenon, and that has to do with the tragedy of John Lennon. Being a kind of Beetle, being a kind of insect in a way, that finds itself in the power position in the world. Saying that the Beatles are more popular than Jesus and then suffering for the rest of one's life in fear of possible hubris, wondering what it is that has happened to one. Lennon surely knew he was a genius, he understood that he was on to something, because everyone reacted to him; on the other hand, he was aware of a kind of Kafka cockroach quality in himself, hence his alliance with Yoko Ono, who, whatever else is wrong with her, doesn't think she's a cockroach, and Lennon's on top, but he's waiting to be shot. So, the Beatles, 1965, is an important concept.

Now, come back to 1952, when my father is writing, "a ceremonial ruler over a quarter of the globe." Well, what is John Lennon doing? He's growing up in Liverpool, in a working-class family—Albert Goldman has documented all of this—and he's wondering what is going on. He has an enormously receptive, sensitive mind; he doesn't just buy what he's being told, and he has this Dionysian quality, the gift of song. Now think of *The Ziegfeld Follies*. Think of George Jessel, and Ed Wynn, and a couple of other enormous comic geniuses of Ziegfeld's day. These men had a marvelous sense of let's call it hyper-vaudeville structure, hyper-music-hall structure. They understood everything about the music hall, everything above vaudeville, and could take it another little step. Jack Benny is, of course, in there. Everyone knows that there's a music-hall quality in what the Beatles did—and I'll interrupt here because here's something I know from five years ago, going to a "rainforest concert" at a time when I was in friendly association with James Taylor. James was performing. James's rise is part of the Beatles story in a way. Elton John was playing certain songs from the thirties. "The Man I Love" is a song Elton sang. After the concert, a party somewhere. A limousine from the concert to the party. We're in the limousine, James and Sting and seven or eight other people, including myself. Suddenly James and Sting, of the Police, talk about the songs of the thirties, and it becomes quite obvious, it's not a secret, they're all just wondering, "Wouldn't it be marvelous to be able to do stuff like that?" Well, it's clear to me that John Lennon would have liked to have been able to do the kind of stuff they did in *The Ziegfeld Follies,* to do the kind of stuff Ed Wynn did. The legitimacy in our time has been a music-hall legitimacy, a show-business legitimacy, and many of our popular avatars of rock-and-roll, including Sting, whose Police songs are very edgy and modern and so forth, go home and listen to Gershwin. Well, it's important, culturally, for us to know that, and no one ever says it, how can they? Sting has to represent the Police, or the post-Police, or whatever it is. He doesn't come out and say, "I'd be Gershwin if I could," it's not in his interest to say it, so he doesn't say it.

Back to John Lennon. What is John Lennon trying to get away from? There's the reality of World War II, the service of the men of Liverpool, the reality of it, the reality of somebody's death at Dunkirk, the reality of the R.A.F., the reality of the nobility of George VI, that's there, but it's not completely there. As presented to him, it's mostly sham. He goes to *Roman Holiday*, and that's just Hollywood—that doesn't seem to have the story—that's just a concrescence. You must understand that Dionysian people have an instinct for what is alive and what is a concrescence. You can't convince a Dionysian person that a concrescence is alive. So John Lennon sees *Roman Holiday*—I don't know that he ever did, but if he did he looks at it and says, "Well, that's just the kind of shit my mother buys. The real story is here with Kerouac, with Elvis." And that's how he goes. What is he trying to get away from? Well, he's not trying to get away from the Old World of masculine honor. No one's ever told him about or introduced him to the Old World of masculine honor; he's just seen the movie. He's a free Western man; he's not going to toady to the gentry around Liverpool who supposedly represent what his mother likes in *Roman Holiday*. His whole working-class culture is against that, anyway. He's been introduced to a concrescence, part of which happens to be real—the real vector of last-chance Western white guys. And he reacts against it. He reacts against my father. "Ceremonial ruler over a quarter of the globe," that kind of thing. Later, his sensational death will be a headline in the *Post*.

Of course it split apart. So, who is Bret Easton Ellis, and what is *Less Than Zero*? It's part of the whole phenomenon of cockroach-Kafka-Beatles; "I'm nothing and nobody, but when I talk, there is, at least, an indication of where the truth is." Of course it split apart. No one was going to live in that *Roman Holiday* myth. It was too appalling. And when Dionysian avatars like James Taylor, John Lennon, came along and said, "You don't have to, I know another way," everyone went, which is why it went.

Here's an unhappy Mainstream Cultural Artifact from October 1, 1995. It's from the *New York Times,* and the headline is AN ATHLETE DIES YOUNG, BUT BY HIS OWN HAND. The picture is of seventeen-year-old Scott Crotow one month before he committed suicide, and the subheadline is FAMILY AND FRIENDS STILL GRIEVE, AND ASK WHY, and I haven't the heart to read it again; I remember it perfectly well. The boy was everyone's hope. Certainly his parents were divorced, separated, certainly his actual life was misery, but when he went to school, it was like a knife cutting through butter. He shone in his football jersey, was he captain of the team?—who knows?—I mean he surely was, and was he straight-A?—he certainly was, and did he have a full scholarship to go somewhere the next year?—well, he surely did have. I know why he died by his own hand. He's my grandfather. "However natural I am, however elegant at everything I do I am, it's trouble for me." This young man, Scott Crotow, from a troubled background, is being schooled to be King George VI. "Spiritual ruler over a quarter of the globe" sort of thing, "vessel for the hopes and dreams of Lewiston, Maine" kind of thing. But he lives in a world where the hit is John Lennon, and the literary truth, when you get to it, is *Less Than Zero,* and he knows it.

FOR FURTHER STUDY

The Patriarchy in the 1950s

I would like to use my very quick reading technique on a story I followed when I was ten, eleven, and thirteen years old, and I'll tell you what I remember of the story now, before I look through the actual clipping, and I should say, what I have in front of me are Xeroxes of the clippings of the Mickey Jelke story from the morgue at the *New York Post*, and I got into the morgue at the *New York Post* by using my father's name, and I acknowledge that, and the *New York Post* was kind to me, to allow me into their files, and I acknowledge that, and it was, in itself, an event for me to see the morgue of the *New York Post*, and the *New York Post* city room, as these rooms are now. The *Post* is now in the old *Journal American* building on South Street, and the city room is lined with television monitors, and when I was there, there were just a few people drifting around, just as though they were working in a bank—a far cry from the city room I remember, which depended for its energy on a kind of crazy, masculine huddle, very like a rugby team: huddling, playing, huddling again, ducking into the composing room, shouting into the telephone, and so forth; I don't really understand how a tabloid newspaper can be put out without that huddle, and I suspect that tabloid newspapers, as opposed to tabloid television programs, suffer a little bit from this modern atmosphere of the hospital environment plus television monitors. Television monitors seem to be telling you that somebody else is doing the job faster than you are, and the whole point of tabloid journalism was that you felt you were doing a job faster than anyone. And I can remember that the morgue at the old *Post* on West Street was Dickensian; I mean, it was piles of clippings and someone named Dexter Teagues, I believe was his name, or there's a story about someone called Dexter Teagues, but it really was Dickensian. Clippings piled on clippings in a tiny space; the modern morgue at the *Post* is quite well organized.

In any case, I went to the *Post,* asked to see the Mickey Jelke files, and there they were, and so, in a way, this for me is the tabloid balance of looking at the 1950 *New York Times,* and here's why. It's a story from 1953–1955, so that is, you know, almost forty-five years ago, isn't it? And here's why the story is important to me. I've discussed—and rather cruelly—the story my father wrote for the *New York Post* when King George VI died. Having been accurate but cruel about that story, I went and read a biography of George VI called *The Reluctant King,* and really what struck me was that George VI and my father were raised alike. I'm not saying that my father was raised in a royal manner; I'm saying that George V raised his sons, namely George and Edward, and the other two dukes, within an old bourgeois, liberal arts, Christian gentleman atmosphere, full of self-denial, modest learning—the idea that inherited status was far more important than money, the idea that there were lots of people you didn't associate with, the idea that other people would finally, necessarily, be depending on you for their values.

My father also had a kind of regality. An important difference here: George VI came by his royalty by virtue of the fact that he was a son of the king of England; my father came to his through a kind of megalomania. But lots of people seem to have that megalomania now, don't they—access to Princess Di and to some throne beyond Elton John. My father was one of the men to have that *first*—I almost want to say, that strange point of view, but then also the aesthetic of their upbringings was remarkably similar—his and George VI's—and this aesthetic was put upon me with full force. There was no other masculine aesthetic for me to embrace; I would not be allowed to embrace any other masculine aesthetic.

My father's education was standard for an upper-middle-class boy of his type at the time, but it seems quite strange now. He went, first of all, to a school called Repton, which was entirely an Anglophile school. I mean, Repton—you can tell the name is meant to sound like Eton. I think it was a rip-off, a clone, a for-profit thing of the kind that used to be advertised in the backs of magazines—you know, "Got a little boy you want to get rid of? Send him to Little Lord Fauntleroy's School for Little Lord Fauntleroys." And he went there for a time, and then he went to the Harvey School, which was a good little boys' school, the real *Tom Brown's Schooldays* of it, which was run by a cousin, and then he went to Exeter, and then he didn't go to college. At Exeter he devoted himself almost entirely to the *Exonian,* the school newspaper of the Phillips Exeter Academy, and then went right into journalism, establishing his two-step, as to what life was. On the one hand, he never went to a public school; he never mixed it up with ordinary Americans; he, in fact, didn't serve in World War II. He just never was in a situation where he was scrambling with other Americans. He spent his life at the *Exonian,* being a WASP boy who happened to want to spend his time not in serious studies but at the school newspaper. That was his aesthetic for his life, and, as far as he was concerned, it held together. There was no contradiction between being this kind of George VI WASP and being a journalist, even a tabloid journalist.

I, on the other hand, saw a contradiction immediately. For instance, I've said that my father presented his friends at the house called Windy Rock as my necessary beginning-and-ending template for the kind of values I must have, the kind of voice I must have, the kind of respect and this and that I must have, the kind of behavior I must exhibit, but it was impossible not to notice that it wasn't a newspaper-reading family at all, that journalism was viewed as something that was forgiven my father, not celebrated in him, and certainly no tabloid paper was ever brought into the house. So when we're talking about the time of this reading of the Mickey Jelke story—I was ten, eleven, twelve, and thirteen, say, just about to go to Exeter—I was in a little bit of a dilemma, because my father would bring home every night a paper that would have a headline like V-DOLLS IN LOVE NEST, or GEORGE DEAD, LIZ QUEEN, and yet, at the same time, I was not being allowed to do anything that was not in, let us call it, the Harvey School–Windy Rock mode. I just wondered—well, I'd already figured out that you couldn't fit the *New York Post* into Windy Rock—I just wondered where Windy Rock fit into the *New York Post,* and Mickey Jelke told me. And so, now, I haven't looked at these; I'll just open the thing—I think I'll do it very quickly. The story, in essence, is of a young prep school boy who gets arrested for being a pimp.

I THOUGHT I'D GET A BREAK. This is from the *Herald Tribune,* April 29, 1955. JELKE GETS TWO TO THREE YEARS, WEEPS IN CELL, WILL APPEAL. "Minot Frazier 'Mickey' Jelke was sentenced yesterday to two to three years in prison, as a procurer"—that's the *Herald Tribune* for you; it's doing it as formally as it can, though it's still reporting the story. "'I thought I was going to get a break,' he sobbed, in a detention cell, after Judge Francis L. Valente imposed punishment in general sessions"—well, we'll go right along, as we're just being associative about it here—and here you have the *New York Post,* doing this thing: "The charges of compulsory prostitution." Let's just keep going right here: "'Then she was in business,' he said, 'From that time on, she made from ten thousand to fifteen thousand over a period of three or four months. Business was good.'" And this had to do with— "Leiber said Pat was taken by Jelke's friend, Ray Russell Davoni, to Barbara Harmon, a call girl described by the prosecution"—well, now, I'm remembering the story. Pat will be a remarkable person called Pat Ward, who was somehow one of Jelke's girls—and Jelke went to the Taft School, as I remember— and the whole point of the story will be to decompose the old patriarchal structure of prep schools and so forth into a Cafe

Society structure, and then decompose that into prostitution, and that was the reportable story, as of the midfifties, as to the old patriarchy. "Demurely garbed Pat Ward arrived to resume her testimony. Pat portrayed the heir to a three million, seven hundred and fifty thousand dollar fortune"—Mickey Jelke was reported to be an oleo heir, and part of the appeal of the story was that, you know, you had oleomargarine in your refrigerator, and guess what, there was this one boy who was heir to every single last bit of oleomargarine money, and this was descended from the days of the trusts; the Vanderbilts owned the railroads, the Havermeyers owned the sugar—you must necessarily be fascinated by what the people who owned these things were like. The fact is that it was always a fake by 1955. I'm sure it will be revealed later that the three million dollars was in some sort of grandmother's trust fund, shared by thirty different people, and there had been four divorces in the meantime. Here's a caption: "Mickey Jelke meditatively puffs cigarette in court corridor." And some text: "Pat testified that she and Mickey began compiling the directories, a black one for him and a red one for her, in 1951."

And there you have the image of a very young prep school boy and a call girl, and this seems a good time to say that at Exeter, when I was there, the boy who ruled my class was named Richard Warren Pershing, and I mean he ruled it, and the first day I was at Exeter I decided that I would begin to smoke cigarettes, because I had to do something to be bad at that school, because I was five feet tall, and there just had to be something a little piratical about me or it just wasn't going to work, and so I decided that I would smoke cigarettes, and I went to the Webster butt room—Webster Hall was the bad boys' dormitory at Exeter in those days, and it was the dormitory to which I was assigned, and there were one hundred boys who entered the freshman class at Exeter, and I don't think I will ever have so clear a visceral sense of any other ninety-nine human avatars as I have of those ninety-nine other boys as they were then. We were cohorted together in a very strong way at that school, and, obviously, we were going to figure out some sort of pecking order—and I should say as I tell the story about Pershing that I never knew him well; I was just one of ninety-nine boys who worshipped him in a way, not slavishly but something more than "admired." This was a boy who had the money, had the status, had the dominance, had the answers, and he let us know that. People have remained fascinated by Pershing; people have written essays about him for graduate school, about, well, how did he do it, and why were we in his thrall, that kind of thing. Well, I can tell you why we were in his thrall; this story will point it out. So, a bunch of us thirteen-year-olds, or fourteen-year-olds, are standing around in the Webster butt room, and one, a rather self-satisfied young boy who's about to be an athlete, he stammers and says that it's going to be tough for him because his father was a famous football player at Exeter in the thirties or the forties or something, and everyone's meant to take this very seriously, at which point Pershing simply jumps up on the table, and says, "I'm Dick Pershing. Do not take my name in vain." Well, it was a little like John Lennon saying he was as famous as Jesus; you know—I mean, it was a very strange and interesting thing for someone to do. Pershing wasn't particularly tall or stocky; he just was dominant—he was alpha, and he didn't see any reason why people shouldn't know this at the get-go.

Now, I'm going to pause to give you my overall take on this whole scene. The old show, the old WASP show, was over. It was just plain over. It was about to be inherited by half-breeds, say, mutant forms, say, or was going to go away completely. Obviously, John Kennedy and Robert Kennedy were the number-one and number-two missiles shot out of this reconfigured WASP gun; their father had not raised them as Irish kids, exactly; he kept the Catholicism, all right, but every time you could go to a WASP school and get a WASP secret and make a WASP alliance, you did, and the Court of St. James was part of that, and so forth. Anything an old WASP had, my sons are gonna have too, was old Joe's p.o.v., and so JFK and RFK are the great avatars of what I'm trying to describe here. But Pershing was the *natural* of it. His grandfather was Black Jack Pershing, who's a very important person in American history; among other things, he mentored George Marshall, who was chief of staff during World War II and put our Military-Industrial Complex together, with *his* protegé, Dwight David Eisenhower, so we're not talking just about a general who did something, but someone who was on the main line of masculine dominance in this century. Dick Pershing was his grandson.

But, as important, his mother was the meanest, most dominant, most stylish Cafe Society woman of a certain type in a certain era. She was Muriel Bache Richards Pershing, and she was called Mo Mo, and this kind of woman has really dropped from the face of the earth, though a lot of young women seem to want to think they can be like this. But there was a certain kind of woman in the 1930s with a drop-dead manner and drop-dead money and a drop-dead point of view, who really did rule, and Dick's mother was like that. And he had a great-aunt named Kitty Miller, who was a daughter of Jules Bache, the financier, and of course, I'm saying that Dick Pershing was partly Jewish, which is really the point. The old WASP thing was one-hundred-percent WASP, but that had passed—and you were just not electable anymore, you were not anything. And Kitty Miller was someone I knew slightly, through Diana Vreeland, and I remember going to dinner once at Mrs. Miller's house, and Mrs. Miller was the almost secret ruler of the remnants of Edwardian New York. In other words, she didn't believe in a house without servants; when she had a house in London, it was a conventional house in London; it was old style, and I can remember one time when Mrs. Miller decided to make a fuss over me, and believe me, I'm not saying I was someone that she was determined to make a fuss over forever; it was just this one time, and it was terribly simple why she was doing it—she wanted to be mean to Diana Vreeland. She was basically saying, "Listen, why are you hanging out with this woman with no money? I've got the money, I've got the style." I mean, it was just for the time of the dinner party, but it was worth her while to do it for the time of that one dinner party, and after that party, I said to

Diana, "Well, Kitty was certainly attentive to me tonight, and I guess it was clear she was feeling a little competitive with you," or something, and Diana said, "I've known her for forty years. She has all the money in the world"—and Diana and Mrs. Miller lived in the same building on Park Avenue—"she has a car and driver available twenty-four hours a day. Do you think once in forty years she'd offer me the use of it? Never."

Well, I'm saying that there was such meanness in that whole world, whether it was the Cafe Society world of Mickey Jelke becoming a kind of a pimp, or whether it was Kitty Miller running her neo-Edwardian house, or whether it was Mrs. Pershing in a very exclusive setting of sort of Cafe Society–descended stuff on Long Island and on Park Avenue. There was such meanness in it, and there was such specificity, and the liberal arts of it had been decomposed to such a point that it was inevitable that it wouldn't work. What we will call the Kennedy experiment of WASP plus something, WASP plus Irish, WASP plus Jew, WASP plus anything finally wasn't gonna work. It was Starbright Park destined to explode.

Anyway, I realize now I don't want to talk about Mickey Jelke and his Cafe Society sex life at all; I want to tell you a story about Exeter and Dick Pershing, which will justify Mickey Jelke in a way. The Pershings lived in what used to be called a maisonette. Maybe it still is called a maisonette. Some of the biggest buildings on Park Avenue and on Fifth were built in such a way that there were a couple of townhouses stuck into the ground floor of them. In other words, you could live in the apartment house, have the service of the apartment house, and yet have a kind of private house too, and there was an entrance right out to Park Avenue—I think it was number 771, but it was somewhere in the seven hundreds on Park Avenue, and Dick had a best friend who committed suicide, a guy named Sam Bragdon, and he'd taken Bragdon down to New York on a weekend, and there used to be, in those days, a madam for prep school boys. Her name was Marge. Marge made it a point not to handle anyone but prep school boys, and Marge sent over a couple of girls to the

maisonette, and Pershing and Bragdon had 'em, and the story
made its way back to Exeter, and it wasn't about Pershing, the
story, it was about Bragdon; and I think Pershing himself spread
the story—he was a kind of magnanimous ruler, maybe it was
Bragdon's first girl—in any case, the whore came out and said,
"You're gonna make some girl very happy some day." Pershing
died in Vietnam.

The Three Caesuras

There have been three great breaks, or caesuras, in American cultural life in this century. The first is the break that took place after the First World War; between the life of *Ah, Wilderness* and Booth Tarkington, on the one hand, and the life of Texas Guinan and Walter Winchell, on the other, there is a great gulf. The gulf is the gulf of the First World War. This caesura remains, in a way, our treasure, for the simple reason that it was visible and acknowledged by almost everyone. You couldn't miss it. It had its effect from bottom to top and from top to bottom. Films documented it almost immediately. This makes it unique in this history of caesuras I'm talking about; that is, Joan Crawford's early film *Our Dancing Daughters* is about the process I'm describing. If you look at almost any silent movie, or any movie at all of the 1920s and into the 1930s, from *Our Dancing Daughters* to *Dinner at Eight*, let's say, the great Kaufman-Ferber-Selznick production, you'll find the record of the story of the caesura, the end of the Booth Tarkington–influenced world, the beginning of the Jazz Age, its effect up and down society, and when I say up and down and top to bottom, I'm reflecting on the fact that the caesura was documented and processed by important literary minds, and the minds that agreed to process this material were immediately accepted as the cultural leaders of the time. I'm thinking of Remarque, of *All Quiet on the Western Front*, to Hemingway—and of course one mentions Fitzgerald as well—back

200

to films here: one has the important social observation to make that socially, within the film community—that is, among studio heads, among creative people, among actors, certainly—the aesthetic established by the processors of the caesura, Remarque to Hemingway, let's say, and Fitzgerald, were established as cultural social leaders, so that although the films of the time reflected all kinds of concerns and met all kinds of entertainment needs, as always, still, the point of view of the overall social construct of Hollywood had been effected by the processors of the caesura. I'll add one other name to the list: Preston Sturges, in comedy, working very late, working into the forties, nonetheless belongs to the tradition of Selznick and Hemingway and Fitzgerald, let's say—people who kept track of American social history, and did not forget that there had been a great sea change after the First World War.

These processors won. That is, after their processing, their honest storytelling, their honest human reactions to the events of the twenties, we were never again to have any serious Booth Tarkington or even any serious Thomas Hardy energy again, at the top of American cultural concern. These processors simply did their job too well. They constantly told stories in terms of remnants of the past and the reactions of the present, and either in social stories or dramas or comedies, and they just got the Booth Tarkington of it put way back where it belonged. Life had moved on.

The second caesura I saw myself, and I'm thinking of myself in Cambridge, either in 1965 or 1966, picking up a copy of an underground newspaper called *Avatar*, and *Avatar* was a smart countercultural publication, smarter than the *East Village Other*, for instance; it was really art-based, and existential-wisdom-influenced and things like that, very radical, and the first issue of *Avatar*, as I remember it—it could have been another issue, but I think it was the first issue—had a centerfold, and the centerfold said, "Fuck, Shit, Piss, Cunt," something like that, just four big swear words, and I remember my shock at seeing it.

And this is something that it's impossible to recapture now, what Harvard was in 1964, say, as against what Harvard was in 1966, and one loss in our era has been any interest in stories told from the top down. Many stories in the 1920s were told from the top down. Hemingway falls into this category. His characters are all educated, and they always bump into a countess or a this or a that. Hemingway was, in a way, establishing a new top. He was saying, my experience in Paris with these people actually constitutes life at the cutting edge of culture now, but there was a drift over from the old system of pre–World War I. That tradition simply ended. The story out of Harvard in the sixties was an extremely meretricious work done for money, it can hardly have been done for any other reason, by Erich Segal called *Love Story*, which embraced ancient archetypes—you know, this working-class girl, and she falls in love with—well, you know the story. In the movie, Ray Milland played a kind of figure who had actually ceased to exist, at least in Ray Milland terms, by that time, and missing from the story were all the dynamics I saw at Harvard in the middle sixties, which have to do with drugs, Leary, Alpert, beginning of contact with Andy Warhol, and let's call it the *Avatar* phenomenon, the really powerful, psychotic reaction to the Eisenhower empire. It was going to go, it didn't matter what you did to get rid of it, it was going to go, and this is the caesura I'm talking about.

The sixties now are presented as mostly motivated by an urge to get Rosa Parks to the front of the bus, on the one hand, and to stop the Vietnam War, on the other. Missing from the story, primarily because the story's never been told from the top down, because that mode of storytelling had simply fallen into disrepute, was that death to the Eisenhower empire. This had been prefigured in *Howl* by Ginsberg: "America, fuck you and your atom bomb." That effort was now taken to the streets, and this caesura was, first of all, very remarkable in that the Eisenhower empire was the empire. It was the control system that produced our money, our dominance, our unique position in the world, and it was remarkable how little it took to kill it. And those two sides of the equation have never really been presented. This caesura was, and still is, largely unprocessed. Why the people who did it, did it, and what the results were—this is a story as yet to be told. I'm looking at a page of notes here, and over the word *avatar* I have written: "No mention in the *New York Times* of this 1960s energy."

Now, I haven't read every single copy of the *New York Times*, but I'll just bet on it. It was a pretty simple situation. The *New York Times* made a point of ignoring what we'll call the avatar energy, the "fuck, piss, cunt, shit" straight through to Kurt Cobain energy. It felt beneath their notice. They decided it could not possibly be true that their own children, for instance, had a homicidal aversion to Eisenhower America. They decided to ignore it, just as parents often now decide to ignore the nature of the video games their children play, or the drugs they're probably taking. They were in, let us say, denial, and denial suited them, because they were in an enormously powerful position, they had a world of their own, and each generation rather likes it when its hegemony is prolonged, and the fact is that the extreme nature of what I'm calling the *Avatar* psychotic energy—and I hope everyone understands that I think that psychoses are interesting things and contain much interesting truth always—there was nothing phony about this energy; it just was psychotic, and filled with hatred, and rage. It suited the hegemony, the *herencia*, the *New York Times*, let's say, to ignore it for these two reasons: first of all, it wasn't something they could process as information, and it suited them to pretend that it was negligible, because by pretending it was negligible they got to keep their positions for perhaps ten or fifteen more years than they would have in an ordinary situation. It's interesting now, when one runs into big organizations, that one often finds they're being run by thirty-five-year-olds. The men, and a few women, but the men of the *New York Times*, in 1966, or 1970, were not thirty-five; they were more likely to be forty-five and fifty, and they were going to get to be in a power position for another ten or fifteen years simply because the *New York Times* wasn't going to entitle the people coming up under them.

So it was in their interest to neglect the story, and neglect it they did. The cultural influence of what I'm calling the *Avatar* energy simply was largely unreported. The Velvet Underground was not put in the Arts and Leisure section—you can imagine the list I'm running down here. Even Dylan was, you know, treated a certain way and not another way. This important, psychotic, homicidal, and very effective energy—the real gestalt of it was just ignored. And another fact that's ignored, because the sixties phenomenon is always presented in a very egalitarian way, and as justification for our egalitarian mood of this moment—there were an awful lot of college boys and girls involved, the Columbia strike being the crucial event that no one has ever done such a thing as make a good film of, and that leads me to a list of American Cultural Artifacts that my reader might want to make use of, in positioning this negative space. Let's call it the unprocessed caesura of the 1960s. Since it was unprocessed, and since there are very few people alive on the face of the earth with whom one can even discuss these issues, what one is left with is a small group of people who had personal social experiences of all of the above, people who had some idea of what Eisenhower's America was like, and then saw the events of the sixties close up, or from further back, and then had some firsthand active ambitious life in the seventies. What one is left with at this point, in terms of social memory of this time, is just those people, people whom one happens to know socially. There is no material broadly accepted by the American public about this extraordinary revolution, and this, in itself, is a marker as to where we are culturally, in terms of denial. Well, here's a list of American Mainstream Cultural artifacts, which, if studied, will give you a sense of the negative space, the undescribed thing, let's call it, remembering that all the things I'm describing were enormously—with one exception, a book—enormously popular, or had recently been enormously popular, and not for intellectual reasons but for social reasons. These artifacts appealed to the significant demography, just as artifacts of today do, so I'm not giving you a list of obscure gospel references from the work of

Walter Benjamin or something; I'm directing your attention to places where, within popular stories, the overall view of the story I'm trying to indicate can be seen. I start with Joe Mankiewicz's film of 1950, *All About Eve.* Mankiewicz, like Selznick, say, and Mankiewicz's brother, Herman, who wrote the screenplay for *Citizen Kane,* belonged to the high end of the twenties, thirties, forties processing group. Like George Kaufman, like Edna Ferber, Joe Mankiewicz was a man who was at the top of the group that had processed the new America of the twenties, thirties, and forties. He was simply in a position to know, and all through this list, I'm dealing very often with people who were in a position to know, able both to make a popular cultural artifact and interested in keeping their artifacts in line somewhat with their own social knowledge, which, I must say, has always been my ambition. In many ways, I've taken my inspiration from exactly those people. One has always known that if you wanted to be in the American mainstream, you weren't going to tell your most extreme personal truth; you wanted to tell a story that was true for a large number of people, but you wanted that story to be in line with what you knew personally, which is a good definition of how a mainstream artist used to work.

All About Eve is a good marker in that it describes the shift from a Broadway and Hollywood studio reality to a television reality, and also a shift from a society of vanity, epitomized by Mankiewicz's heroine, Margo Channing, played by Bette Davis, to a society of narcissism, the Anne Baxter character, Eve Harrington. Marilyn Monroe was used as the television avatar, and she doesn't make it in the Broadway world, certainly, and George Sanders says that her next move ought to be in television, and Marilyn Monroe says, "Are there auditions in television?" She's just flunked an audition for a Broadway play, and George Sanders says, "Yes, there are auditions in television. In fact, that's all television is." All auditions. Well, so it was in 1950, and it's just a useful social marker, and I always want to refer to Diana Vreeland's famous remark, "I loathe narcissism; I approve of vanity." The shift from a society of vanity to a society of narcissism—not a small shift, vanity being one of those things, like sexuality itself, that humans are called upon to accept as part of their condition, and narcissism being something from another planet—you know, a situation in which you deny the existence of all other people—and Mankiewicz is indicating not just that there's a devolution in American character but that this devolution is henceforth going to be at the top of the American cultural hierarchy. I take Mankiewicz's film very seriously, more seriously than I take *Citizen Kane*, for instance, which is a theatrical fantasy.

The second artifact is *Rear Window,* by Hitchcock. It's his most theatrical film. It really is a stage set he's working from. Jimmy Stewart is on one side of a courtyard, and there were Broadway shows in the fifties that were lit like the back of the buildings that Stewart is looking at. It was quite common, really, into the sixties, to go to a Broadway theater and see something like that panoply of buildings. *Dead End* had such a set. It was a treat in the theater to see this kind of architecture lit that way, and Hitchcock knew how to do it, and did it, and the way he pans across the buildings is extremely theatrical, and the main point of the movie is that the photographer's camera is now a weapon. First of all, it's a weapon of intrusion; again, in terms of shifts, let's say that the shift from vanity to narcissism, as when Stewart moves from looking at his neighbor across the way with binoculars to looking with his telephoto lens, is quite a shift. One visual aspect of that: it's a move from looking with two eyes, with two lenses, to looking through one lens, which is enormously elongated, or like a phallus, like an erect phallus, it just changes the scale of intrusion, and at the end of the film this is put in other terms: the villain has actually killed someone, and Stewart is defending himself; nonetheless, he uses the flashbulbs of his camera to defeat his adversary, who, actually, is presented a little sympathetically. If one wants to look at it carefully, there's a sense in which this man, played by Raymond Burr, is a villain, a murderer, and yet a human being, and there's just a remarkable sense of Burr's vulnerability at the end of the movie. Somehow,

Jimmy Stewart, even in a cast, even on this side of the law, is presented as someone who is winning through very extraordinary means. The means are the explosion of lightbulbs, of intense flashbulbs, one after the other, in a man's face. That's echoed in what you see on the screen. You are, for a moment, and this never happened before in a movie, you're asked to identify with Raymond Burr. In other words, you're suddenly Burr, and Burr is seeing this blast of flashbulbs. He's blinded by it, and you, as a member of the audience, are blinded by it. It's a marker; Hitchcock is the most intuitive and prophetic of all our popular artists. He was absolutely right for the moment; every detail is on track, and in fact it's the only Hitchcock film that I regard as realistic. There's very little myth in it, and very little real film vocabulary. It's theatrical, and it's very accurate as to the social life of New York at that moment, and he goes so far as to introduce the name of Leland Hayward's wife, and so forth and so on. He's invented a theatrical juxtaposition in which the social realism of the context of the film makes the use of the camera equipment even more extraordinary.

The third artifact I've already referred to, and it's the *Elvis '56* film, so I won't go into it here, except to refer again to a frame in which Dwight Eisenhower is used as a kind of silly old ninny. He, too, has a camera; it's a little Kodak Instamatic, or, they weren't called Instamatics in those days, but you know, a cheap camera, and he's taking a picture of something, and the filmmakers immediately identify what he's taking a picture of as sort of a white-bread American family. Well, Ike never did anything like that; whatever he was snapping, it certainly wasn't an advertisement for Wonder Bread, which is what the sense of *Elvis '56* would give you, so at this moment I'm just introducing the idea of the triumph of rock-and-roll, so complete that it obliterated any real sense of the context to which it was juxtaposed.

So I'm trying to give you a sense here of the lack of processing that was going on in America about the climaxing social revolution that was taking place, and so, after *Elvis '56*, the next artifact to be aware of—I wouldn't recommend that anyone look at it—is *Love Story*, the 1970 or '71 movie in which all of the above is denied, and the point here is that this began to introduce the process, very different from real processing, of pretending that it all already had been processed, which is where we're at now. I call it hyper-denial. This is where you pretend that you have understood the past, walked through it, and are in established human modes, but even stronger and better than before. I can't help mentioning that last night I looked at the Garth Brooks concert in New York City, and I had to turn it off when he began to schmooze about his personal feelings in the song he sings called "The Dance," which is about the dance of human life and all its complexity and so forth and so on, and I thought, well, you haven't danced anywhere near Merle Haggard, and until you have, I don't want to hear that particular story from you. I mean, Merle Haggard is a very great American, and he's certainly danced and danced and danced, and we've never had a song from him about how he's reached some final reconciliation with life, because Haggard, having experienced so much, would be too modest and too repulsed by bunk ever to do such a thing. Yet Garth Brooks is here to tell us that he's done it all, and I have to note that Billy Joel was at his side, telling his audience that he'd done it all too, in terms of New York City—well, it's just not something I believe. I don't believe those two men have done it all, or even very much, but this process of pretending that you have processed it, you know, has always been with us, but it began to really escalate in the seventies, and precisely because the sixties revolution was so hard to witness and to understand, and *Love Story*, by my perception, is particularly meretricious, simply because Erich Segal knew better, he was at Harvard, his own friends were people who were living a very different way from this template story of Ali MacGraw and whoever it was. It was cynical of him to write this story, but he wrote it, it worked, it was a big hit, and introduced that lovely thing of love meaning never having to—whatever it is, the meretricious slogan of that moment. But it was a step into telling people that they still lived in a recognizable world, and that it all had been processed, when, in fact, it hadn't been.

Mentioning Ali MacGraw leads me to my next artifact, which is the only book on my list: *The Kid Stays in the Picture*, by Bob Evans. Here you have the example of a man who did, in fact, see it all, was there, did do it, was a big part of inventing the aesthetic of the seventies, yet apparently none of it touched him in any intelligent way. It's a fascinating book; Evans began as a radio actor on a show called *The Aldrich Family* or *Young Widder Brown*, even, which were artifacts for popular consumption that continued to evoke an old America that had actually vanished; one can see a cynical young actor going to a radio show in the late forties, being somebody in *Young Widder Brown* or someone on *Henry Aldrich*, and all the time knowing that that was a completely fucked reality, and that something else was going to matter to him, and Evans documents his drift through all of this; I mean, he even meets Alfred Lunt and Lynn Fontanne, and he does this, and he's a movie star for a while, and he certainly knows the studio, and he walks right through all this social history and none of it touches him anywhere, I expect because he's not a vain man but a narcissist, so none of it has ever had any social meaning for him. It's a fascinating book, and also a marker as to how far down the garden path we've gone all these decades. It includes the single most chilling paragraph I've ever read in any printed work, and I mean that because I'm an American; I mean, someone else would have a reaction to some other kind of thing, but he talks about the high point of his life being the premiere of *The Godfather*, a movie he produced at Paramount, and he's married to Ali MacGraw at the time, and he gets Henry Kissinger to fly up from Nixon's Washington to attend the premiere. And, one has to say, all this is in the tone of a narcissistic child—he's writing this book as a man of fifty-something, having been through a great deal of pain and a lot of triumph, and all the things that are supposed to form a person into a reflective being, and yet the tone of the passage I'm about to refer to is that of a ten-year-old radio actor who's just thrilled that he was part of an event that was so cataclysmic, from so many different points of view. He reflects that he persuaded Kissinger to come up even though he was very busy in Washington, and that after attending the premiere Kissinger went to a meeting in Washington in which he ordered the bombing of Haiphong.

Well, this is just not something that a sensitive man would write. Anyone in any reflective mood would juxtapose the vanity of a movie premiere and the horror of this event and come up with some notes on the character of Henry Kissinger; but simply to present it as a social triumph is something too ghastly. You really can't imagine, moving back in history, someone from the Broadway of 1917—I have no analysis for it—I'm trying to come up with some sense of some Broadway impresario taking pleasure in the fact that a secretary of state had come to his Broadway premiere and the next day had ordered a hundred thousand soldiers to the trenches. I mean, you can't—I'm having enormous difficulty using that metaphor, although in a certain way an exact metaphor, because it's so impossible as to human personality as it was during that period. The Broadway producer would be thinking more like *All Quiet on the Western Front*. He would be having some simple human reaction to what was going on. Evans apparently didn't and doesn't; it's a matter of image, and it's a matter of what goes on only in his head. The whole book, which is, indeed, an impressive march through entertainment history from the late forties, is shocking, and eye-opening as to how far we've gone down the path toward self-involvement and refusal to process experience. So, having laid that out as my overview of the situation, here are a few more artifacts.

A movie called *Drive, He Said,* a Jack Nicholson movie, an attempt to process the real social experiences of people who were in a position to know, and to experience the events of those days, an attempt to present the actual mind-set of someone who really was experiencing the horror of the psychosis of what society was going through. It failed as a movie—I mean, commercially—and my reference here is back to the enormous usefulness social history had for the writers and, to some extent, the filmmakers of the twenties and thirties, and to the fact that the real social experience of the 1960s proved to be nearly useless commercially, and hence wasn't explored. *Two-Lane Blacktop,* a movie by Rudy Wurlitzer and Monty Hellman, with James Taylor, is another example of an attempt, a strong attempt, to give a real feel to what was happening for some people. And, of course, *Five Easy Pieces,* dancing two or three steps away from the real hot energy, was a success. But actually, in general, the subtext of anger, epitomized by Nicholson's long rap in *Five Easy Pieces* with a waitress, finally proved to be useful to filmmakers, floating all the way through to *Pulp Fiction,* though the story itself, in any of its fullness, proved to be useless.

My next cultural artifact is a television program. It's *The Monkees. The Monkees* is a *Love Story* for the Beatles. The real story of the mind of John Lennon is something no one has bothered to try to deal with, not even his life as it was led, really, although there have been beginning attempts now; but *The Monkees* was a way of saying that it all had been processed, it all was easy. Essentially, it was *Love Story,* on the one hand, and amusing moppets on the other, our dancing sons of the sixties; as if our Rolling Stones and our Beatles are essentially just the Andrews Sisters another way, and, indeed, our wish for memory loss is so extreme now that when MTV did a documentary on the seventies last year, it asked people like Donny Osmond to remember the seventies—well, Donny has no memories of the seventies as such; he has memories of being in a process like the *Love Story* process, or *The Monkees* process.

Next on my list: *The Rose,* with Bette Midler, in theory the story of Janis Joplin. Once again, it's telling us that we understand. Well, in fact, there is no understanding in the movie as to who Janis Joplin really was, or is, and it is rather more a cooption of Janis Joplin's energy by Bette Midler, corresponding exactly to the vanity-narcissism problem. You get to think that Janis Joplin's energy in some way resembled Bette Midler's, which it in no way did. Not possible for one second for Bette Midler to approach the ferocity, and the wish for death, and the wish for total validity and authenticity, within the context of something like madness, that Janis Joplin possessed. It's told in terms of the familiar kind of too much too soon, or *I'll Cry Tomorrow*, it really is presented a little in the *I'll Cry Tomorrow* mode—*I'll Cry Tomorrow* is the story of Lillian Roth, who was an entertainer, similarly from a troubled background, who had a great success and trouble with liquor and so forth—it's presented in that template, and with no sense, for instance, of what Janis destroyed, an important part of Janis's story. Janis was someone who fought demons every single day of her life, and won a lot of the time, and in the process of winning, destroyed a lot. Not a simple entertainer by any means.

I'll go a little faster now, because I'm making arbitrary choices in a way, with no intention of giving a complete history of the era but to create this sense for you, my reader, of the negative space of what wasn't said, and hasn't been said. For my next artifact, we jump ahead to television, to *Dallas*. *Dallas* is a very interesting thing. I think it's unparalleled; I don't think there was anything like it before. I don't think that in American history, an unabashed interest, even worship, of rich people with no redeeming social value—I think *Dallas* was a first in that department, and I think it was made possible by the emerging cynicism within the demography, having to do with exactly the process I'm describing, the process of not having processed it, the process of beginning to understand you're living in a story that hadn't been told, that had been incorrectly presented, or not presented at all, that you'd been asked to watch *Love Story* when the real facts at Harvard were different, that you had been asked to watch *The Monkees* when the real facts about the Beatles were very different, and so forth and so on. So that there began to be, in the demography, a kind of deep cynicism about how people really acted, especially at the top, and this, then, became an available energy source to tap, and it was tapped in *Dallas*, and then, of course, in all the other ones.

Now, I understand that this sort of rich person's saga has always been with us, and I'm sure that someone doing a history of rich people's sagas in what I call the vertical way, moving right along from this to that and the other, will note that Edna Ferber wrote *Giant*, and *Giant* was made into a film of the 1950s, and I'm prepared to agree with that, and I just think that almost the two most useful things you can do in using this list, after looking at the *Elvis '56* story, which really is probably the most useful artifact, is just to juxtapose that Rock Hudson–Elizabeth Taylor–James Dean movie with any episode of *Dallas*. The *Giant* story, especially as presented in the fifties film, is our official attitude toward rich people. On the one hand, they were pioneers and were brave, and on the other hand they are neurotic. There's something wrong with the way they earn their money, they pay for it over time, and they pay for it by being suddenly uptight, or restrained, or in an artificial social atmosphere; they are, on the one hand, on top of the social order while, on the other hand, they are vulnerable to the social order, because they have stopped walking across the landscape they created, and there's a little truth in that basic way of looking at things, and Edna Ferber was a person who knew a lot about these things. By the 1950s it was presented in a kind of official, glossy version, with the James Dean character as the point of audience identification.

This is wildly different from *Dallas*; in *Dallas*, history has been removed. These people actually struggled across the plains in Conestoga wagons, and in a certain way proved their fitness to have an appropriate role in the history of Texas—but that's not really presented. In fact, it's indicated that that probably wasn't the case. The *Dallas* people just sort of appeared from Mars, with piles of money and ranch land and oil land and so forth; and, similarly, the real social background, which gave rise to the neurosis presented in the Edna Ferber story, has been eliminated. We have no way of reaching back into social history to these characters. But what's interesting is that the neurosis has been transformed into a psychosis. These people are psychotic. They, in a certain way, have no life. They are not just narcissists, they're homicidal narcissists, and even in the intimacy of their family they continue to behave as, indeed, Hollywood agents behave at the office, if not at home. And in a way, I think that's the appeal of it. It appealed to the American public's instinct; but in fact, this whole thing had been going down another way; you know, Eisenhower's America wasn't what Eisenhower said it was, there was a control group behind it, and the sixties wasn't anything like *The Monkees*, there was some other way, and someone's always been behind it, and so on, and not only that—and this is my major point—there was a caesura out there, there was a great psychotic event that went undescribed, and I think it was a relief to the American public to see psychosis celebrated and brought together with the morals of the worse sort of Hollywood agent, and presented week after week. I think it seemed socially real, and I don't say that the series is negligible at all. Any time someone accurately describes social reality it's impressive, and *Dallas* was, in certain ways, impressive, as well as extremely depressing.

Now I think I'll just jump to the present. So now three artifacts from the moment of this moment. First of all, *My Best Friend's Wedding*. As I've said, I liked it very much, and in some ways it's the most socially retrograde artifact I've ever seen. The biggest lie in the movie—and it's a movie filled with lies—is that we still have what we used to have. Here we are in Eisenhower's America again, the young man in the film is a kind of deutero-Hemingway guy who's, you know, being a poor sportswriter instead of doing something else, and the girl belongs to one of the richest families in America, but they happen to be terribly nice people, they're billionaires, everything is just as lush as it ever was, and none of that is true. And the other side of it has to do with a moment at the end, where the billionaire's daughter confronts Julia Roberts in a women's room filled with poor people; it takes place at a baseball park, and all the poor people applaud the rich girl for standing up for herself, and this is another one of those moments that tell us, we've done our work, you know? We are all one, we went through the sixties, did what we needed to do, went through the seventies, and so on and so forth, and it's just a lie. We didn't, and we aren't in that position, and it's just a lie. And you can say, well, entertainment always deals in fiction, but the moment when a certain kind of fiction becomes useful is what I'm trying to direct your attention to here. That movie was not available to be made in 1975, or in 1965. It's available to be made now precisely because it is a lie, and it happens to be a lie we need to like.

The second artifact is *Conair*, which is about a 1970s psychosis at large in the world today, and it presents our ambivalent attitude to that world. It's a biker bar taken into movie hyperspace. Just as movies take a fist fight and make it into rocket launchers exploding in your face, so has *Conair* taken a pretty accurate view of a biker bar of today, and rocketed into hyperspace. Our ambivalent attitude toward our own social subtext is visible here. This is, to some extent, who we are, the kind of people we are, and we're fascinated by that, but it really is pretty horrifying too, and introduced into this context, as a way of making some sort of contact with the *My Best Friend's Wedding* world, is an old American hero, a kind of down-by-the-bayou veteran—actually, it's someone who's in jail for the wrong reason, something lifted from a 1940s prison film.

And the third is *Pulp Fiction*. Quentin Tarantino is someone who has caught a whiff of it. He wasn't there in the sixties and the seventies, but he knows pretty much what went down, and he knows that people's reactions to it are fucked, and he knows that psychosis was and is involved, and he feels himself to be the legitimate heir of that, and to some extent, I believe he is. I believe that he feels in his mind pretty much what sixties and seventies people sometimes felt in their minds. He just happens to belong to another generation, and he has every right to tell the story. The point I'm going to make here is that there's one part of the movie—and this will lead us to caesura number three—that doesn't work, and it's the World War II reference. Christopher Walken comes—it's a dream sequence that Bruce Willis is dreaming, and I won't describe the scene, because it's really quite repulsive—I don't mean the scatology of it, but the point of view. It's not from the film. It's from something else. It's something Quentin Tarantino doesn't know about, he didn't know how to deal with it, and he dealt with it in a very simple way. He used a literary template; the literary template is mostly from *Catch-22*, say, some sort of absurdist treatment of World War II, earned on the part of Joseph Heller, unearned on the part of Quentin Tarantino, and he's done a very typical sort of directorial thing. He's not real familiar with the material, he doesn't have any instinct for the material, but he finds a very good actor, Mr. Walken, to carry it off for him, and, to some extent, Walken does. But it's wrong. It stands outside the values of the film, precisely because it's been brought inside the values of the film. And that leads me, then, to caesura number three, which is World War II.

I'm going to describe, again, my own feeling in my early childhood, which was 1946, '47, '48; exactly, but exactly, postwar. Walter Savage Landor, an important nineteenth-century man, said that after the storm is the time to find little pieces of sincerity. Landor was cynical about human nature overall; I think I am too. What he said was a little like what Schopenhauer said: "Finally, I think you must be pessimistic about human nature and human life." I'm all with Mr. Landor and Mr. Schopenhauer; nonetheless, I opt for Mr. Landor, to the extent of agreeing that after a storm there are, indeed, pieces of sincerity, and they give you hope, and a sense of wonder, and I think I've said elsewhere that my feeling, in my earliest life, was that something enormous had just happened—there'd been a story—and the air was clear, as it was after a storm, but everyone was silent. I thought at the time that there was a kind of dignity in the silence, and I think there was, but I think really what there was, also, was shame. I think people did have some dignity, but I think they had an enormous amount of shame. I can't describe this, because I didn't experience it directly. I've experienced it over my life through various members of the older generation, for whom a dance between dignity and shame seemed to be definitive. Nonetheless, after World War II there was something in the air. The air had cleared; it seemed to have cleared for a purpose, but the world was strangely silent about what that purpose could possibly be.

So, I'll just end with a reference to a cultural artifact I caught a glimpse of; I'm embarrassed to say I don't know the filmmaker's name; it was something I caught while surfing television in Canada. I didn't pay enough attention to it at the time; it was one of those things you pass by, look at for a while, and then wish you'd seen more of. It was a documentary; the central figure, the speaker in the documentary, was a man named Berliner, and he'd served in World War II, and he was being interviewed by a male relative of the next generation, perhaps a nephew, about his family's experience. His family was from Poland, Jewish, and his father—Mr. Berliner, the World War II veteran's father—had come very early in his life from Poland, sent from an interesting but impoverished context to this country, with the idea that he should make a lot of money, or so one gathered from the documentary—I won't go on about it, except to say it's extraordinarily interesting to me, and the best documentary about World War II I've ever seen. Mr. Berliner, the veteran, was someone for whom I had an instinctive liking; he just kept on, with an air of command, a little like Jesse Helms in another way, he kept on saying, "No, that doesn't interest me," "No, I don't want to hear about that," "No, of course I don't know who they were," and the member of the next generation—and I sympathize with this man too, because I've spent a lot of my life struggling very hard to make real connections to my past, with the World War II generation— he was saying, "But don't you find it interesting, this letter that your grandfather wrote to your father?" And then he read a letter that was, indeed, very moving, and intelligent, and full of feeling, and the World War II veteran kept saying, "I don't know anything about that. Who cares about that?" And I won't go on, because I think I've made my point. The World War II generation really did something. It's never been described. A sense of being arose, especially for the eleven million men who served—and some women too, of course—and a sense of appropriate modesty, so different from either vanity or narcissism. At one point, the member of the younger generation says to Mr. Berliner, the veteran, something about throwing World War II into the conversation with respect, and Mr. Berliner says, "Well, there were eleven million men there; what do you wanna hear *my* story for?" And that, of course, was the other point—the enormous silence. The fact that every other subject was lesser, of lesser intensity, and in a certain way, contemptible, from the point of view of men who'd served intensely in that conflict; on the other hand, if you tried to get at their experience of that conflict, well, then, they'd say, "There were eleven million men—what are you asking *me* for? It was just something we did." And that's been a big social dynamic of our time, leading right on down to *Pulp Fiction*. The exalted experience of World War II, with its attendant silence, was, and still is, a problem for this civilization—and I feel sympathy for Mr. Tarantino; none of us really know how to present it, in our civilian context, not even at this distance. We have, of course, the war stories of the time, but the war stories of the time are for that moment, and a certain amount of propaganda adheres to them, and when the generation passed that had a taste for those stories, we began to get less and less, and finally nothing, and so, again, sympathy for Mr. Tarantino; you come to that part of your story, and you just don't know what to say.

The Future of Tabloid

The future of tabloid—by which I mean not only tabloid journalism, but also the tabloid mind, the sensational mind that
both loathes and loves authority—the future of tabloid has risen
to the surface this month, because of the death of Princess Diana.
It's impossible to ignore that event. Given my very, very long-
range experience, exposure, study, whatever you want to call it,
of the tabloid sensibility, I have to put it together in my mind with
a section of this book I wrote almost a year ago about the film
Roman Holiday, a film that took for its inspiration the vogue for
the young Princess Elizabeth, now the queen, who's not at all in
vogue at this moment, and I think it's worthwhile for anyone
who's immersed himself, or herself, in the coverage of the funeral
and death of Princess Diana, and the attendant discussions about
the role of the media and the tabloid or something, to go and have
a look at *Roman Holiday* and see how ironic, but how fitting also,
the plot is—how Gregory Peck, in a moment of decency and
manly valor, presents the princess with the pictures he took, and
so forth, and declines to publish the story. Well, that just gives
you a little bit of the arc of the social change from the early 1950s
to September of 1997. But of course *Roman Holiday* was a film,
and the death of the Princess of Wales is a real event.

Nonetheless, there are things to notice about it. It's cruel to a
person to discuss her death in terms of an information-delivery

template, but nonetheless it's an issue before us, and it's one I've laid out in this book already, so let's do it. Well, there's one remarkably underreported aspect of this story, and again, the reader will forgive me if my very long-range mind goes back to an old children's book called *Little Lord Fauntleroy*. Now, *Little Lord Fauntleroy* involves some of the issues involved in the current drama within the House of Windsor—roughly speaking, the difference between spontaneous feeling and hidebound old ways that refuse to change. And the irony I'm noting—the result of my too-great exposure to Anglophile culture (not entirely my fault, by the way)—is that the old curmudgeon in the Lord Fauntleroy story is a Belted Earl. Earls were often called Belted Earls in those days. I don't know quite what it means; I don't think there's such a thing as an Unbelted Earl, but I think what it means is, when you get to earl, you really are in a different category from viscount, baron, etc., you really are somewhere, and earls go back to—you know, it's an ancient English title and so forth. Well, Princess Diana's father was a Belted Earl, and it's really not much mentioned in the coverage. There are a couple of ironies here. One is that the princess's story is by no means a Cinderella story, and it's by no means a contemporary story, in any real way. She was a daughter of the aristocracy who married the heir to the throne. It wouldn't usually be so terribly dramatic, except for one reason. Between Little Lord Fauntleroy and Lord Litchfield, who I think was also an earl, but maybe a viscount, but he was the fashion photographer who jumped into the mod world of the sixties and seventies—in that time the aristocracy really lost its power to impress and inhibit, and so you really can't get much mileage out of it. I mean, if Lord Litchfield's young child were to become a punk-rocker, I think people would say, "So what?" I think that's actually what they would say; you might get a little publicity out of it, but not much.

The point I'm trying to make is that the tabloid sensibility absolutely requires this back-and-forth of loathe and love of old authority. Well, here's one prop that the tabloid sensibility is not going to have much longer. What I mean is, in 1910, you could get quite a lot of mileage out of a story about a little American boy and an earl, but today you can't get that kind of mileage out of any story except a story about the actual royal family, and I mean those particular people who live in Buckingham Palace. I don't think you can get that kind of mileage, for the American public, out of the Saudi royal family, or the Sultan of Brunei, who certainly lives a very Cafe Society life—that particular thread of the original tabloid template will have frayed now, and now you see where I'm heading. I'm saying that we may have seen the absolute heyday of the tabloid sensibility. We may now begin to see—because every system carries within it the something-or-others of its own demise—we may begin to see certain internal contradictions within the tabloid sensibility begin to bring about a criticism of, and also a weakening of the power of, the tabloid sensibility. It may turn out, again, to be a sensibility not for all of us but for those of us who are least willing to take a look at anything like the real story, and this has to do with the likely crumbling of our seventies subtext in American life, visible also in *Conair,* into which was introduced a traditional American hero—you can't just have a seventies-subtext, biker-bar sensibility put flat on the screen anymore; there's been too much pain associated with it, there's too much criminality, too much drug use, so there has to be something to countervail it. And it was our seventies subtext that was so marvelously vulnerable to a resurgence of a tabloid sensibility. So with the seventies subtext crumbling, on the one hand, and the simple, pure absence of the old-fashioned-spontaneity-versus-old-authority dynamic, on the other, then you have two props taken away from our twenty-year climax of tabloidism, which is what we've had.

I want to mention here a film I'd thought of putting on my list of Important Artifacts, but it really belongs here: *Dog Day Afternoon,* a Sidney Lumet film with Al Pacino. This is kind of an ur-tabloid production, and it was my viewing of this film that helped me decide in the late 1970s, when I wrote *Within the Context of*

No Context, that, indeed, this thing would happen. In other words, a seventies subtext would deteriorate the social structure to a certain point, which would encourage cultural productions of a certain kind that got energy from glamorizing a certain kind of cultural deterioration. That is one part of what I meant by "within the context of no context." In other words, one saw that stories that were categorically unhappy stories, and about failure, in a way, and about a completely missed opportunity, and a bad take on life, and so forth, could be given a kind of antihero spin, and be useful to Hollywood; that had begun by the time of *Dog Day Afternoon,* and there are lots of other films that have drawn on that over the decades, but *Dog Day Afternoon* was a kind of perfect tabloid story of that moment, one that could be raised to the level of *zeitgeist production* and begin the spin of you-too-are-like-this-man; you too, perhaps, have a transsexual friend, or you don't fit into society yourself; you may, for all that, feel that you can rob a bank and still be a good person, or something.

That dynamic cracked, I think, during the course of the O. J. Simpson case. It cracked, for me, over the issue of Kato Kaelin. Kato Kaelin is a kind of *Dog Day Afternoon* guy, in my opinion. In other words, he's one of our new Huckleberry Finns, because, you know, Twain kind of gave us our national character in that book, and we all are, or love to think of ourselves as, Huckleberry Finn. But when I looked at Kato Kaelin in the middle of that O. J. Simpson story, I thought maybe it's over in a way for Huck. Bad guys—good-bad guys of the Huckleberry Finn sort—are really supposed to know the ropes and take you somewhere interesting. Well, Kato Kaelin was not going to do that for anyone; he was going to be a houseguest. Now, an awful lot of the tabloid sensibility has to do with a huge market for the new Huck Finns, so that a problem in Huck Finn appeal can be a problem for the tabloids—if Donald Trump goes broke, for instance, or if Kato Kaelin is just a sponge. To this, the princess's death adds. There's been too much carnage, and it simply will begin to be difficult to market the carnage as glamorous, and carnage has been marketed as glamorous since *Dog Day Afternoon,* to use my very simple marker for that. Al Pacino in *Dog Day Afternoon* was a Huck Finn mutant and was accepted as an appropriate New American on our new Mississippi. In *Conair* we see a cast of mutant Huck Finns gone mad on a toxic Mississippi, and the straight guy stands out in the crowd.

Let Reagan Be Reagan *versus* I Like Ike

This chapter is called "I Like Ike," as opposed to, and versus, "Let Reagan Be Reagan." Who on earth was Ronald Reagan? The key is in the reaction of other Republicans to Mr. Reagan. They didn't know who he was. But they knew that when Reagan was allowed to be Reagan, something happened. What was that something? A kind of forgiveness, a kind of exit from every single difficult issue I've raised in this book. When Reagan was Reagan, you didn't have to think about it.

Insight into the Mystery of Ronald Reagan

"OH, DEM GOLDEN SLIPPERS" Well, it's an old, corny song, "Oh, Dem Golden Slippers," and that seemed to be one part of Ronald Reagan. There are a lot of seem-to-be's about him. He seemed to be an old Irish kind of guy, he seemed to be a musical-comedy kind of character, and he seemed to be a movie star, but when you came down to it, you didn't remember him as a movie star, and you never saw him at the Blarney Stone, but he had the seems-to-be of it all right. He sang a song in notes way above the scale we could hear, but it came across as "Oh, Dem Golden Slippers." I'm going to suggest a Grimm's Fairy Tale here, to explain the unexplainable. It really does seem possible to me now, listening to the way people talk about a global economy, and also the new role of the American military as something that's never going to have to wage a war, that we've entered a period of serious self-reverential madness, i.e., a kind of nonhuman state. Well, that's impossible; how could it possibly be? There are six billion people on the planet. God, in his infinite wisdom, reminds us of our humanity every day. The military is something other than an organization designed to do battle? Well, how absurd. Ten minutes in a Bengali village, seeing the conflicts there, will tell you that human conflict bubbles, bubbles, bubbles everywhere, all the time, and death is still a factor in human life, and so are the pangs of childbirth and all the other things that remind us that we are one with nature, with the animal kingdom. So how could it be that our country, intensively, and the planet as a whole, at least superficially, are in this period of self-reverential madness, where, it would seem, even a Bengali villager, up close and personal, against conflict, the pangs of birth, and the evidence of death, puts aside common sense in hopes of getting ahold of a Seiko watch, or a watch that would seem to be a Seiko watch? Well, of course, a lot of it has to do with mechanization, and with promise.

Now, that's just my little prologue. Let's see if I can invent a fairy tale of people who enter into a period of something like unexampled prosperity, where, for a time, more people have access to nonstarvation than ever before, and this despite their proliferation, and despite the fact that a very significant group of people enters into real prosperity, and another group, more impressively large than ever before in human history, enters into a period of hyperprosperity, and all this absent any organizing aesthetic that could offend anyone. And here I'm suggesting access into the mystery of Ronald Reagan, because when you got to him, the fount of this aesthetic, there was nothing to offend you. If you didn't happen to like an old-fashioned Irishman, well, he wasn't really that, and if you didn't happen to like a movie star, well, he wasn't really that either; he really had no power to offend. This in counterdistinction to Dwight Eisenhower, whom you liked, and that's a big difference between our real 1950s and our self-reverential 1950s of the moment. You loved Ike, you liked him. When you got to Ronald Reagan, you weren't offended, and that, by my perception, is indication of a serious step down in the evolution, or devolution, of human personality. Sorry to have exited my fairy tale for that insight, but there you are. So, in this atmosphere of fewer people starving on a planet where there are many, many more people than there have ever been before, and a new hierarchy, in hyperspace, let's say, of mythical, prosperous people, and within that group of mythical prosperous people, a significant group of people who are really very, very, very prosperous, and all this within an atmosphere of nonoffense. Well, you begin to get something like the aesthetic of this moment, but how do you project this aesthetic? Every aesthetic must be projected if it is to be successful, with utter confidence, based on a real human life of triumph. You can't just suggest a worldview as possibly possible. People have to see that worldview embodied, and often, and they have to see their fellow citizens, especially the fellow citizens they envy, as being in a mode of acceptance. So, now to my fairy tale. We're now on Planet X, in the kind of aesthetic I've laid out as the one ruling this planet at this moment, and there's a small tribe of people on Planet X who fall in love with a pair of golden slippers. It's real love. It's what they really like. They like it better than sex, they like it better than anything. They like to be near and around those golden slippers. And these people are on television.

My Experience Behind Palace Walls

I'm writing this in the old American town of Worcester, Massachusetts, a town that is partly new and shiny and partly not new and not shiny, and yesterday on the street I saw a man wearing a T-shirt, and it said, "Royal Majesty," in big letters, and then under it, "Cruises," and then there was some additional information about the happiness attending someone who had taken, or was going to take, a Royal Majesty Cruise. The man was, by my perception, homeless, or nearly so, at least he was pushing a grocery cart full of his personal belongings; he wasn't, in any case, a fully functioning citizen, by my perception, and I thought, well, how interesting. The man was African-American, he might have had a T-shirt that said, "Give a Damn," or one of the civil-rights slogans from another day, or he might have had a T-shirt that said, "Give a Man a Job," or "Give a Man a Break," or just a T-shirt that said nothing at all, but he didn't; he had a Royal Majesty Cruise T-shirt. It was a sweatshirt, actually; I'll correct myself. And I thought, well, what is this new vogue—and it is a new vogue—for the royals? I remember when Prince Charles and Princess Anne visited the Nixon White House, and members of my generation thought it was less interesting than the new Crosby, Stills, Nash, and Young album by about a hundred billion miles. I mean, they couldn't get arrested. So, what is this new fascination with the royals? If we wanted 'em, we coulda had 'em. We didn't want 'em; they went away a long time ago. In my mind, it's a little like a vote for the Merovingians. I mean, any time you say you want something, and you say you're interested in something, it's kind of nice if the thing involved is actually around, so you can interact with it, see if you want it, test it out, and see if it's of use to you, and so forth. This stuff is, to my mind, very strange and insubstantial, and somehow in mysterious relationship both to Ronald Reagan and to the global economy, but I'll leave that to someone else.

I'm here to tell you about my experience behind palace walls, and it was brought to my mind by a Mainstream American Cultural Artifact, and I'm particularly motivated to tell you this story by my extreme resistance to someone named Stone Phillips, who is one of the anchorpersons on *Dateline NBC*, the one that comes to you with thundering announcement from Rockefeller Center, as though it were really located right at the very heart of things, and so forth and so on. That's going to be part of our aesthetic now. Anyway, Stone was the host this week of a journalistic artifact about the Sultan of Brunei, the world's richest man, and, indeed, the phrase "behind palace walls" appeared a couple of times—this is a phrase that has crept into journalism over the last years, especially in relation to the story of the Princess of Wales, and her death—and now, by my perception, the crapola-ridden journalists who understand they're not going to have the princess to show them in, around, beyond, or through palace walls and are going to have to be a little circumspect about her sons, the young princes, for a while, at least, are looking for new palace walls to get in, under, behind, and through, and have fixed on the Sultan of Brunei.

The story reported was pretty simple; it included one remarkable tangential interview, which I'll discuss here. Seems there's a man in Los Angeles, he's forty-five, he's an ordinary American who's taken his chance and done well; his job is to book American girls who have some kind of title, they're Miss Kawasaki Motorcycle, they're Miss Maytime, they're Miss Front Door, they're Miss Back Door, they're Miss Anybody; preferably they're royal, Miss Royal Front Door, Miss Royal Back Door, because the titles matter, but if they have some kind of title, they're bookable to Asia. Well, this man is doing show business work on the very dimmest fringes of show business; one step down is pimping, and these girls are, you know, dealing with someone who is booking girls—not on the basis of any talent, certainly, and the clients are apparently Asian for the most part. He's booked, he reported—and it was the one interesting fact in this broadcast—many thousands of these visits by titled American girls to Asia, and that's the background of the story. The front of the story is that the Sultan of Brunei has flown over, for his own pleasure and that of his brother Jeffrey, the really titled ones, including a former Miss USA, who arrived horrified to discover that she wasn't going to have dinner with Henry Kissinger every night but was going to be asked to dance, or be in a harem situation. There were upfront discussions by more realistic young women, who said, yes, they understood what was going on, and yes, it was a harem situation, and indeed, some of the young women were selected to sleep with the richest man in the world and his brother, and some of the young women who were thus selected were very pleased by the favor shown them, and so forth and so on. They showed pictures of the palace, the one with the palace walls; it looked very much like the Kennedy Center gone a little awry; you know, really corny 1960s modern architecture, full of gilt and chandeliers, and so forth, exactly what one doesn't want in a hotel.

Now, before I tell you my experience behind palace walls, let me clarify: yes, it was an experience with the Sultan of Brunei—the father, as I believe it, of the current sultan and his brother, and my memory is that the current sultan overthrew his father in some way, but that wasn't mentioned on Stone Phillips's broadcast, but I'm almost certain that that is the case, that the father was, perhaps, impeding progress or something, or not encouraging this sixteen-hundred-room palace, with its Kennedy Center walls, to be built, I forget the specifics of it.

So now my story. In *Within the Context of No Context* I've given a rather extended account of the one job I ever had that wasn't at *The New Yorker*. As I've mentioned before, it was as a protocol guide at the New York World's Fair, in 1964 and '65, and I mentioned some of the people I met at that time, and some of the people who came through our office were exotic, and I mentioned in that story Mar Shamoon, the Patriarch of the East, who was the spiritual leader of x number of Asian Christians. As a courtesy, we handled their visits. There they were, the exotically titled people. Mar Shamoon was called "His Holiness"; you couldn't just let him go out on the site, you know? You had to give him some level of protection, even though no one in America really knew who he was. Well, the Sultan of Brunei, at that time, fell into that category. Here he was, he was a sultan; we didn't know exactly who he was, but it seemed that he had reason to expect a certain courtesy, and we gave it to him. He wasn't viewed as anyone very important or I wouldn't have been assigned to him, alone, as I was. I was just a guide, and if he'd been very important, one of my bosses would have gone out with him. As it was, there he was, he was the sultan, and I think I had a little bit of a reputation as kind of a sultan's guy, you know? I liked that kind of thing, and I knew how to behave, and so, give it to George, and so it was given to me.

It was a two-day visit, and the sultan arrived. He was not a tall man; he was an extremely cheerful and friendly man. It was obvious to me immediately that this was fun for him. Ordinarily, he didn't get to do stuff like this; here was a display of America all in one place, he was going to be treated well; this was time off for the sultan. He came with a British equerry, a nice young British lieutenant of some kind, who was obviously on permanent assignment to him in some way, and it was quite obvious that the sultan liked the equerry, and the equerry liked the sultan, and frankly, they both liked me, and I liked them, and so the three of us spent two days together. By that time, I really knew how to show anyone at any level the fair, and I just did what I did. We went to the best pavilions, and the sultan was polite—that's what I want to say. He saw, he liked, he said, and then, halfway through the second day, he whispered something to the equerry, and the equerry took me aside, and what the equerry said, in essence, was, "The sultan wonders, could we, is there"—and the meaning was, is there anything more? Is there any real thing here? Well, this was a problem of the 1964 World's Fair. I had an intuition, and I acted on it, and I took the sultan to an exhibit we hadn't yet visited. It was the Belgian Village. The Belgian Village wasn't an official pavilion in the sense of having been endorsed by Belgium; it was a speculation by some people who wanted to make money by creating a little version of a neighborhood in Brabant or something, and in the Belgian Village you wandered over cobblestone streets and into little shops, and you could have Belgian waffles, a delicacy not generally known around North America then. If we were taking around the vice president of General Motors or someone high up in the Spanish government or something, it would not have occurred to us for one moment to take them anywhere near the Belgian Village. We were a tiny bit ashamed of it, but I thought maybe the sultan would like it, and he did. This corresponded to what he wanted. It was—let's call it easy Belgium, you know? It was Belgium all in one spot, it was there for his fun, and he would go in and out of little shops, and buy things, and have fun, and eat Belgian waffles. And we did that.

I remember quite clearly that I was astonished just how many of those tiny shops the sultan wanted to have a look into. It was miniature. It was a fantasy. It was, of course, Disneyland, in a way, but this only took forty-five minutes. I mean, the Belgian Village wasn't something you could stay in forever, and by moment twenty, I thought to myself, oh, my God, why don't we just take him to the entertainment zone? We had one. It was over a bridge. We kept it out of the official fair, it was something called the Entertainment Area. I don't remember much about it, except that there was, I think, the Florida Citrus Tower, and some other things. I don't remember much about it, because when I suggested it the sultan immediately said yes, and when we got there the first thing we saw was a dodgem car arena, and the sultan just took to it like a duck to water. We didn't have a chance to do any of the other interesting displays available within the entertainment zone; this was what the sultan had come to America for; someone had delivered the goods, and we stayed, and we stayed, and we stayed. The equerry in one dodgem car, me in another dodgem car, and the sultan in his. He'd never been in a dodgem car. He didn't know there was such a thing as a dodgem car, and he loved it, and the equerry and I both tried to keep him a little bit reined in, but he liked very much the fact that you were authorized to slam your car into other people's cars, and he did it. After a time, I understood that it would be rude not to slam him every once in a while, so I did. Gently, of course—he was still the sultan—but every once in a while, I would take my dodgem car and slam it into the sultan's dodgem car. So it was a happy day, and I'd done my job, and as we began to exit the fair, the equerry came over to me and said, "His Highness"—I think he was called His Highness—"very much wants you to come back to New York with us."

Well, I said yes; we went back to New York, and I thought, well, how interesting, I wonder what's going to happen now. It does amuse me now to compare this to those poor girls being shipped abroad and so forth; I didn't have any contract or any concerns; I was with a gentleman who had asked me to come back with him to New York for some reason that I knew would be attractive and appropriate. And we went to the Waldorf Towers, which is where he was staying, and nothing remarkable happened; I don't have a big climax to the story, except in the sequence of events, and in the nature of his personality, and, frankly, of mine. We got to the Waldorf; we went up to his suite, and when we entered his suite, his manner changed. This was, for the time being, his palace. The Waldorf Astoria had provided palace walls for a person who was, in fact, royalty, of the right kind; where he is, is his palace, and when he entered his suite at the Waldorf Towers his manner changed. He was no longer a person in dodgem cars; he was the sultan, and there was, in fact, a big drawing room in typical Waldorf style—you know, good furniture, but nothing you could auction off at Sotheby's—and then he left the room, leaving me to sit in the drawing room. Again, he was now a royal person, and I was someone to whom something was about to happen, within his context, and I was allowed to cool my heels for a while. In fact, it had a practical aspect; he changed his clothes, or at least his jacket, or something, and when he came back, he was a different person. He sat on a Waldorf Astoria sofa at the end of the room; there was a table in front of him, the equerry put a little box in front of him, the equerry gave me a sign that it was time for me to come into the royal presence, and the sultan gave me the box. Really, that's it. The box was a silver cigarette case that was silverish rather than silver, and not studded in gems, and it had a little something on it—I rather think that there is, or was, a kind of a very low-level order of distinguished, happy-to-have-you-in-Brunei kind of thing, with the seal of Brunei on it—and that's what I got. I think I still have it somewhere. The point is only that he was trying, and successfully, to give me something back, of which the box was merely a token. I had shown him what America could be like when it was fun, and he wanted to show me what it was like to be in a friendly relationship to a royal person.

Ronald Reagan;
or, A New Dawn for America;
or, I Still Like Ike

The Mainstream American Popular Artifact we're dealing with today, end of September 1997, is something on last night's evening news that really caused me to laugh and cry and get angry. Photographers—beneficiaries of the worldwide First Amendment, freedom-of-the-press egalitarianism, which is something that ought to be handled carefully and with great respect—downed their tools. They refused to take pictures of the president of France—or was it the mayor of Paris? In any case, someone important in Paris—because of the investigation, a quite right and proper investigation based on established laws, around an automobile accident, of those paparazzi who pursued the car in which Princess Diana was fatally hurt. Photographers were appalled. How could this happen to them, being subjected to an investigation? And with particular horror it was noted that press passes of two of the photographers were being withheld during this time, and they couldn't work, and so they weren't going to take pictures of the president of France. Well, of course, it's interesting where and when a person decides to down tools. The photographers weren't refusing to take pictures of Elton John—that wouldn't be practical for them—but they know perfectly well that pictures of the president of France, or the mayor of Paris, or whoever it was—it was outside the Lycée Palace, so it must have been the president or the premier, you know, these photographs don't ignite the popular imagination, so it's a little like denying themselves nothing in making their defiant protest. It's their power card. They feel that politicians need to be in the newspapers, and here they are, they're downing their tools, but this is the day when I down tools over this work of intense exploration of the aesthetic of Dwight David Eisenhower and FDR.

I'm going to go back just a moment to the photographers and the automobile accident in Paris, and Paris itself, because in a way it makes part of my point. There ought to be some real rules in life, and one of the real rules for us ought to be, don't mention Hitler, Nazis, and anything to do with World War II unless you know what you're talking about, or are prepared to act with proper respect and distance toward that enormous, still unexplored, still not-available-for-full-discussion topic. A nonmainstream British cultural artifact to mention here is Carlyle's history of the French Revolution, written in the 1830s, as I remember. In any case, at one point in his history, written forty years after the Terror, Carlyle says that, getting a visceral sense of what the terror was like, it's natural to indulge a tendency to screech and to scream, but we're human beings, and isn't it time to reason? Well, it's fifty years after the end of the Second World War, and I don't think we've even begun to really reason about what the overall impact of that war was.

And so, two points: one, these press photographers, acting really out of enormous arrogance and ignorance, in my opinion, without any respect for the history of the civilization they service, the detritus of which they service, decided that they could note that the Nazis occupying Paris also interfered with freedom of the press, and . . . I can't go on with it, because it's just too absurd: paparazzi doing really very dirty work, trying to sabotage a completely legitimate action of the French polity—and I remind my reader that that's the basis of the action of the French authorities in this case; if there's been an automobile accident, there are certain rules to follow, and so forth, a completely legitimate investigation—by raising the spectre of Hitler. My immediate thought—because I know something about Paris, about the landscape of the city—is, "Oh my God, how could they!"—for a landscape reason, and I'm a landscape boy. I take very seriously the real, built, lived-in landscape as an expression of the natural landscape, and also I take the dead very seriously, and I'm very cautious about the dead, and I think everyone should be. If you walk around Paris, you will see etched into stone, and sometimes the stone of very famous, important buildings, some testament to a man or a woman who acted with ferocious bravery during the time of the Nazi occupation, as a member of the French Resistance. The event is noted; the name of the person is given, honor is given. These are monuments I walk by with considerable respect, knowing full well that, the kind of man I am, I might have done it, might have acted that bravely, but I can't assume I would have done it. It's too much for any person to assume that he or she would, under those circumstances, have been member of a group that brave and that ferocious, and my thought was, as I watched these pathetic photographers putting their tools down—and what an easy tool it is, you know? heavy lifting it isn't—in front of the palace of authority in Paris, and I thought, not half a mile or a quarter of a mile away, maybe not five hundred feet away, there is one of these etched testaments to a real hero.

And another thing is, as to my downing my own tools, as to the most serious aspect of this cultural explication of mine—and I'm certainly going to go on with cultural explication, I like it— but this business of tackling the World War II heroes, and what was Roosevelt really up to, and so forth, this is going to be over for me as of today. And frankly, I'm glad, and that has to do with a perception of mine that came two minutes ago; it's, my God, why is it *me* thinking about these issues? I'm not the kind of guy who—and it's me because no one else is doing it, and I thought, what is the metaphor for this, and I said, well, George, you've lived a privileged life, you've always been in the room where the most interesting people, where the thing is going on, and so forth, and I said, well, you're like a person who was in the room where it was all happening, and you were there as a kind of special social guest, and twenty years later you discover that none of the really powerful people at the party have ever come clean about it, on any level. They've just gone on and on and on with the template they were working from originally, trying to justify it, expand it, not lose too much, not lose face, and I said, well, that's your answer. You went to a party, you learned a lot, you discovered that other people at the party weren't coming clean, you told the story, now go home—and that's my story. I just note that probably the person who's done best with all of this is Robert McNamara, and look how little he's done. After enormous soul searching, he's decided that, yes, the Vietnam War wasn't that great an idea. But even then he hasn't just done that, which he certainly might have done; he's decided, "Well, my apology has to be met with some kind of apology from you North Vietnamese, some kind of quid pro quo."

And now I'm going to give myself a little treat. I'm going to put Dwight David Eisenhower, my hero, in context and perspective, as Dan Rather likes to say—and Dan has never put anything in the first C of context, let alone the first P of perspective. It's a little bit of a love story here, I warn my reader; a reporter's supposed to confess his bias, and I don't just like Ike; I love him. I think he's the guy of guys, I think he's uniquely American, and I'm sorry we're not going to have him anymore. So, I'm going to try to tell his uniquely American story, using my authority, which is the authority of social history, and, frankly, of style—how people do things, who the guy really is, even how he dresses, how he makes his impression on other people. *That* I know down to the ground. You'll have to trust me on that one. And I'm just going to indicate that there ought to be a few other people out there who know a little about Ike and the changes in our America in the last forty years who can pick up some other aspects of the tale. So I've made a little list, a list of items that would fall comfortably under the heading "The Aesthetic of Dwight David Eisenhower"—and I love his full name; I think it's a really dignified American name, and I urge my reader to remember that Eisenhower is a German name, and that Ike took full responsibility for an utter defeat of the people of his heritage. I just might remind my reader that life is so strange that it might turn out to be that an African-American general might have to be part of a military operation against an African nation. It's entirely possible. Anyway, Ike did that. That's what it takes to be an American, by the way, in case anyone's interested.

So, now just a discussion of the aesthetic of Dwight David Eisenhower. Number one—you've had this—the rag soaked in oil. There's a famous photograph of Ike at the summit, and it was the summit of Ike as well as Ike's summit with Nikita Khrushchev. It was 1955. Smiling, looking great, by my perception, wearing his famous homburg, tipping it, taking his hat off. But beside him is a darker figure. Of course it's a Secret Service man, and I understand the objective correlative of this, but you know by now, my dear reader, that that's not the way I think, and I look at that picture, and I see things a little mystically. I say, well, that's Ike with his dark side; that's what I like of that picture—of course he had one. We're talking about a man who sent other men into battle, and four hundred thousand Americans died in World War II. Ike was aware of that. You don't do that if you're the old fuddy-duddy with the spun-sugar society of the fifties in your blood. That wasn't Ike. He lived to preside over that society, but that's not who he was. He was a man who was comfortable in a march—oh yes, it was an American political march, but he would have been comfortable in another kind of march, too, lit by a flaming torch of rags soaked in oil. That's number one for Ike. You don't get Ike the soldier without that, and you don't get Ike the president without Ike the soldier. And that leads to something that isn't quite a digression but just something that naturally spins off that thought. I recently, within the last six months, heard someone on television say that the role of the military was evolving, and it was no longer just to fight wars. I won't say too much about this, because it's just too absurd. The role of the military *is* to fight a war, and my only thought is, dear reader, what thought of yours is as crazy as that one? Let's say you're a currency trader; do you imagine that when you buy and sell currency, when you drive down the deutschemark to drive up the yen so you can make some money for yourself or your bosses—do you convince yourself that you're doing something other than trading in money? Have you convinced yourself that you're part of some evolving world civilization of economics that is finally going to benefit everyone because you are making a hundred million dollars? Just how far has this craziness gone? That, too, is a question for someone else to answer.

My second item says, "The Eisenhower style," and it has, in quotes, the words, "Let's not be corny," and this comes from a *Life* magazine of 1956, the same year as Elvis Presley's dance onto the world stage, with Ike running for reelection, and *Life* did a big spread; it was more like a celebration of Tom Cruise than any of the kind of political stuff we get now, and my generation— quite logically, I want to say, or necessarily—reacted against this kind of thing because there really was a lot of celebration of Ike that was wildly uncritical. On the other hand, now I think it's great, given what's happened in the last forty years. Ike is out shooting and the photographers are there, and one of the photographers says—the shooting's finished, the day is over, and Ike is standing there with his shotgun no longer in firing position, and so forth—and the photographer says, "Oh, won't you bring the shotgun back up into firing position so we can get a better shot?" and Ike says, "Let's not be corny," and the reporters at *Life*—and this is to show a little of what I've called the deutero-Hemingway style in the 1950s reportage and media life, reflecting you back to *Roman Holiday,* where the photographer gives the pictures back to the princess—the reporters note this with a little pride; the guy said, "Oh, come on. I'm not playing that game, and why should you?" And so Ike didn't have to do that, didn't have to photo-op it, and the reporters didn't have to feel that they had been part of something second-rate. They got a little bit of amusement back; they got something better than the photographs. They got a laugh on themselves, and in terms of that laugh on themselves they got to show themselves as, "Hey, we're like Ike. We're not corny, we're people who do a real job." So Ike wasn't corny. He just wasn't. Never anyone less corny, and he had a fashion sense. It amuses me to use that word in relation to him, but he had fashion sense. There's a particular item of clothes with his name on it; it's the Eisenhower jacket. It's a battle jacket he liked, and people took as much an interest in that battle jacket as at another moment they took in the Windsor tie. Ike set a fashion trend, but the particular clothing item identified with him at this period is the homburg hat, and you see a really good one in the photo of Ike at the summit I mentioned. It wasn't a fedora; it was far more formal than anything Harry Truman would have felt comfortable in, far less formal than Woodrow Wilson's inauguration high hat, and so forth, although morning clothes continued, in and out, to be used at inaugurations. It was a homburg. It was his crown, the one he earned.

Under the Homburg; or, The Summit

Well, who was Ike when he went to the summit to meet Khrushchev in 1955? What were the stakes, and what was his approach to the event? You, Mr. Thirty-Five-Year-Old Businessman, know how you approach your next meeting—are you selling promotional items to someone? You need to know who the other man is. You need to know what your relationship to the other man is. Well, here's how Ike wasn't going to the summit. He wasn't going in the kind of style you so like now, the royal stuff—for instance, Diana in her tiara, anyone in their tiara, anyone in their royal title, whatever it is. That was corny. It was corny in particular in 1955 in Geneva, because the Soviet Russians, you know, felt quite clear about their relation to royalty, to our royal past, and quite unrepentant about their torture and murder of the Russian royal family. So it really wasn't going to do to arrive at Geneva claiming that one's masculine authority, one's ability to negotiate, was based on royal title, the corniness of ancient anything. And what else wasn't going to do, from the point of view of that moment? Limousines. Oh, a big stretch limousine, with twelve doors instead of merely ten, and half a mile long instead of—the biggest limo in town, the most money in the world; well, the Russians, the Soviet Russians, were pretty clear about that too. They thought rich people ought to have all their money taken away from them. So these two particular dominance vectors, let's call them, were so unpopular in the world at the moment that the royals—what goes on beyond, or behind, or beneath palace walls—and all the money in the world, these two fabulous dominance vectors we're all so fond of now, lifestyles of the corny and cornier, let's call it, weren't available to Ike. How was he going to arrive? Well, he was going to arrive as the Number-One Guy in the World, period. Khrushchev was quite clear that that was what was being fought over, there wasn't any of today's attractive we-are-all-a-thousand-billion-flowers-blooming; it was quite clearly who's the number-one guy in the world, and who gets to say. Well, Ike was going to arrive as the Number-One Guy in the World. That was going to be under his homburg. Well, what did that mean?

Now I get to go to items three and four. Number three is: unexampled dominance well held. So now I get to tell my absolute favorite story about Ike, and it involves a man who deserves to be discussed, but not by me, except a very little bit, and that's General George Marshall, his boss. The story is simply this: naturally, all ultradominant men—and both Marshall and Eisenhower fit in that category—please, this business about the military, or anything being a career opportunity, or a career being about—well, whatever nonsense it is that people talk—of course, they were two pack leaders, one of whom was going to actually lead the pack, and the other be number two, in some important way. Marshall picked Ike up out of his cohort, and raised him up. Eisenhower was Marshall's protegé, so that, of course, was part of the mix; and Marshall—and here's my very brief discussion of him—came from a tradition I know quite a bit about, and do not embody. Hence, my reluctance to discuss it at length. It's the tradition of the Traditional Christian Gentleman, the man who gets to the top and who makes it a point to step aside. Not that all of us don't have to make a point of it, to step aside at various moments, but the tradition of the Christian Gentleman is such that it's almost number one on his list, that he's the expert on stepping aside and still wielding considerable power. I don't think it's a useful tradition anymore; I think our life has to be about honest, decent, relentless conflict. That's what I think, and I think the sooner we acknowledge that, the better, and the sooner we put the decent in number-two place and the honest in number-one place, the better we'll be in our competition, and the less likely it will happen that we'll just throw everything away, which is what it seems we're doing now. But, in any case, through access to a wonderful old cousin of my grandfather's, named Ernest Trow Carter, and through the family of Windy Rock, and a lot of other people, too, I know quite a lot about this tradition of stepping aside, and it does help make sense of this story.

Marshall was the chief of staff, and a very hidden, powerful man he was, but what he wanted, wanted for himself, was to command the invasion of Europe. He'd done all the staff work, he'd stayed in Washington, he really wanted to show what he was made of on the battlefield, and he wanted to command Overlord. I now refer to Ike's book *Crusade in Europe,* because Ike's description of the events I'm about to recount is as important, in my mind, as the events themselves, and it's the style of the description that will tell you, dear reader, what was under the homburg, and what Ike went to, in terms of balls, and how testosterone and the history of your balls is reflected in the look in your eyes and in your facial expression. For instance, the style in which Ike writes about the events I'm about to recount tells you what he went to Geneva with, in those terms, and—I hate to do this, because it's so pathetic, it takes us so far down, but it's really necessary to ask you, dear reader, after you read *Crusade in Europe,* to pick up a copy of, oh, let's say *The Art of the Deal,* by Donald Trump, and see what it is he's recommending you bring with you to your next meeting. I'm not betting on you—as against the Chinese, or the Indonesians, or the Dutch—at your next really important business meeting if all you're going to that meeting with is what Donald Trump is recommending. I think you'd better have a little of what Ike had.

So, anyway, the story he's telling in *Crusade in Europe* is about when the art of the deal went his way, when Roosevelt decided that he, Dwight Eisenhower, not Marshall, would command the invasion of Europe, and the circumstances are pretty interesting. Roosevelt's dealing with Stalin, not a nobody to deal with, and credit please for the enormous suffered bravery of FDR, and his extraordinary optimism. He's in a wheelchair, he's at the end of his life, and he's dealing with a psychotic madman as an ally. I really do think that enough time has passed so that we can stop looking at all of these events from the point of view of the propaganda of the time and begin to look at what it was like, in terms of the personalities of the people who were actually involved in this thing. How would you like to be FDR, that old, that crippled, that everything, and one of your jobs is to deal appropriately with the madman Stalin? In any case, he has to tell Stalin what's going on as to the invasion of Europe, and he's telling Stalin—perhaps he's told Stalin in person, my memory is so bad—and we're talking about Casablanca here—I'll check it later—or I won't—but Roosevelt is telling Stalin that it's going to be Ike and not Marshall, and Marshall is right there. I believe it's a telegram, actually, being sent to Stalin, and Roosevelt is dictating the telegram to Marshall—I'm almost sure that's what it is—and Marshall is sitting there with the destruction of all his personal hopes, actually. He wants to be in the Soldiers' Hall of Fame, and he's not gonna get to be. He's not there yet, by the way; his name is hardly mentioned. A soldier accepts this. It does take an enormous battlefield victory to get your name remembered, and Marshall never had that, and I'm telling you the story of the moment in which it was to be decided that he was never going to have that. And he sits there and takes this dictation from President Roosevelt, saying, in essence, "You, General Marshall, aren't going to get what you wanted, and your protegé is going to get what you wanted"—never an easy thing for a man—and I'm going to switch to Marshall just briefly here, because I do, without knowing one single thing about what it is to be a military officer at that high level, I do know something about what it is to be a

Christian Gentleman, and he does a very remarkable thing. He decides—quite correctly, by the way—that no one single thing must be done to undermine the confidence of Dwight Eisenhower. Eisenhower is going to command these men, these are real human beings, real American men, who are going into battle, and they depend, for their effectiveness, on their absolute trust in the absolute confidence of General Eisenhower. He, General Marshall, must not do one single thing to undermine, for one second, the confidence of the man who will command this operation. So, what he does, General Marshall, is to step aside with maximum gentlemanly grace. This is not something I'm recommending to you, dear reader, because you don't know how to do it, and probably it would be of no use to do it anymore, but it used to be done, and it really was quite simple. He took the copy of the cablegram to be sent to Stalin, and wrote on it: "Dear General Eisenhower, This has been sent to Stalin today, and I thought you might like to have this token for your memory book."

Now, I haven't given the exact words, but really, it's like that. And Eisenhower—to come back now to Ike, and his style, which was Caesar-like, Julius Caesar–like, Caesar's Gallic wars–like, in presentation not flat, exactly, but without any emphasis at all—he tells this story, and there's a picture of the document, which is really saying, "You, Ike, are going to be one of the hits of all time"—because that's really what it said. I mean, given the better than fifty-fifty chance that the war was, in fact, drawing to a close, and that Overlord would be an operation remembered throughout history, as long as there would be a history, this document was simply saying, you, General Eisenhower, have more than a fifty-fifty chance to be one of the heroes in the history of Western Civilization. I thought you might like to have this telegram for your scrapbook, and Ike's remark is, "This is one of my favorite mementos"—it really is something like that, and you see that's why he was a hit, because he was just slightly less formal and conventional than General Marshall; his phrasing again—I might be getting the words slightly off, but not by much, "This is one of my favorite mementos," or "one of my favorite

things"—there's sort of a Rodgers and Hammerstein aspect to
Ike in this way, which Rodgers and Hammerstein made sure they
understood, and, my God, one of my favorite mementos? You
know? That's what Ike had under his homburg.

My fourth item is, "The eye must travel"—and this brings
me back to myself as a man in the world of pleasure, which is
certainly where I've always been, except for a few years here,
where I've been considering serious issues somewhat out of my
depth. "The eye must travel" is my friend Diana Vreeland's
remark, really about life, period. It's a very interesting phrase,
the eye must travel. It means, you have to be the person you are.
You have to be utterly natural, whether you're the tsarina of fashion, or the president of the United States, or a person sewing a
hem, or a buck private. Whoever you are, in whatever condition
of life, you have to be secure enough in yourself so your eye, the
window to your soul, and also the way you take the world in, is
secure about where it goes. Your eye goes here as opposed to
there, and the meaning you need to take comes to you. It's a very
serious power. Ike had it. Nixon didn't—that's why he stumbled
and fell. If you don't have the eye, the eye that inspires trust in
other people, sooner or later you stumble and fall.

Natural human life is the inevitable, desirable condition for
all humans. Ike had it, and here's how I know. It's another one of
these wonderful Julius Caesar moments in *Crusade in Europe.*
Ike is conferring with General Alexander and Winston Churchill
about the invasion of Italy, Sicily first. They are on Malta. It's a
different moment from the Overlord moment; it's tougher, more
beleaguered, more medieval, in a way. He's given a medal,
together with Alexander and Churchill, struck at the command of
King George VI, a gold medal, never to be given to any other man.

Well, here you have, again, one of these tokens, those extraordinary World War II artifacts, and I want to refer a little to anthropology here, and compassion for all of us, in this situation, because
an anthropologist going to a Samoan island knows how to read the
artifacts. This king won a battle, this man did this; ordinarily, in
our human life, we're able to read our markers. We're able to read

them again, and I want to back off just an inch from my criticism of our current situation, because it is healthy that, once again, we regard the president of a Baby Bell as a person who deserves respect, because we need to have many head men and women. It's just healthier. What we need to understand about the World War II situation is, we didn't have that then. And we have anthropological artifacts from that time that are very difficult to read.

What do you do with the fact of those three gold medals presented to Alexander, Eisenhower, and Churchill? Never to be struck again, one-time-only honor, for the saviors of Western Civilization—it's just too high a thing to aspire to. You can't raise your child by saying, "Dear Lavinia, dear Edward, you must do your best so that one day, you can get a token of this kind, as you struggle to save Western Civilization"; it just isn't a practical thing to enter into the equation, so we don't enter it into the equation, but at least we can read the artifacts right. These gold coins are really quite remarkable. But the point is that Ike stayed natural during all this, and for that reason he's one of our really great Americans. Not only wasn't he a monster, not only wasn't he a dictator, not only was he not megalomaniacal, he was natural. And because I take the dead so seriously, I take note of the fact that when Ike retired he went to Gettysburg, where all the suffering of the Civil War is around you; and also please note that the really fairly modest house the Eisenhowers lived in in Gettysburg was the first house Ike ever owned. This isn't a guy in a mansion on a hill. He was just Ike, but that was plenty. So in that situation, which might well have been identified with megalomania or a lot of other ugly things, Ike was still natural. He was still observing, his eye was still traveling, and he records this, just as he noted the television set in the 1952 convention situation. He noticed something about his own situation other than that he was being singled out as one of the coolest guys ever in the world. He looked around the hall and noticed that at another moment, many centuries earlier, it would have been filled with roistering knights. And this is the greatness of Ike: that the height of power could be achieved in this way, and that his eye could still travel.

NOTES TOWARD
AN OVERVIEW

My Pilgrim's Progress

As I say, this book is the story of an Irish soul (mine by right) struggling with a great deal of Anglo-Saxon cultural information (also mine by right—but *struggled* for; you don't come into your *language* inheritance without a struggle).

So, who *is* my English language hero, then, me being Irish and not Irish? Well, it's William Butler Yeats. First of all, he has been my guide as to what to say and what not to say in this book. Yeats's *Autobiographies* are *the* road map, in my opinion, and so have I used them. I read in them that Yeats wanted (when he died) to "sup with Landor and with Donne," and I immediately got to know Walter Savage Landor, since I already knew Donne. Also, in his *Autobiographies* Yeats says that he has "omitted nothing necessary for understanding," and this I have tried to do.

The sentence I puzzled longest over in the *Autobiographies* has to do with President Woodrow Wilson. "When I saw his face," Yeats says, "I knew that the moon had entered the Fourth Quarter." It took me many years to understand that this "Fourth Quarter" was the end of the line as to *civilized masculine dominance energy*. Yeats found something unsettling about Wilson *as a man*.

Traditions have their problems. A person might read this book and say to himself or herself, "Why is he complaining? His father read good books to him and told him he had a legitimate, almost personal connection to Franklin Delano Roosevelt. I wish *I'd* had that."

Well and good. *But the conversation had grown corrupt.*

Conversation is a big word, actually. A child hears differently from an adult. A child hears trouble. He incorporates it in his own being as a problem to be solved—or dropped.

I wasn't allowed to drop the problem. It kept resurfacing and resurfacing—and the Fourth Quarter was *waning* all the time.

Finally, it resurfaced one last time in my father's conversation; and it presented itself as a control system.

A Parallel Life

Walter Winchell had a son: Walter Winchell, Jr. I have always been vaguely aware of the fact, and known that Winchell Jr. killed himself. What else could he have done? What were his *options*? His *opportunities*?

His father, an extreme narcissist, naturally expected him to toe the line. With such a father, if you altered the received text in any way, you were dead. How to *replicate* the received text, then?

Walter Winchell was a member of a vaudeville troupe called Gus Edwards' School Days. Amusing little moppets on the stage—Huck Finn in a way, on the stage. George Jessel was in the troupe also. These were the rhythm-and-blues boys of their days; they were *there* when the rock-and-roll of the twenties was first thought of. Like Alfred Sloan's "Whizzer" at the Hotel Pontchartrain in 1910. If you did anything to disrespect Gus Edwards' School Days, you were *dead* in Winchell's eyes. If you didn't have the *whiz* of Gus Edwards' School Days, you were *dead* in Winchell's eyes.

Winchell then went on to invent the modern tabloid gossip style, killing off a good part of Gus Edwards' School Days in the process. If you did anything to indicate that the gossip column was not a good thing—was a little tough on the nice old Gus Edwards moppets concept, for instance—you were *dead* in Winchell's eyes.

Walter Winchell, Jr., would have been, you known, *shown off* for a while. Dolores Del Rio would have planted a kiss on his infant brow right there at table one at the Stork Club. Should Walter Jr. have decided to become an actor, say, he would have had to rise to the Dolores Del Rio level *fast.* If he had decided to join the *contemporary* version of Gus Edwards' School Days (by then a jazz combo, the Broadway-Winchell style having killed off the Edwards stuff), Winchell would have put a stop to it as violating—oh, something; not being good enough; not being *innocent* like *his* first stuff had been; not being up to the Dolores Del Rio level where Winchell Jr. had, in theory, been placed.

What if Winchell Jr., with the mind of an infant sage, had understood that it would not be possible to replicate his father's life because history had obliterated the rituals that had formed his father (history having been given a hand in this by Winchell Sr.) and had recognized as absurd the idea that he should function from moment one at the Dolores Del Rio level. Well, had he had the extraordinary powers of an infant sage, he might have decided to take, you know, a *third way*; just become, you know, a *doctor.* How *square!* Do you think anyone so *pedestrian* as a *doctor* could win Winchell's respect? So, first, *acting out.* Then, *over and out.*

A PREDICTION: Stupid television in the 1950s drove smart people crazy. In the future, smart television will drive simple people crazy.

A Second Parallel Life

The Phillips Exeter Academy, when I was there, 1957–1961, was a *swirl* of many of the social and intellectual vectors I have laid out and *swirled* in this book. A tiny thread of the Old Patriarchal (as in my own family life); an anticipation of the end (the wished-for end) of the Eisenhower regency; a frenzy of ambition as to the Kennedy possibility, along with a jittery aspect of Cafe Society energy; what our classmate Dick Pershing had so strongly in *his* family, the old warrior aesthetic morphed into a mean (but not so lean) Park Avenue maisonette. I like *maisonette* in this context, because a maisonette isn't quite a real house, you know.

Well, that was just our world, and it didn't occur to us that the *next* world wouldn't be morphed out of *all of the above*. We had the Last Patriarchal Thread; we had the Kennedy Brains; and we (some of us) had New York City, too.

Well, it didn't happen, and the *real aesthetic winner* (socially, I mean) from my Exeter class of '61 was—and is—a perfectly nice, unprepossessing boy (now man) named Bob Tuttle. Bob's father, Holmes Tuttle, was (maybe still is) *the biggest Ford dealer in Los Angeles.* And one day, Mr. Holmes Tuttle turned on his television and saw Ronald Reagan; and he said to himself, "This guy can do it" (whatever "it" was in his mind), and Republicans were called together and *made aware,* and the rest is history—or rather *not* history but something else—Faye Emerson another way.

Intermezzo: What We Need to Do (As People Say Now)

We need to understand (as people say now) that the important issue in human history is the human mind. We need to understand how our mind has evolved. We need to understand, for instance, that Dwight David Eisenhower (growing up, also, in the age of the telephone and the McCormick reaper) had his mind formed within the atmosphere that gave rise, also, to the oratory of William Jennings Bryan. Bryan was *Gilligan's Island* for Ike. Later on in his life, Ike could pick up the phone and get the president of the McCormick Harvesting Machine Company (and the president of American Telephone and Telegraph, too) on the line *tout de suite,* but his first mind wasn't a reaper mind or a telephone mind, it was a mind formed on the American *steppes.* Later on, children would have their first mind formed within the *mechanical atmosphere* of the reaper and the phone. Nowadays, children have their first mind formed within the *atmosphere* of the Candice Bergen Sprint *advertisements*. Really, it's as simple as that.

We need to understand the sixties. Our mind (my generation's mind) was already on its way to Mediaville. "Vim, Vim, Vim, Vim, Vim for Value" comes to my mind, and no poem by Longfellow does. William Jennings Bryan I don't remember. A rag soaked in coal oil and set ablaze I never saw. However, we (my generation) did have a kind of *nostalgia* for the rag soaked in coal oil and set ablaze. We liked the *look*, and sometimes the *feel*. And we *did* really loathe the mechanical. However, it was Mediaville ("Vim, Vim, Vim, Vim, Vim for Value") that was really strongest in us; let us call it the *pull to the future*. Let's just say that on the basis of a kind of nostalgia for something real, we fire-bombed Detroit (that nice feel of a rag soaked in coal oil for a while) and ended up in Hollywood.

We also need (as people say now) to set the *seventies aside as an unexampled time deserving of a very particular kind of study.* Let's use our common sense here. Golden-tongued orator in 1890—you're a hit. Later on, you'd better have other assets too. In 1890 if you've got a *great visual sense,* you might end up painting signs on the sides of barns; with those talents today your *options and opportunities* are almost unlimited. Who you are *when* matters. Because of the particular and *peculiar* history of my generation, outlined above (French Communards, acting in an atmosphere of nostalgia for the Revolution, firebomb Detroit but spare Hollywood), show-business trivia from the seventies has an importance show-business trivia didn't have before and won't have again. Nothing to do with the quality of the stuff within the history of show business; everything to do with the formation of our First Media Mind.

For instance, the show-business cabaret act named Caesar and Cleo. Pure corn. Three steps down from Xavier Cugat and Abbe Lane, whom they somewhat resembled. In the history of show business you've got Valentino as a god; Xavier Cugat and Abbe Lane as members of the chorus; and Caesar and Cleo out there on the road, playing Paducah. But not quite. Caesar and Cleo surfaced *at the right moment* as Sonny and Cher. The right moment was the firebombing of Detroit. They looked anarchic (said or did nothing to defend Detroit), but they had a friendly cabaret energy. Lou Walters' Latin Quarter in a way. Because they were *there* when our First Media Mind was being formed (no steppes of Kansas, no McCormick reaper, just *pure light and sound* going into the brain moments after Detroit went up in flames), they are with us forever. *You don't get a second chance to make a first impression,* as people say now, and every seventies hit was written on a slate that had been swept clean of *text.* And there they are: in every barroom in America you find the raspy-voiced man who thinks he's Caesar, and the more-talented-than-he-is girl who really *does* look like Cleo, in a way.

Something Happened—And Here's What (A Not Completely Facetious Response to Joseph Heller's Book)

In the earliest 1970s I was one of a very small handful of mainstream journalists who attended rock-and-roll concerts and parties. I'd go—to the Fillmore East, say, and there it would be, my name on a secret, tiny press list. Hippies everywhere, dressed in velvet, anything; a golden marijuana haze; and, somewhere at the ticket seller's side—a secret, tiny press list. Thirty names on it, twenty-eight of them from *Billboard, Tiger Beat,* and so on. I'm exaggerating. The people from the *Voice* and *Rolling Stone* were there too, of course; but the number of mainstream journalists was really very small. Maureen Orth was sometimes in attendance, and a few established freelancers who would try to sell something to a mainstream journal, but no one on the staff of the *Times,* for instance.

Well, I lived that life for a time, and then I dropped it, and then, about ten years later, I thought I would *have another look.* I

decided to write a story for "The Talk of the Town" about a performer named Adam Ant. Adam Ant was the kind of performer
who, in my day, would have been set, jewel-like, in the back room
of Max's Kansas City, but now he was at a (then) new venue called
the Ritz. I went to the Ritz. No hippies in velvet, but four hundred souls bedraggled in a *new* way, milling about outside. I
glided to the ticket seller. "I'm George Trow. I'll be on your press
list," I said. A woman looked up, bemused. She waved toward the
bedraggled ones. "That *is* the press list," she said.

Now, real human social life is *tough* because in a demographic democracy you *never* criticize the subtext of your market.
If fifty percent of your audience is made up of semiliterate farmers you do *not* set about to critique the manners and mores of
semiliterate sons and daughters of the soil; you just work that
semiliterate soil into your *style* and your *approach*. Now, in the
America of *aujourd'hui* (and I promise you, this is true), a full
fifty percent of our demography is made up of semiliterate sons
and daughters of rock-and-roll—a fact *never to be mentioned*
since it is sacred *subtext;* i.e., what the *New York Times* needs to
be cognizant of (and silent about) now. The fact is that fifty percent of our national mind is a giant, explosive *blowup* of a *Xerox*
of a 1970s rock-and-roll press list.

Some Sympathy (but Not Much) for the Sixties

I once was in a room with "Mama" Cass Elliot, who was making
an appearance in favor of something called "Earth People's
Park." People talk of the sixties in terms of wild, free expression,
but there was a murderous catatonia abroad as well. Some bed
partners: the obligation toward wild, free expression lying down
with murderous *don't you dare ask;* and that was what it was like
at the Earth People's Park party. Mama Cass seemed to feel the
contradiction. She looked a little depressed. Maybe that's why
she died young. Maybe that's why everyone died young. Some
of the questions you *didn't dare ask* about Earth People's Park

were: Where is it? Who will run it? Will anyone want to do the real work? Like the global economy now, it was just something assumed, and the people in the room were there to embody the zeitgeist of it and kill the people who didn't belong (or seem to belong) in the body of the zeitgeist.

Well, I'm Mr. Contrary. At the time, I was one of a very few people in my social group who thought that questions to do with social status, money, and practical arrangements *would out.* But there was *something* there—at that time I mean: a real psychosis, real defiance, and a red-hot (if crazy) link back to the preindustrial past. We shouldn't throw all of that away *now;* in our memory, I mean. It wasn't about Dylan playing for the pope, or Elton John and Princess Di or anything like that. We should try to remember what it *was* about. Since we gave up half of what we had (at least) by *acquiescing* to it, we should make a point of getting what we paid for.

Negative Space

I am trying to indicate a *negative space* here; a story told in silences. The link between Earth People's Park and the global economy is *there*—in murderous catatonia: don't you dare ask where the global economy *is,* or who is there to really promise that it will work, or what the *authority* of that global economy promiser really is—you just sit down and watch us try to *embody* it. People who get to embody a powerful zeitgeist get to have a very superior social position, by the way, which is the key to the whole thing. Embody *any* powerful zeitgeist and you get to be a regent of the University of California later on, and some of your youthful pain will have been healed—maybe. Maybe that was why Mama Cass Elliot was a little depressed. Looking around at the rock-and-roll world she was in (the managers and the money men, on the one hand, and the Earth People's Park rangers, on the other), maybe she intuited that it was going to result in a few people moving way up a new social ladder—but not her. And, after all, she was an intelligent woman.

Lively Purveyors of Silence

Well, if our real history is there—somewhere in the Silent Zone (forget *Twilight*: *Silent* is the really scary zone)—then we must look for our Real Rulers there, among people who are most comfortable when most silent; and as for Frontpersons, we must look for those individuals who are Inoffensive to People Who Love Silence, on the one hand, but who are Marvelously Authoritative and Lively, on the other. My nominees for Most Important American in the Silent but Lively Zone, 1950–1997, Frontperson's Division, are . . . Oprah Winfrey and Ronald Reagan. Faye Emerson, open the envelope, please.

EPILOGUE

My Life in a House in Flames

1. The Vanderbilts Won

One of the good things my father did for me was to interest me in Franklin Roosevelt, the man, and to show me the life he lived and the place where he lived that life. One day, when I was ten or eleven—this would have been 1953 or '54—we piled into a car and went to Hyde Park; I juxtapose this in my own mind with the moment in 1940, before I was born, when my mother and father went to Windy Rock in Westchester to watch King George VI make his progress with Franklin Roosevelt toward Hyde Park. Hyde Park was, in our family, a Mecca, what is now called a *tourist destination,* and I was shown it early, and in the right atmosphere, and it stayed with me. Later, when I got the chance, I moved to the Hudson Valley myself, and, in fact, I have lived all my life in and on the East Coast landscape Franklin Roosevelt knew and loved. Many of my friends have been people who have had some connection to him: a spiritual connection, a family connection, or a social connection. When I was in my early twenties I was introduced by my friend John Winthrop Aldrich to Daisy Suckley, a lady who came from my social background—that is, not the people who came from the great landed families along the Hudson (although she did, come to think of it, have a connection in that direction), but from high-bourgeois people from New York

City. Miss Suckley had served for many years as Franklin Roosevelt's confidante and secretary. She was with Franklin Roosevelt when he died. Fala, Roosevelt's dog, was a gift from Daisy, I think. She lived to be almost a hundred, and I can remember the day, not so long ago, when she died. I was with my friend Winty Aldrich at his house, Rokeby, on the Hudson—Rokeby being a very fine and interesting old nineteenth-century house. We were having a picnic. I think it was the birthday of Winty's brother Ricky, and we were looking out toward the Hudson River, across a landscape that is still unchanged, really, from the eighteenth—or even the seventeenth—century; the land has been in cultivation that long. And we heard that Daisy had died. An interesting footnote here is that Winty Aldrich has been the spirit behind the preservation of Daisy Suckley's house, Wilderstein, and, shortly before she died, Miss Suckley—and she was Miss Suckley, she never married—indicated to Winty that there might be something under her bed of interest to him, and after she died Winty found a cache of letters written to Daisy by FDR during World War II, and which were clearly meant to be the starting ground for some autobiography, some autobiographical work that Roosevelt projected writing after his retirement. This book has been published. In any case, that landscape, and that presence of Franklin Roosevelt, has been with me all my life, and it took palpable form on the day my father took me to Hyde Park; it was the complement, in a way, of his taking me to Windy Rock, the house he regarded as his home; here was the intellectual and social and even the political reference I was to have. The house Hyde Park matched the spirit, the social spirit, of Windy Rock in some way; a house of deep probity and old-fashioned manners.

We visited another house on that day, as well. There are two properties in Hyde Park, New York, that are owned and maintained by the federal government: one is Hyde Park, FDR's house; the other is the house of Frederick Vanderbilt, a grandson of Commodore Vanderbilt—a kind of American palace, built by McKim, Mead and White. It looks a little like a railroad station; I like it for that reason. My father made a point, when he showed it to me, of not liking it, and in this my father was Black Roosevelt, as always. I don't think there was ever an opinion held by my father that wasn't in perfect coincidence with what FDR had said ought to have been true. And FDR's fairly *cunning* idea about the Vanderbilt house, which he caused to be preserved by the federal government, was that Americans should first come and see what a real aristocrat's house was—Hyde Park being that—and afterward, have an opportunity to tour a money-power house, the idea being that Hyde Park would come out ahead.

It must have looked like a pretty safe bet, as of the 1940s, because, although this has been forgotten now, in the 1940s the biggest American houses, those palaces of the robber barons, were goin' a-beggin'. They were goin' a-beggin' in terms of money; Rosecliff, the house in Newport owned by the Oelrichs family, which was used as a background for the film version of *The Great Gatsby,* a house that has become a kind of symbol for American grandeur, sold, I think, in the 1940s, for thirty or forty thousand dollars; these were houses that had been built for two million dollars, or three or five million dollars, at the turn of the century, when a million dollars was worth twenty times what it is now; and they had gone terribly out of vogue. At a time—it was wartime—when people had ration coupons; when people had family members who were dying abroad, when soldiers were receiving pay, and I don't know exactly what a GI's pay was during World War II, but was it sometimes fifty dollars a month for a private?—and all of this sitting on top of the Great Depression; in the early 1940s, say, a big marble house built by a robber baron forty years before was—almost an object of terror, one wants to say; a lesson as to a mistake that had been made and suffered through. And remember, too, that the other great force in the world opposed to Hitler was Stalin's Russia, just a fact, and we were all aware that in the Western world we would be competing for the minds and hearts of unaffiliated peoples, let's say; the poor people of India; the poor people of anywhere; and we were not about to represent ourselves as the country of money power, of big marble palaces, of people who lived off the income of their income, which is an old formula for how the richest people lived—it was said that they lived on the income of their income while other people were earning fifteen dollars a week. It was not acceptable to Americans, living with the idea of America, to think that some people would be earning fifteen dollars a week and that other people would have what amounted to infinitely more by virtue of living off the income of their income. This was all within the context of public relations; within the context of our fight with communism. So, all forces in the 1940s worked against the aesthetic of these big palaces.

And another thing: the families living in these houses had very often been unhappy; there are many great American palaces that look pretty good today, or very good, very shiny, and are emulated, but were lived in for only twenty years or so. They were ego monuments to the founder; the founder organized his family around a life of grandeur; the children were psychologically unhappy; refer here, perhaps, to the Princess Diana phenomenon; they were regimented, kept away from the free life of this country; the children rebelled. The founding of Cafe Society is almost entirely a result of that reaction; a big part of Cafe Society had to do with the children of these income-of-their-income people who fled the big marble palaces to go have fun in nightclubs. This is, in a way, the reason you don't have Cafe Society in the old way today; that element is missing. It isn't just gangsters, actors, and people with cash in their pocket who make up Cafe Society; an important part of the mix was that interesting moral vector of the young heirs and heiresses of these big marble-palace families deciding against a hyper-privileged aesthetic of that kind, and choosing to mix it up with their fellow citizens.

And all of this showed in the big marble palaces that were available to be viewed in the early fifties, say; and I saw some of them then. And they were tatty; ratty; and I remember, on touring the Vanderbilt house in 1953, thinking first of all that it was fun—an illicit reaction on my part; my father meant me to be horrified—but also that the house had the feel, which, by the way the Plaza Hotel also had in the early 1950s, of being something for old women; the furniture hadn't been re-covered in forty years; the velvet hangings were bedraggled; it looked as if the place hadn't been thoroughly cleaned in a while. That added to the atmosphere of *overness* for this whole aesthetic.

And, of course, over the years, I have revisited the Vanderbilt house and Hyde Park. About three years ago I noticed an extraordinary change at the Vanderbilt house; when I'd first visited it, the guides were in that spirit, which is gone completely, of the 1953 policeman; the 1953 public librarian; those stolid, not particularly well educated, very businesslike, very firm and human presences of the early fifties; people who were fifty years old, who had been born in 1900, say, and had a very simple American authority; people doin' their job without any curatorial nonsense about them, without any interior-decorator nonsense about them; they just showed you around. Well, that went on for a while, because people in the civil service stay on, and there was an intermediate period when things weren't all that different, but on my last visit to the Vanderbilt house—my, what a change. The guides were all young; not particularly well informed as to the overall flow of American history, but wildly well informed as to the history of the Vanderbilt family; and suddenly, out of the woodwork, or out of some books, came all kinds of facts and figures about the Vanderbilts, in terms of how much money they had and how many houses and how many yachts and so forth, which showed that the Vanderbilts, at least in the minds of the guides, and I guess, probably, everyone else, had lately been put on a new kind of Mount Rushmore; these were people who had invented the aesthetic that everyone at this recent moment had decided to embrace. This, of course, represented a kind of defeat for FDR's intent. I didn't see one horrified face or one disapproving face as the young guides described plutocracy in its old form.

Well, Reagan did that, didn't he? But how on earth did it happen, I wondered, as I went around in a kind of post-Proustian mood, taking the official tour of the Frederick Vanderbilt house two or three years ago; I say post-Proustian, because I'm not Proustian, insofar as I've determined for myself not to get bushwhacked by the way the wheel goes around; not to be shocked that Madame Verdurin has married the Prince de Guermantes, and so forth, this is all just part of life, and our great artist Fellini has given us a clue to it; but nonetheless, there was a kind of *swirl* going on in my mind as I walked around the Vanderbilt house three years ago, observing this new attitude on the part of my fellow citizens; I had to think about it. One reason I had to think about it was personal; there had been very few members of my generation who, during the sixties and seventies, were in any way in touch with or at home with the idea of our former plutocracy, though I was, ironically, one of them; I say ironically because I began to let it go after Reagan came along. But I can remember, for instance, a friend of mine taking me to a left-wing meeting in the late sixties—a meeting of journalists, and I was then a journalist, and so was this man—at which an action was projected that would get *Time* magazine to be worker-owned, like *Le Monde*. I mean, this is the kind of thing that went on in my generation; the sixties weren't an easy time, and they weren't just about feminism as currently projected, or civil rights as currently projected; there was a real left-wing element, and there was a real anti-money element; but I can remember thinking how strange it was that for some reason it was okay for me to go with this friend to hear this—to me—silly idea that *Time* magazine should be worker-owned, and, at the same time, to go around town with people whose grandfathers or great-grandfathers had been a part of the old plutocratic construct, and who, to some extent, kept up the manners of that construct. But that was just my life, and the reason it was allowable in my mind at that time that I should do both things was that I was a son of New York, and was entitled in some way to know what was going on in New York.

In any case, in attending that meeting of young left-wingers of 1969, I was very aware of being solitary, in a way, of having a different view of social history from that of anyone else in the room, and being aware that one of the things that made me different from everyone else in the room was that I was in some sense at ease with the descendants of plutocrats; I found many of them to be attractive, sympathetic, sophisticated people. And there I was, twenty-something years later, in something like the same position of isolation, but in a completely different atmosphere as I toured the Vanderbilt house, watching my fellow citizens make mental notes about just how rich the Vanderbilts were, and how many yachts they had; I found myself isolated again, feeling that it was very silly what my fellow citizens were doing. But this time, I found, my isolation was not *nonce* isolation, but an isolation that was taking a kind of permanent form. On the one hand, in 1969, participating, in a way, in the life of the sixties, while allowing myself to have my simple personal reaction as to the personal attractiveness of people who had had some plutocratic or aristocratic background—that was just a fact of my life; I was only temporarily isolated in that meeting at which *Time* magazine was going to be like *Le Monde;* I could just go back out on the street and be part of the swirl of life. Whereas at the Vanderbilt house three years ago, I began to feel a real isolation come over me in a Proustian way; I was aware, for instance, that the friend who had taken me to that left-wing meeting in 1969 was now in sympathetic relation to our new plutocracy, whereas I was not. He had gone from *"Time* magazine ought to be like *Le Monde"* to being at the party for the man who thought that Time-Warner ought to triple in size, perhaps. This was just a fact as to what had happened to that man; so that I began to feel my options, as to healthy life, narrow. And so, as I have said, I had to think about it: How did this happen? And, yes, Reagan did it, but how did he do it?

About this time, by coincidence, Richard Avedon, the photographer, sent me a photograph that I had to look at very closely, it was so remarkable. I don't have it in front of me, but believe me, I can tell you what it was. It was a photograph of Diana Vreeland taken, I think, by Avedon himself, at the Reagan White House, and Richard Avedon knew that I had been a good friend of Diana's and he had sent me the photograph for that reason—so that I would be amused, and I was. It was Diana, the Reagans, Prince Charles, and a man whom I'll mention in a moment. And Diana, in the most impressive way, was curtsying to Prince Charles, who had a bemused, pleased smile on his face. Because—guess what—Diana really knew how to curtsy. Diana had a very remarkable neck; her neck was *muscular*, one wants to say; she could thrust it back and *up* at the same time; and that's what she was doing in the photograph. Well, I don't know what's involved in doing a curtsy, but I knew it was a real one I was seeing in this photograph. I knew from the expression on Prince Charles's face that he didn't often see a real curtsy; it was like running into someone who really knew how to play the bagpipes, or someone who really knew to make haggis; someone who really knew how to do some old thing. It is a very amusing photograph, and I will take this opportunity to thank Richard Avedon for sending it to me. It was just a piece of private social information that was useful to me. And Nancy Reagan and Ronald Reagan were standing by, and in the background was someone I knew quite well—the man I said I would describe—and here's my description. His name was Jerry Zipkin, and he's dead now, but he was really the worst of a group of men in New York who were called "walkers"—and I was always very careful in my relationship with Diana Vreeland to distance myself from these men. I didn't want to be in the same category as Jerry Zipkin—it was a personal ambition of mine; and I achieved that ambition. I just happened to adore Diana Vreeland. She was an older woman, I was a younger man, and that just happened to be the terms of the friendship. But I didn't want to be confused with Jerry Zipkin. Jerry Zipkin was called by my friend Ahmet Ertegun "the social moth"; and so he was; he flitted and he burrowed, he was everywhere, and I don't think he ever did anyone any real good. He was someone I particularly disliked. But he was in my world for a while, and I knew him quite well, in a way. And I looked at that photograph and I thought, "Oh, God, Studio 54." And that's how Reagan did it.

A big part of American history in recent decades has been about the social life of New York City; I'm just sorry if anyone doesn't want to believe that, but it's true. As I said at the start of this book, each media event takes place within a real moment in someone's life, and that moment is affected by the social atmosphere around that person in that real moment, so that in 1950, when people were inventing television, there were certain real people doing that work, and they were involved in the social life of New York City. They had their will to power; their ambitions; their limitations; their own particular brand of meretriciousness; their particular sense of what the American people would fall for. And since, in the minds of these people, the ultimate thing would be to achieve something like ultimate social authority, that sense would have been infused into all their aesthetic choices; so that the particular artifacts being projected onto the American public, whether it was in the *Journal American* or on CBS, whether it was in a newspaper or in a magazine or on television, would carry with it that little gene of social information—what the creator of the artifact would himself, or herself, find romantic.

So here's a short essay on Studio 54—my life at Studio 54; my brief life at Studio 54. I went to Studio 54 for the first time shortly after it opened. It was Bianca Jagger's birthday; I went with Mrs. Vreeland. There was a party first at Halston's. Diana and I sat in the VIP gallery. I didn't like it. It was the first time I'd been out with Diana and I did not have a good time. We were sitting in the balcony of what had been an old movie theater, and we were looking at a scrim, a bit of decorative art that was promoting cocaine; there was a spoon going up into the nose of the man in the moon, or something. I didn't like that. I was in the process of losing a friend, and a cooperative building that I shared with that friend, on account of his cocaine use; I saw him turn his young son into a caretaker for him, which, in fact, mirrored what had happened between me and my father; I'd had to become the adult male in my family; and I had just made a private decision against cocaine; and I found myself looking at this scrim that was promoting cocaine use, and I didn't like it. I said to myself, "This thing is getting out of hand." I began to understand that what had been my private social life, in what I conceived to be the private context of the current version of Cafe Society, was going public, and that it was something that everyone was going to want to embrace. That is, I had been aware of how 1950s cultural artifacts had been formed in New York City—I'll refer you back, for instance, to the Elvis Presley–Hy Gardner interview of 1956; I had come to an understanding that the career of Elvis Presley had in some way been influenced by his relationship to New York City, to Hal Wallis, to lots of specific people whose social values I had come to know pretty well; I'd come to understand that genius was often deformed in America, and that Dionysian energy was always the big story, and that Dionysian energy—always an admirable thing, to be admired and enjoyed—was nonetheless subject to processes of deformation within the filter or template work of media life. And I began to understand, on the VIP balcony of Studio 54, that I was watching a new media template in formation.

When, then, fifteen years later I looked at the photograph Richard Avedon had sent me of Diana Vreeland, the Reagans, Prince Charles, and Jerry Zipkin at the White House, I began to see that that Studio 54 (the sixties reconfigured as the seventies) Cafe Society template had opened the door to the Reagans. As of 1978, New York had run out of specific cultural information; Roosevelt had died and had been buried; Winchell could be Army Archerd from the *Hollywood Reporter* or any other angry tabloid person; there was no reason Walter Winchell, dancing on Roosevelt's grave, couldn't be that loathesome man who gave us *Lifestyles of the Rich and Famous.* As to Hyde Park versus the Vanderbilt house, the Vanderbilts had won.

2. Franklin Roosevelt—Man and Template

So, a little abstract thinking here. Franklin Roosevelt was two things: a man and a template; a man and an information delivery system; a man and a *suggestion* as to how men and women in the future might want to be. He was a man and a *suggestion.* His most powerful idea was: you, ordinary man and woman, listening as you do to Walter Winchell, with perfect pleasure, can also listen to *me.* He suggested a possible ground for a permanent linkage between a decent American past (pre–money-power, in fact; more than a little preindustrial, in fact; almost *agrarian*, in fact) and the ordinary Americans of his day. Ordinary Americans of his day had suffered economic privation, many of them; they were of recent arrival in this country, many of them. His suggested linkage, projected with the marvelous power of his marvelous personality, was determinative for many people. And why shouldn't he have done it, after all? We live in a mass society, after all. We are not—cannot be—in touch with one another in any direct way; our life has been and will continue to be about *suggested connections* and information delivery templates.

FDR invented the first big-time information delivery template. His fireside chats on the radio really inaugurated our media age. His alliance with Walter Winchell (Marilyn singing "Happy Birthday, Mr. President" another way) lent a jittery excitement to the enterprise. People began to forget (my father certainly did forget) that Roosevelt was improvising; making a *suggestion.* The roots of human life are in human life, after all, not in any suggestion, however persuasive, as to what human life ought to be. God, I want to say, has his ideas too, also firmly held.

The intermediate figures between the spectacle of Roosevelt and Winchell dancing happily together and the devolved situation we live in now, where political figures of every stripe and at every level struggle to find the next camera angle, are of course the Kennedys. Personally, I think we really have to stop mourning them and look, rather, at the flow from FDR to our own real situation here on the earth in the last years of the century (also, of course, the last years of the millennium). We've been in a thirty-five-year depression about a possibility that just never took shape. The promise—very seductive—born in 1932 and revivified, let us say, in the early 1960s for a while—that we could take ourselves, just as we are, as moral authority *and* have the moral authority of the real deep past on our side, urging us uncritically on—this promise may have become demonized now.

As to what should be done. Well, first of all the president of the United States could stop hanging out with celebrities. I see a president entertaining one gray bureaucrat after another and reporting to us on what transpired. Today he entertains Mr. Anonymous Nobody from Philadelphia, who happens to run a school where no student now carries a gun. Tomorrow Mr. Anonymous Nobody is Mr. Not-So-Anonymous Somebody, and *he* then has the power to raise someone *else* up out of obscurity into public notice. That is how it works, you know. I think it could be quite striking—the sight of the president with an endless succession of noncelebrated people who happen to be doing their job. *Not* the symbolical photo-op people, but rather the ones whom everyone finds *un*glamorous but who happen *professionally* to be on the front lines. And *not* from the goddamned role-model point of view, which is the *worst* thing we have left from the Roosevelt-Kennedy attempt: "Every one of you ought to be like *this* remarkable avatar." *No. No more Universal Avatar suggestions, please.* We have, whether we acknowledge it or not, come to *loathe* universal avatar suggestions. What we need to know is that there is one great cop on the beat in Philadelphia and that next year there will be two. Like that, as they say in the gossip columns.

Of course I am thinking about Dwight Eisenhower here. Ike sent the National Guard to Little Rock, you know. The man who gave us D-Day also gave us the National Guard outside Central High School in Little Rock for the purpose of getting African-American students in the door. That made a rather strong point, don't you think? I don't think Ike would have stood for a permanent homeless population or children bringing firearms to school. Fuck the overview or the historical reasons for the problem, just get those guns *out* of all schools *now*. And why *wouldn't* the National Guard be called out to guard the homeless population—the homeless are housed in armories, after all; and why *wouldn't* that population be culled, or cull itself, the mentally disturbed people being sent to mental institutions. Common sense.

♦　♦　♦

I'm being a little easy on FDR here, because why not? But if it had been Nixon in league with Winchell at the height of his power, oh, boy. Winchell was psychotic. The man was mad and brought into our national life a way of thinking and talking that has done us nothing but harm. I saw the Biography (I mean the TV show) version of Winchell's life the other night. The show had personal meaning for me, of course. My father was at the *New York Post* when the *Post* ran the series that began to bring Winchell down. The bylines on those articles have a personal resonance for me. Alvin Davis, for instance. I knew these men. At a distance of almost fifty years, I have to say that the whole thing was fucked. There is no such thing as *good* tabloid journalism. That was one of the strange aesthetic conflicts I had to untangle for myself, over decades. The *Post* didn't go after Winchell until Winchell was ready to fall, you know. And he was brought to his knees on the basis of, well, irrelevancies; kind of like arresting Capone for tax evasion. There is no *good* tabloid approach; and there is no *linkage* between fine and pretty ancient patriarchal forms and the tabloid approach. The feverishness of this book, the *swirl* of my own literary style, will serve as partial proof of what I am saying, perhaps. The intricacies of my mental database will serve as partial proof of what I am saying, perhaps. "This man had to take in *that* much information, and develop *that* complicated a literary style—and over decades—in order to process the Roosevelt Tabloid Template." That is what I hope my readers' reaction will have been.

I had to do it. Do or die—I mean really die. My grandfather was a suicide, and my father's attraction to the neurosis—and psychosis—of tabloid journalism had to do with the ocean of denial a journalist gets to live in forever if he plays his cards right—and I mean Dan Rather and Abe Rosenthal, too. And Barbara Walters, and Larry King. Nearly *all* of them, as they say in the gossip columns. A child of this thing you don't want to be. And there he was last night: Walter Winchell, Jr. I knew the demented sparkle in his eyes—I've seen it in my own eyes, though not recently. Winchell Jr. died by his own hand, and America will die by *its* own hand unless it puts the tabloid mind away. If you have a tabloid addiction, if you swim in its ocean of denial, Walter Winchell is *your* father too.

3. Dwight Eisenhower—Man and Home

Before I tell you about Ike's house in Gettysburg, which is *not* a house in flames, both in the sense of not being a house that's wildly fashionable and popular, and also in the sense of "it's still there," I'll just tell you one last time about Windy Rock, the house of deep probity I was introduced to as a child, thinking again of Mr. Allen Coggeshall, the head of the house—"The Aged P" he was called (*P* for *pater*), who in 1948 sponsored a fund-raising party for Henry Wallace. If you can get a sense of what that house was like in 1948 you begin to touch on a lot of cultural concerns that have been written about by the Big Boys— by which I mean Windy Rock *was* Heartbreak House. I allude to the Bernard Shaw play; and anyone who wants to read that great play in connection with this work—a cat may look at a king— but it would be one of my ambitions that you could read this book, and then read *Heartbreak House* and see some connection between our Roosevelt–Anglophile–Old American world and what Bernard Shaw was writing about in *Heartbreak House.* And even Thomas Hardy—*Tess of the d'Urbervilles,* anything you want—because Henry Wallace was someone who was keeping up an agrarian, preindustrial view; and some people, and in the East as late as the 1940s, were thinking that what they wanted out of the Roosevelt tradition wasn't Walter Winchell, thank you, not at all; what they wanted was some sense of preindustrial probity.

The story that's coming to my mind now is of Windy Rock as Heartbreak House—and I guess I'm thinking of this because it was the first moment in which I got an idea that maybe there was something wrong with Windy Rock and that maybe it *was* Heartbreak House, because, naturally, it presented itself to me as something that was friendly to me, and something I was meant to learn from, and aspire to, and when something is presented to you in that fashion, and you're a child, any difficulty that comes to you, you feel has to do with your own ignorance, not to do with the thing you're aspiring to.

But I got a glimpse of the Heartbreak House of it through a stranger who came into the context; and this would have been, I think, in the middle or late fifties. I was just at Exeter, I think, or just about to go. But in any case, one of the Boys of the house— and they were always called "the Boys"—Bancroft Coggeshall— one of the Boys got married. Bancroft had been the son who had left the place and the construct—he had gone to the South; and I now understand that he wanted to escape it—he was the smartest of the Boys and he was the one who left; but it's hard to leave, I can promise you. It's taken me my lifetime to leave what I'm discussing here—and Bancroft's leaving wasn't so easy or so complete. He met a young southern woman in North Carolina and brought her north to meet his family, and this was a party at which the extended family met the new Mrs. Coggeshall. It was a very striking thing, this party, in that the southern woman stood out so. It was as though she were black or Asian or from another planet. She didn't know how it went second by second, and in that kind of old context it does go second by second, you know. Conversation is an entirely ritualized thing, mechanical at a very high level, kind of high-priced yard goods against which the occasional witty remark or surprising reference can be seen. If you don't know the yard goods, you can't get to the occasional (or very occasional) witty remark, and if you don't know all the references going back three generations (including the history of the occasional—or very occasional—witty remarks that have at other times been made), then a strange silence surrounds you and you feel, quite correctly, that you are under a microscope. (There may be a link, it occurs to me, between this Anglophile conversational phenomenon and the gossip-column style. Come to think of it, this language cruelty may be the *real* linkage between the old Roosevelt context and Walter Winchell.)

In any case, the southern woman was in *alarm*. We were

daunting to her; she was deeply afraid of us. And she fastened on to me; it was very striking. I think—in fact I know—at different times during the day she went upstairs and took a slug of booze. And part of the party was a skating party, and she was already a little drunk by that time. And this would have been at the Choate pond, the Choate house being next door to Windy Rock—it occurs to me to tell you that all this patch of ground—Windy Rock and the Choate place—is now Pace College, in lower Westchester—and I guess you could do an etching of that party in the late 1950s and it would look like Currier and Ives; the Choate house was, and is, something with columns, and the pond is in front, and everyone there was—you know—but it wasn't a Currier and Ives party; it was about panic. The southern woman threw us all into relief, I want to say; *we* became the foreground as framed against *her* panic, and the possibility as to *our* panic rising to the surface *forever* came before us, and it wasn't a successful skating party. And I can remember, out of the blue, this person I'd never met—this southern woman—taking me to skate with, and clinging to me.

◆　◆　◆

Well, that's a sad story, so let me tell you a happy one. I guess it's clear to my reader by this time that I just went on and on and on with a certain level of concern—keeping my mind's eye open; I wouldn't ever let anyone close my mind's eye—but, nonetheless, accepting this ancient Black Roosevelt template and the preindustrial concerns behind that template, because in my own life I was following if not the Henry Wallace of it, then certainly the Hyde Park of it; the idea that there was something back there, in some preindustrial America, that had to be kept going in a part of one's mind—I just kept on with it. So now I'll tell you the story of a happy time.

This has to do with my friend Hélène Walker, who's alive on the face of the earth at this moment; she's in her nineties; an aristocratic woman of Boston and elsewhere, the mother of one of my college roommates; I just made friends with her, that's all; I went to see my friend Owen Walker over Christmas in 1962, I think it was, and his mother was there, and it was the cure for Windy Rock. I don't want my reader to think I've spent my life breaking my heart; although my heart's been broken often enough. For every bad thing that's happened there's been a good.

Hélène Walker had a house on Fifty-third Street—243 East Fifty-third Street—and she didn't have a lot of money at the time she bought it; at the time she bought it it was a rooming house; and she kind of frontiered it—the Third Avenue El was still up, and, as she liked to say, when she bought that house there was a man who sold ice at one end of the street and a man who sold coal at the other. And, well, where Hélène lives now, in Ashfield, Massachusetts, it's still like that; Hélène is a kind of aristocratic frontierswoman, and, as far as I'm concerned, that's one of the best possible ways to go. And I lived in that Fifty-third Street house for a number of years, and then the house was sold, and Hélène moved to Ashfield, Massachusetts, and I saw less of her. And then my friend Owen got married for the second time, and there was a party. A wedding party. At Ashfield. And, having been away from that house, and Mrs. Walker, for a number of years, I looked around; and, my God, didn't I love it; it was a very attractive party—full of old friends; my friend Owen was marrying happily, and there was Mrs. Walker, and I hadn't really seen her in a number of years; and in the Irish-immigrant side of my soul I just said, Oh my God, I love her, and I just couldn't help myself, I went over and said, "Hélène, I just adore you." And I gave her a kiss. And she looked up at me—and I guess I'm presenting this to you as the very good side of the old preindustrial way of acting; it wasn't all—or always—about repression and panic; the toughness wasn't all—or always—cruel. She looked up at me and said in the nicest possible way, in a way that didn't interfere at all with the flow of affection back and forth from her to me and from me to her—she said, "Well, George, you can't help who you love."

Well, that's me and Ike. I'm telling that story because when I walked into his house at Gettysburg, that phrase came back to me. I said to myself, "Well, George, you can't help who you love." That phrase came back to me at the moment when I was looking at two portraits—and I'm laughing at myself now because they're not very good portraits; it's Ike in uniform, and Mamie, his beloved lady, and they're just not very good portraits. At the age of fifteen I would have known what to say about them—and cruelly. And I looked at those portraits—yes, at Mamie, but then finally at Ike, and I laughed as I thought to myself, "Well, you can't help who you love."

About the Author

Born in New York in 1943, George W. S. Trow attended Exeter and Harvard, was a founding editor of *The National Lampoon,* and was a *New Yorker* staff writer from 1966 to 1994. He has published a collection of satiric pieces (*Bullies,* 1979), and a novel (*The City in the Mist,* 1982), as well as his highly regarded *Within the Context of No Context* (1981, revised 1997). Several of his plays have been staged in New York, and he has written the screenplay for two movies. He lives in Columbia County, New York.